'Napoleon is Dead'

'Napoleon is Dead'

LORD COCHRANE
AND THE GREAT
STOCK EXCHANGE SCANDAL

RICHARD DALE

SUTTON PUBLISHING

First published in the United Kingdom in 2006 by
Sutton Publishing Limited · Phoenix Mill
Thrupp · Stroud · Gloucestershire · GL5 2BU

British Library Cataloguing in Publication Data
A catalogue record for this book is available from the British Library.

ISBN 0-7509-4381-5

Typeset in 11/14.5pt Sabon.
Typesetting and origination by
Sutton Publishing Limited.
Printed and bound in England by
J.H. Haynes & Co. Ltd, Sparkford.

To the memory of my father,
1911–2006

Contents

Contents

List of Illustrations

Preface

The name of Thomas Cochrane should be better known. He commanded no great fleets, he was associated with no single large-scale action on which the fate of nations turned and he served for much of his active life as a mercenary under foreign flags. Yet Cochrane was one of the most brilliant naval commanders the world has known – and certainly unrivalled in his time in single-ship combat and as a leader of small battle squadrons. He wrought havoc on the French, Spanish and Portuguese navies in Channel waters, the Mediterranean, the Atlantic and the Pacific, he terrorised onshore garrisons and fortified anchorages along the French, Spanish and South American coasts and he was accorded high honours by the governments of Brazil, Chile and Greece – as well as Britain – in recognition of his exceptional contribution to the cause of freedom and independence in these countries. This book, however, does not set out to eulogise Cochrane's extraordinary achievements at sea. Instead, it focuses on a darker chapter in the naval hero's career – one that drove him from his native country, changed the course of his life and cast a long shadow over his later years.

Acknowledgements

I would like to thank the Earl of Dundonald for his generosity in allowing me free use of the Dundonald family papers deposited with the National Archives of Scotland, including in particular the trial documents previously held by Farrer & Co., Lord Cochrane's solicitors in 1814. I would like also to thank the staff of the National Archives of Scotland and especially David Brown, who offered helpful insights on the interpretation of certain documents. I also received valuable assistance from the staff of the Inner Temple Library, the British Library and the Plymouth Naval Studies Library. Finally, I would like to express my gratitude to Farrer & Co., who were most helpful in guiding me towards relevant documentary sources and in making available material from their own legal archives.

13 Green Street

Map of Mayfair showing 13 Green Street. Cochrane's Green Street home was de Berenger's final destination after his long coach journey from Dover. It was here that he was entertained to breakfast by Lady Cochrane. *(A to Z of Regency London, Guildhall Library)*

Author's Note

The main source for the Stock Exchange trial is the published transcript of the court proceedings taken down by William Gurney, who was short-hand writer to both Houses of Parliament. In describing the trial and the events preceding it I have adhered closely to the verbatim evidence of witnesses and the speeches of counsel presented in this transcript, although grammar and style have been adjusted occasionally to help the modern reader. The italics and underlining in quoted material indicate original emphasis unless otherwise stated.

I have quoted from the personal letters of Cochrane and his wife, Kitty, which are to be found in the Dundonald family papers deposited with the National Archives of Scotland, although much of this correspondence is also cited by Ian Grimble in his biography of Cochrane. The letters from de Berenger to Cochrane from which I have quoted are published as appendices to de Berenger's book *The Noble Stockjobber*. The quotations from Henry Crabb Robinson's diary for 1814 are cited by Henry Cecil in his book *A Matter of Speculation*.

The new evidence I have drawn upon is to be found in the trial papers lent to the National Archives of Scotland by the Earl of Dundonald, which were formerly held by Farrer & Co. These documents include the defence briefs prepared for Cochrane, Cochrane Johnstone and Butt, pre-trial correspondence between Cochrane and his solicitors, depositions and affidavits, case notes, various trial-related memoranda and Cochrane's charges against Farrers as well as their response.

ONE

February 1814

For England the year 1814 opened with great promise. There was at long last a real prospect that Napoleon would finally be crushed by the Allies' massively superior forces under the command of Blücher and Schwarzenburg. Indeed, so confident of victory were the Allied leaders that they had begun to compile seating plans for dinner parties to be held at the Palais Royal in Paris. Yet, against all the odds, Napoleon was able to exploit a fleeting opportunity that presented itself in early February, when the Allied armies separated, to inflict a series of lightning defeats, first on the Silesian army of Blücher and then on the Russo-Austrian forces of Schwarzenburg. It was in the context of these bewildering changes of fortune on the battlefield, as well as uncertainties surrounding the parallel peace negotiations taking place in Châtillon, that rumours and counter-rumours swept through London and its financial markets in mid-February.

The market in government bonds was especially sensitive to military and political developments across the Channel, and during these crucial weeks the two most actively traded government securities – Consols and Omnium – fluctuated in response to every rumour. On Thursday 10 February, for instance, the afternoon edition of *The Courier* reported unsubstantiated rumours of Napoleon's downfall: 'some say that Bonaparte has been killed in battle, others that he has been assassinated, that Paris is surrounded by the Allies . . . and that the Senate is in Treaty with the Allied Sovereigns.' Over the next three days, the premium on Omnium increased from 20 per cent to 28 per cent and Consols rose by 7 per cent to 71¾. Yet on Monday 14 February the news was reversed: *The Courier* reported information received from Dover, based on contacts between fishing boats off Saint-Valery, that Bonaparte had won a great victory. The premium on Omnium fell back to 25 per cent and Consols dropped by 4 per cent, while across the Channel French funds rose by 3–4 per cent.

Although government bonds may have fluctuated by only a few percentage points, the gains or losses represented by these movements were hugely magnified by the practice of buying stock without immediately paying for it. An investor might, for instance, buy Omnium for the account, in which case the purchase price would not have to be settled until the next Stock Exchange account date – by which time the purchaser would hope to have made a successful offsetting sale. Alternatively, a forward contract, specifying some other longer-term settlement date, might be entered into. Sales of stock could also be 'for time', so that the seller need not be in possession of the stock at the time of sale: a seller who had sold forward in this way would be hoping to buy the stock more cheaply before the settlement date.

Given the vital importance of news from the Continent, Stock Exchange speculators, or 'plungers' as they were called, were prompted to develop their own sources of information – as Rothschild was to demonstrate the following year when he famously benefited from being first with the news of Waterloo. Some investors, as well as newspapers, maintained agents at the Channel ports to relay information to them in London as soon as it was brought ashore – whether from fishing vessels, merchant ships or naval patrols. Messages could then be rushed up to London in a matter of hours, either by express rider or, if to be delivered in person, by post-chaise.

The Admiralty, however, had its own communication system based on semaphoric or 'line-of-sight' telegraph. This consisted of a network of semaphore towers linking the Admiralty in London to Portsmouth, Deal, Great Yarmouth and Plymouth. Telegraphs were sited on suitable hills at intervals of 6 or 7 miles. Ropes controlled six pivoted 'shutters' which were attached to a raised frame, and these could be moved either into a horizontal (invisible) or vertical (visible) position. The telegraph network, which could be effective only in daylight and clear weather, was manned by sentinels who were not allowed to leave their telescopes for more than two minutes at a time during the day. The Deal telegraph, which is especially relevant to the story that is about to unfold, was linked to the Admiralty along a relay of fifteen stations: short messages could be transmitted through this network in only a few minutes, weather permitting.

As the military fortunes of the embattled European powers ebbed and flowed across the Channel in these early weeks of 1814, England was on heightened alert. The Admiralty communications system was primed, innkeepers along the main coach road into London anxiously awaited messengers carrying news of the war and in every Channel port there was an air of expectancy. In this febrile atmosphere, stock-market 'plungers' bought and sold on every scrap of news while a group of more serious speculators positioned themselves for the announcement of great events.

TWO

The Officer in Red

At around 1 a.m. on the morning of 21 February a striking figure could be seen in the dim light walking through the streets of Dover. The gentleman, who wore a red uniform under a grey greatcoat, appeared to be a military officer, and his bearing suggested that he had travelled far and was near exhaustion. The officer stopped at the Ship Inn and knocked loudly at the door – loudly enough to attract the attention of the landlord of the neighbouring Packet Boat public house, who came with candles to see what the commotion was about.

The night porter of the Ship opened the door to the officer, and there ensued, in the presence of the Packet Boat landlord, an agitated conversation in the hallway of the inn. The officer spoke brusquely and in terms that discouraged further questioning: 'I have this last hour been landed on a beach from France after travelling for two nights and I am the bearer of dispatches that are the most important to be brought to England these past twenty years. I must have horses and in the meantime I would be obliged if you would bring me pen and paper so that I can inform the authorities of what has passed.' On being asked the nature of his news, he waved his interrogator aside: 'Do not pester me with questions. You will know it tomorrow from the Post-Admiral.'

Mr Wright, the landlord, was roused, and he, together with certain guests who had been woken by the knocking, joined the officer in the parlour. Among these was Mr William St John, who was staying in Dover as an agent of *The Traveller* newspaper: he was there to obtain intelligence for the paper on developments in France but he also hoped to use such information for his own Stock Exchange dealings. Clearly the City spies were out that night in Dover.

4

Once candles had been brought into the parlour, the officer's full regalia could be seen by those present. It consisted of a scarlet uniform coat with long skirts buttoned across, a red silk sash, grey pantaloons and a fawn-coloured fur cap circled with a gold band. He wore several ornaments, the most prominent being a star on his breast and a silver medal suspended from his neck, and he carried a small portmanteau. The officer requested privacy and addressed himself to the landlord:

I am the bearer of sensational and glorious news – the best that could possibly be wished. But I cannot say more. I must ask you to arrange with great urgency an express horse and rider to carry a message to the Admiral at Deal as well as a post-chaise and four to take me to London. For the present I need pen, paper and ink and I would be obliged if you could also provide some refreshment to sustain me.

Once writing materials and a bottle of Madeira had been supplied, the unexpected visitor proceeded to draft a hasty dispatch, as follows:

To the Honourable T. Foley,
    Post Admiral, Deal

Dover, one o'clock am
February 21st, 1814.

Sir,

I have the honour to acquaint you that the *L'Aigle* from Calais, Pierre Duquin, Master, has this moment landed me near Dover, to proceed to the capital with dispatches of the happiest nature. I have pledged my honour that no harm shall come to the crew of the *L'Aigle*; even with a flag of truce they immediately stood for sea. Should they be taken, I have to entreat you immediately to liberate them. My anxiety will not allow me to say more for your gratification than that the allies obtained a final victory; that Bonaparte was overtaken by a party of Sacken's Cossacks, who immediately slaid [*sic*] him, and divided his body between them.

General Platoff saved Paris from being reduced to ashes. The Allied Sovereigns are there, and the white cockade is universal, and immediate peace is certain. In the utmost haste, I entreat your consideration and have the honour to be,

    Sir,

    Your most obedient humble Servant,

      R. du Bourg

    Lieut-Colonel and Aide-de-Camp to Lord Cathcart.

Wright took the letter and entrusted it to one of his own boys with instructions that it be delivered to Admiral Foley personally at Deal. At about the same time a chaise and four was brought to the door of the Ship by two postboys to convey Colonel du Bourg (as we may now call him) to London – first staging post the Fountain Inn at Canterbury.

Du Bourg had offered to pay the Ship's landlord in gold Napoleons, as might be expected from a traveller newly arrived from France. Wright, however, preferred to receive Bank of England notes, and these were duly produced. From now on, however, du Bourg paid his way along the route to London in gold Napoleons, which the various postboys were happy to accept. The next staging post after the Fountain Inn was the Rose at Sittingbourne and thereafter the Crown at Rochester, where, at around 5.30 a.m., du Bourg entered the parlour to refresh himself with a little chicken and beef provided by the landlord, William Wright, who happened to be the brother of the landlord of the Ship Inn at Dover. Wright was already aware that important news was about to break, since a postboy from Dover carrying an urgent letter to be delivered in London had just passed through with the information that an official messenger was en route. Clearly, du Bourg's sensational news was preceding him to the metropolis.

Wright was understandably curious to know more about the dispatches brought by the officer in red. 'I am led to suppose that you are the bearer of some very good news for this country,' he tentatively began. Du Bourg answered him with a perfunctory 'He's dead,' as he took his refreshment. 'Who do you mean, Sir?' Wright asked. 'The tyrant Bonaparte,' was the reply. When Wright asked whether this was really true, du Bourg replied curtly: 'If you doubt my word you had better not ask me any more questions.' Whereupon Wright apologised for presuming to doubt him and asked whether he might know the dispatches, given the anxious state of the country and of Rochester in particular.

Du Bourg deigned to give a more informative reply:

There has been a very general battle between the French and the whole of the Allied Powers commanded by Schwarzenburg in person. The French being completely defeated Bonaparte fled for safety. He was overtaken by the Cossacks, however, six leagues from Paris at the village of Rushaw. Having there come up with him they literally tore him to pieces. I myself have come from the field of battle as aide-de-camp of Lord Cathcart. The Allies have been invited to Paris and the Bourbons to the Throne of France.

After this brief ten-minute stopover at Rochester the same chaise drove du Bourg to the Crown and Anchor at Dartford. The landlord here had once again been alerted to the breaking news by a preceding postboy, and du Bourg elaborated again on Napoleon's downfall: 'The Allies are in Paris, Bonaparte is dead, destroyed by the Cossacks, and literally torn in a thousand pieces; the Cossacks fought for a share of him as if they were fighting for gold. The country can expect a speedy peace.'

As dawn broke on a cold and misty morning the coach was on its final stage between Dartford and London. Du Bourg gave the remains of his bottle of Madeira to the postboys and engaged them in conversation. He shared with them his sensational news, which he asked them not to repeat to anyone until their return from London, and said that he had had to walk 2 miles after he came ashore because his French crew were afraid of coming too near to Dover. He then addressed one of the drivers: 'Postboy, you have had a great deal of snow here, I understand. Here is a delightful morning, I have not seen old England for a long while.'

As they approached London the officer evidently wished to avoid attracting attention to himself. At Bexley Heath he asked the postboys to moderate the pace of the horses. Past Shooters Hill he asked them where the first hackney coach stand was located. On being told that this was the Bricklayers Arms, he said it was too public; they were without luck at the Three Stags in Lambeth Road, but, finding a solitary coach at Marsh Gate, du Bourg asked that the chaise be drawn up alongside. After pulling up the window blind, he was able to transfer directly to the coach without stepping out. The coachman was then instructed to drive to 13 Green Street, Grosvenor Square, the private residence of Lord Cochrane, where du Bourg arrived just before 9 a.m.

Despite his precautions, du Bourg's arrival in London did not go entirely unnoticed. Richard Barwick, clerk to Messrs Paxtons and Company, Bankers of Pall Mall, was passing by Marsh Gate on his way to work when he noticed a man getting into a hackney coach from a post-chaise. The horses of the chaise were sweating profusely from their exertions, and the postboys told him that the gentleman was a general officer carrying news from France. Knowing, as a banker, the value of inside information, Barwick decided to follow the hackney coach. This he did as far as the Little Theatre at the Haymarket, when he had to turn off in order to be at his office by 9 a.m. (Presumably he had in mind personal rather than corporate gain, since the latter might have justified his being late for work.)

While sensational news was spreading along the coach road from Dover to London, the other avenue of communication that du Bourg had opened up was encountering difficulties. The postboy arrived in Deal with du Bourg's message to Admiral Foley at about 3 a.m. Thomas Foley was woken and asked the maid to bring him the letter so that he could read it in bed. Doubting the veracity of the sensational contents, he then questioned the postboy in his dressing room. He remained highly sceptical, but in any event, when daylight came, thick mist obstructed line-of-sight communication. Foley therefore decided not to try the telegraph but instead sent du Bourg's letter to the Secretary of the Admiralty, accompanied by a note of his own.

Notwithstanding the failure of the telegraph at Deal, du Bourg's reports from the battlefield, first communicated by postboys and coaching-inn landlords along the London Road, were shortly after breakfast time on the morning of 21 February beginning to multiply among merchants, dealers and brokers in the City of London. When the stock market opened that Monday at 10 a.m., government bonds were quoted at around the levels they had reached at close of business the previous Saturday. But soon the market began to stir as news spread of the officer in red and his extraordinary dispatches. The leading government trading stock, Omnium, having opened at 26½ premium soon rose to 30¼, but towards midday, when there was no official confirmation of the reported Allied victory, doubts crept in and stock prices began to fall back. At this point, between midday and 1 p.m., the market was given dramatic renewed impetus by the appearance in the City of a post-chaise drawn by four horses decorated with laurels, the two gentlemen passengers wearing blue greatcoats with white lining and cocked hats with white cockades – the uniform of French royalist officers. This impressive cortège came over London Bridge, down Lombard Street, along Cheapside and over Blackfriars Bridge, the occupants scattering paper billets inscribed with 'Vive le Roi!' and 'Vivent les Bourbons!' The City saw the triumphal display as corroboration of Napoleon's downfall, and Omnium, reversing its earlier decline, touched 32½.

In the early afternoon, the City still awaited official confirmation of the news, and an expectant crowd gathered outside the Mansion House in anticipation of an announcement from the Lord Mayor. But, when messengers were sent to the West End, it was found that no dispatches had been received by the office of the Secretary of State. At this point it became clear that investors had fallen victim to an elaborate hoax, and government bond prices began to subside. Omnium sank back to 28 by the close of business, and there was a further fall to 26½ the following day, bringing quotations back to the level prevailing before the appearance of Colonel du Bourg.

Since ordinary investors had been duped on a large scale, there was an immediate outcry, and calls for an investigation to identify and prosecute the culprits. In its leading article of Tuesday 22 February

The Times thundered against the 'fraud of the most impudent and nefarious description', expressing the hope that 'Great exertions will . . . be made by the frequenters of the Stock Exchange to detect the criminal'. On that same day the Committee of the Stock Exchange, with its reputation now at stake, met and appointed a subcommittee to enquire into the hoax and to bring to justice those responsible. The subcommittee appears to have pursued its investigations with great energy over the next ten days, because on 4 March the Exchange posted a notice asking whether 'all those members of the Stock Exchange who transacted business either directly or indirectly for any of the persons undermentioned on Monday 21st February last, would favour the Committee with an interview'. There followed the names of the Honourable Cochrane Johnstone, Mr R.G. Butt, Lord Cochrane, Mr Holloway, Mr Sanders and Mr M'Rae. At the same time a reward of £250 was advertised for the discovery of Colonel du Bourg. The wheels had been set in motion for the preparation of an indictment for conspiracy and a sensational trial that would not only hold London's population in thrall for its duration but whose outcome was bitterly contested for more than a century afterwards.

THREE

The Stock Exchange Investigation

The Stock Exchange Committee charged with investigating the
fraud carried out on the morning of 21 February had three main
lines of enquiry. First, there were the fictitious 'French officers' who
had been carried in a triumphal progress through the City; second,
there was the identity of the mysterious Colonel du Bourg who had
been the chief perpetrator of the hoax; and, finally, there were the beneficiaries of the fraud who had created a false market in government
stock in order to generate profits for themselves. It was this last group
who had presumably funded and instigated the whole charade.

The sub-plot revolving around the French officers was the first to
be unravelled, although some of the detail recounted below was not
revealed until the trial. Four men were involved – Mr Sandom, a
spirit merchant who had fallen on hard times, Mr Lyte, a navy
agent, Mr M'Rae, described in court as a 'person in the most
desperate circumstances', and Mr Holloway, a wine merchant who
appeared to have acquired the services of the other three.

The French officers' post-chaise was traced to the Rose Inn at
Dartford, whose landlord, Mr Foxall, said that he had received a
letter at 7 a.m. on Monday morning from Sandom, a regular
customer, asking him straightaway to provide a chaise and pair to be
sent to Northfleet to collect some gentlemen. These would return to
Dartford, where four good horses were to be made ready to drive
them at full speed to London. According to Foxall, the chaise, when
it returned from Northfleet, drove furiously into his yard carrying
Sandom and two other gentlemen who were dressed in blue and
wore large cocked hats with white cockades.

Foxall asked Sandom whether the gentlemen wanted breakfast.
He replied: 'No, they have breakfasted at my home, they have been

11

in an open boat all night and they are very much fatigued.' On being asked who they were, he added: 'I do not know who they are but they have news of the utmost consequence and I beg you to let them have the best horses you can provide.' Foxall then provided four fresh horses and harnessed them to a new chaise, since the wheels of the first vehicle were insufficiently well greased for a fast drive to London.

The postboys from the Rose Inn then drove the three gentlemen towards the metropolis. As they approached Shooters Hill, however, Sandom got out with one of the others and walked. He explained to the postboys: 'My lads we do not want you to distress your horses up this hill but when you get up you may get on a little . . . I shall give you twelve shillings apiece for driving.' The *équipe* then made its dashing tour round the City via London Bridge, Lombard Street and Cheapside, before moving off towards Marsh Gate. Here the three gentlemen descended from the chaise, changed their cocked hats for round ones and disappeared from view.

A certain Sarah Alexander, who had lodged on the same floor in Fetter Lane as M'Rae and his wife, was able to throw further light on the officers' dress. Because they were all hard up and coal was dear, Sarah often shared a fire with the M'Raes. According to Sarah, on Sunday 20 February M'Rae brought back two dark blue officers' coats with ornamental braiding and lined with white silk, together with two opera hats, one having a gold tassle at each corner and a brass plate. M'Rae told his wife to make two white cockades, and, being asked the purpose, he said they were 'to deceive the flats' (speculators). The following day, he brought back only one coat and asked for the white lining to be removed before taking it to the dyers to be dyed black. The white cockades and the paper they were quilled on were thrown onto the fire. M'Rae, who had been almost penniless, now had in his possession £10, £2 and £1 notes, explaining that he had gained £50 for what he had done. Soon after, he disappeared without leaving an address.

M'Rae's role in the affair was further elaborated on by an acquaintance of his, Mr Vinn. In mid-February Vinn had received a letter as follows:

February 14, 1814

Mr Vinn,

Please meet me at the Carolina Coffee House, Burchin Lane, about eleven tomorrow, upon very particular interesting business.

Yours very respectfully,
Alexander M'Rae

Vinn went to the Carolina Coffee House at the appointed time and met M'Rae, who confided that he, Vinn, could make his fortune if he was prepared to participate in a scheme that was being planned by men of consequence and affluence where his knowledge of French would be particularly useful. On being asked whether there was any moral turpitude attached to the scheme, M'Rae replied:

Not at all. What is contemplated is practised daily by men of the first consequence. It involves nothing more or less than biting the biters or, in other words, a hoax upon the Stock Exchange. It is to be performed by going down to Dartford, Folkestone or Dover, as may be instructed and on the appointed evening it will be necessary for you and I to have dresses appropriate to the character of French officers.

Vinn claimed that at this point he insisted on having nothing to do with the project, although he did go so far as to provide two French phrases in writing at M'Rae's particular request. The phrases were 'Vive le Roi' and 'Vivent les Bourbons'. Vinn left and immediately made the story public but without mentioning M'Rae's name. Some people may therefore have been alerted to the fact that a Stock Exchange scam was in the offing.

Given the facts that were coming to light about the French officers' dash through the City, it is perhaps not surprising that towards the end of April both Mr Holloway and Mr Lyte, on whom suspicion had already fallen, approached the Stock Exchange with a full confession of the sub-plot and the identity of those who had participated. Holloway, however, insisted that he had acted

13

independently and denied any connection with Lord Cochrane, Cochrane Johnstone or Butt. His sole motive, he said, had been to profit from a rise in price of government stock (he had indeed sold out his entire £40,000 holding in Omnium on the morning of 21 February). Holloway and Lyte hoped that by confessing before the impending trial they could avoid prosecution – in vain as it turned out.

The Stock Exchange's second line of enquiry focused on the person of Colonel du Bourg and his red uniform. Here again events moved rapidly. As early as 6 March an undisclosed person, quite possibly one of Lord Cochrane's servants, claimed and received the £250 reward that had been offered for the identification of du Bourg. The informer named a certain Charles Random de Berenger as the imposter. A few days later on 11 March Lord Cochrane published an affidavit (see p. 22) stating, *inter alia*, that the gentleman in uniform who had been seen visiting his house in Green Street was none other than this very same de Berenger. On 26 March the Stock Exchange revealed that a waterman, dredging for coal with a drag above Old Swan Stairs, had recovered a scarlet regimental coat from the Thames. This had been cut into pieces and bundled together with an embroidered silver star and a silver badge, weighed down with pieces of lead and brass, and tied up in the covers of a white chair cushion. At around this time de Berenger was heard of in Sunderland, where he was apparently aiming to leave the country under an assumed name. Finally, on 8 April the fugitive was arrested in Leith. His possessions included a portable writing desk, various personal papers, a bugle, some Napoleon coins and a large number of bank notes. De Berenger was then brought to London on 12 April and committed to Newgate to await his trial.

Charles Random de Berenger, a 42-year-old adventurer in straitened financial circumstances, was a remarkable individual. In physical appearance he was unprepossessing: of middling height, he was described by one witness as having a large red nose, large whiskers and a rather blotched face. His father was a native of Germany who had been an aide-de-camp to Frederick the Great of

Prussia during the Seven Years War. His family had then settled in North America after inheriting landed property there but, because they sided with the Crown, they subsequently lost this in the War of Independence. De Berenger had then moved to London, where he tried without great success to earn a living as a draughtsman, designer and inventor. By 1814 he was confined as an insolvent debtor under the rules of the King's Bench, which meant that his movements were restricted to a short distance from his lodgings in Lambeth. De Berenger had considerable military experience, belonged to a volunteer corps of sharpshooters under the command of Lord Yarmouth and was an acknowledged crack shot, weapons expert and specialist in pyrotechnics. He also had wider interests and was often to be heard playing the trumpet or violin in his rooms in the morning. All in all, de Berenger's military background, audacity and inventiveness made him an ideal candidate to play the role of Colonel du Bourg.

De Berenger was connected to Lord Cochrane through his friendship with the latter's uncle, Mr Cochrane Johnstone, and they had from time to time dined at the same table. The precise extent of the intimacy between Cochrane and de Berenger was to become a key issue, Cochrane claiming in his affidavit that de Berenger's visit to his house on the morning of 21 February was motivated solely by the desire to discuss the possibility of a naval appointment. In any event, de Berenger was sufficiently familiar with Cochrane's domestic arrangements to know that he had just taken up residence at 13 Green Street, Mayfair, even though the house had been acquired only three days before the events of 21 February.

The third line of enquiry conducted by the Stock Exchange focused on the identity of those who had profited from the surge in government stock values on the morning of the hoax. Suspicion immediately fell on an investment syndicate comprising Lord Cochrane, Cochrane Johnstone and Mr R.G. Butt. It transpired that these three gentlemen, transacting mainly through a broker named Joseph Fearn, had invested heavily in government stock in the days immediately preceding the great hoax and that as of 19 February their holdings were as follows:

	Omnium (£)	Consols (£)
Lord Cochrane	139,000	–
Mr Cochrane Johnstone	410,000	100,000
Mr Butt	224,000	168,000
	773,000	268,000

Furthermore, these purchases had been paid for on account and not for cash, the next settlement day being 23 February. Any profits realised before that date would therefore represent a windfall return obtained with no capital outlay (although the syndicate of course faced heavy losses if prices moved down rather than up). As it happened, the syndicate, for whom Butt acted as investment manager, sold out the entirety of their combined holdings in a series of hectic transactions between 10 a.m. and noon on Monday 21 February – so hectic, indeed, that in the confusion Mr Fearn sold 10,000 Consols too few and 24,000 Omnium too many.

Lord Cochrane had been dabbling on the Stock Exchange, with advice from Mr Butt, since October 1813. However, as of 11 February he appears to have held no government securities. Then on 12 February he contracted to buy £100,000 Omnium, a holding increased by further purchases to £139,000 as of Saturday 19 February, the whole amount being sold the following Monday morning at a profit of just under £2,500.

Who, then, was Lord Cochrane and who were his fellow partners in the investment syndicate Messrs Cochrane Johnstone and Butt? Sir Thomas Cochrane enjoyed the courtesy title of Lord Cochrane, being the eldest son of the 9th Earl of Dundonald, whom he later succeeded as the 10th Earl. Tall, impressive, intemperate, with flaming red hair, Cochrane was, at the age of 39, a major national figure, an aristocratic grandee, renowned both for his brilliant naval exploits and for his fiery performances as a populist Member of Parliament, representing first Honiton and then Westminster.

The Cochranes were an ancient Scottish family descended from the Vikings whose estates had been considerably reduced over time. The

9th Earl of Dundonald had added to the family's financial problems by giving up a naval career to become a professional inventor. But his inventions and scientific experiments came to nothing, with the result that Cochrane and his siblings were brought up in penury.

Joining the navy at the beginning of the revolutionary wars with France and Spain, Cochrane was quick to make a name. In 1800, aged 25, he was given command of the *Speedy*, a diminutive vessel of 158 tons, with fourteen 4-pounder guns and 90 officers and men – later reduced to little more than 50. Ordered to cruise off the Spanish coast and disrupt enemy shipping, Cochrane created havoc: during the thirteen months of his command the *Speedy*, once described as a 'burlesque on a ship of war', captured over 50 vessels, 122 guns and 534 prisoners, the biggest catch by far being a large Spanish frigate (over 600 tons, 32 heavy guns and 319 men), which was forced to surrender when the *Speedy* manœuvred under its guns and fired successive broadsides at point-blank range.

Following the Peace of Amiens in 1801, Cochrane, like many other naval officers, became temporarily redundant, and he decided to use this period of enforced leisure by enrolling at Edinburgh University to further his education, first in ethics and then in chemistry. After hostilities had been resumed, Cochrane, in 1805, was appointed captain of the *Pallas*, a new 32-gun frigate. Cruising off the Azores, he succeeded in securing several rich prize vessels before returning triumphantly to Portsmouth with enormous Mexican gold candlesticks, 5-feet high, attached to each masthead. When the *Pallas* suffered severe damage in an encounter with the French, Cochrane and his crew were transferred to the frigate *Impérieuse*, initially with a roving commission 'to harass the Spanish and French coast as opportunity served'. Once again, Cochrane wrought havoc, although this time the damage was inflicted mainly on French coastal communications. By breaking down roads and bridges and blowing up batteries, towers and signal stations, this one frigate severely disrupted the inland movement of French armies and their supplies. Cochrane also demonstrated his familiarity with the importance of the new telegraphic communication systems when he reported to Lord Collingwood that he had blown up and completely demolished 'the newly constructed semaphoric telegraphs, which are of the utmost importance to the safety of the numerous convoys that pass along the coast of France . . .'.

However, Cochrane's greatest achievement came in 1809 when an English fleet under Lord Gambier was instructed to attack the French fleet in the Basque Roads. Cochrane's mission was to organise fireships to drive the French fleet ashore and leave them stranded and helpless – an objective that he achieved with total success. He organised and led a frontal attack by night on the French battle fleet of fifteen ships, which were moored in what was thought to be an impregnable anchorage protected by heavy shore batteries. Five French ships were destroyed, with most of the rest driven ashore and forced to discard their guns. The destruction might have been complete were it not for a delayed follow-up by the English fleet that allowed many of the French vessels to heave off and escape. Nevertheless, for his signal services on this occasion, Cochrane was decorated with the Order of the Bath, an almost unprecedented distinction for anyone below the rank of admiral. He was also acclaimed as a national hero.

It is worth noting that throughout his naval career Cochrane showed himself to be a master of deception. When commanding the *Speedy* he had avoided detection by painting his vessel as a Danish brig, and hiring a Danish quartermaster who could be passed off as captain. He had also made use of the quarantine flag to keep enemy vessels at a distance, claiming he had sailed from Algiers, where the plague was rife. Some years after the trial of 1814, when Cochrane found himself fighting for the Brasilians against the Portuguese, he was to engage in a monstrous double bluff. Attacking the province of Maranham with a single fighting ship, he came in under Portuguese colours, and those on shore, believing him to be a reinforcement from Portugal, sent out a messenger with dispatches and congratulations on his safe arrival. Cochrane then told the messenger who he really was, explaining also that he was the vanguard of a powerful naval squadron coming up behind. Cochrane sent a message back to the Portuguese commander of Port Bahia to the effect that the commander could prevent the destruction of his city and forts by overwhelming force if he would accept reasonable terms for capitulation. The terms were accepted and Cochrane took the surrender with one ship under his command.

Cochrane's activities at sea were also characterised by a determined quest for prize money – a motivation that reflected his desire to restore the Dundonald family fortunes. Although he is understood to have collected prizes running into several tens of thousands of pounds, Cochrane objected strongly to the more democratic rules for the distribution of booty introduced by the new regulations of 1808. Under the old rules, £20,000 of prize money distributed among the ship's crew of a first rate would be allocated as follows: £2,500 for the fleet admiral, £5,000 for the ship's captain and about £6 15s per man for the seamen and marines. Under the new regulations, the distribution was £1,666 for the admiral, £3,333 for the captain and £10 5s per man for the remaining crew. Cochrane complained bitterly about this reduction in the financial incentive enjoyed by captains, and in 1812 he claimed in the House of Commons 'that it was the diminution of the prize money by recent regulations which principally induced me to leave the profession for the last two or three years'.

After his Basque Roads exploit Cochrane did indeed decline to continue in service with the *Impérieuse*, whereupon he was placed on half-pay. For the next three years he devoted himself to his parliamentary career and in particular to the exposure in the House of Commons of naval abuses and maladministration, the wretched financial provision made for wounded officers and the alleged maltreatment of French prisoners. He also appears to have developed an interest, like his father, in patenting inventions, his pet scheme at the time of the Stock Exchange hoax being the manufacture of a ship's lantern, with an intensified glare, on which he had been working for the past year. Cochrane's design was a major improvement on the standard Argand oil lamps whose globe had a single aperture. The resulting mixture of atmospheric and consumed air retarded the light. Cochrane was able to intensify the light by providing two apertures, one admitting atmospheric air to the burner and the other expelling consumed air.

Cochrane showed the romantic side to his nature when he fell in love with a 16-year-old beauty, Katherine Barnes, who was an orphan with a modest family background. He whisked her off to Scotland, where, in August 1812, the couple went through a marriage ceremony at the Queensbury Arms at Annan, with two servants acting as witnesses. To remove any doubt about the legitimacy of this union, Cochrane and his bride were remarried in an Anglican church in 1818, at the specific request of Kitty's guardian.

Towards the end of 1813, war having broken out with the United States, Cochrane's uncle, Sir Alexander Cochrane, was appointed commander of the British fleet on the North American station. Sir Alexander departed immediately in a frigate, leaving his flagship, the *Tonnant*, to be fitted out at Chatham and brought out by his nephew who returned to service as flag captain. However, having joined his ship on 8 February 1814, Cochrane successfully applied for two weeks' leave of absence to put his domestic affairs in order and to complete the process for patenting his lantern. Accordingly he arrived back in London on 14 February, and it was here at his new residence in Green Street that de Berenger found him on that fateful Monday morning one week later.

Cochrane's two investment partners on the Stock Exchange's 'wanted' list were the Honourable Andrew James Cochrane Johnstone and Richard Gathorne Butt. Cochrane Johnstone was a younger son of the 8th Earl of Dundonald and therefore Cochrane's uncle, although only eight years his senior. He was both a charmer and a rogue. From 1797 until 1803 he had been governor of the island of Dominica in the West Indies – a post that he used for his own personal enrichment. He dabbled in the slave trade, as well as in the sale of arms, and he was eventually cashiered by the Army for his underhand financial dealings. When he married the daughter of the Earl of Hopetown, he added the name of Johnstone to his own, and after her death he married another heiress – the daughter of Baron de Clugny, Governor of Guadeloupe – from whom he was later divorced. After his forced resignation from the army, Cochrane Johnstone bought the parliamentary seat of Grampound, a notoriously corrupt constituency that was to be abolished in 1822. He continued to engage in multifarious business projects, most of which turned sour: on one occasion he bought sheep and wool in Spain which were to be paid for by exports of muskets from England. However, his London agent could not obtain export licences for the muskets, while the sheep failed to sell at the price expected, the result being a disastrous loss. At the time of the Stock Exchange fraud Cochrane Johnstone had debts of around £16,000, and it was only his status as a member of Parliament that kept him from a debtor's prison and allowed him to live in some comfort, first in Harley Street and later in Great Cumberland Street.

Richard Butt, a man in his late thirties, had previously been pay clerk in Portsmouth Dockyard. By 1813 he had become what might be described as a 'day trader' and investment adviser – that is, he had no regular job but was reputed to speculate successfully on the Stock Exchange while acting as investment adviser to others, including Cochrane. He lived in some style, having bought a house in Cumberland Place.

These, then, were the prime suspects to emerge from the initial Stock Exchange investigation into the hoax of 21 February. De Berenger was cast in the role of chief perpetrator, while Cochrane and Cochrane Johnstone were the alleged originators, along with Butt, the stock-market expert. The gentlemen concerned were not, however, prepared to wait on events. In keeping with Cochrane's favoured naval tactics, they launched an immediate pre-emptive counter-attack.

FOUR

Protestations of Innocence

On 7 March the Stock Exchange issued a preliminary report on its enquiry into the hoax perpetrated on 21 February. This showed that Colonel du Bourg's journey from Dover had ended at Cochrane's house at 13 Green Street. When the investigating police officer, a Mr Sayer, had called at this address, he was told that the manservant who had opened the door to du Bourg had been sent into the country and that the maidservant 'is not allowed to be seen or spoken to'. The report pointed the finger at Cochrane and his alleged collaborators but it did not formulate specific charges nor, according to Cochrane's own solicitors, did its cautious language provide a basis for a libel action by which he might have cleared his name. However, given the report's damaging implications and the fact that newspapers and street posters were claiming that the person who had committed the stock-exchange fraud had visited his house on 21 February 'in open day, and in the dress in which he had committed the fraud', Cochrane decided to publish a vigorous defence by way of voluntary affidavit.

Cochrane's affidavit, dated 11 March, became his public defence, since he took the trouble to have it printed, circulated and published in the newspapers. Because it provides the key elements of his subsequent trial defence, it is reproduced in full as Exhibit 1, but the following is a summary of its contents:

> My reappointment to active naval service being unexpected, I had obtained leave of absence from the Admiralty to settle my private affairs, including in particular the supervision of work on my lantern for which I am seeking a patent.
>
> On the morning of 21 February I breakfasted with my uncle, Cochrane Johnstone, in Cumberland Street so that I could share

the coach in which he drove daily to the City. I was dropped together with Mr Butt (who was also in the coach) on Snow Hill at about 10 a.m. I had been at Mr King's workshop at 1 Cock Lane for about forty-five minutes when I received a note from my servant asking me to return immediately to my house. I could not read the signature on the note because it was written too close to the bottom of the page but I was told by my servant that it was from an army officer and since I feared that an accident might have befallen my brother, who was serving with the army in Spain, I hurried back to my house. There I found Captain Berenger, who apologised for imposing on me. He explained the desperate financial circumstances that had prompted him to come to ask whether I would allow him to serve with me on the *Tonnant*, and to provide rifle training to the marines. I replied that this was not immediately possible because the *Tonnant* was still being made ready and in any case de Berenger, as a foreigner, would have to obtain authorisation from the Admiralty. However, knowing him to be a man of great talent, I went on to say that if he could obtain Admiralty clearance he would be welcome to join the *Tonnant* when it was brought to Portsmouth.

De Berenger then said that in anticipation of possibly coming on board the *Tonnant* straightaway he had come in military dress. He could not, however, go to Lord Yarmouth, or to any of his friends, in this dress or return to his lodgings where it would excite suspicion (he being confined under the King's Bench). He therefore requested a great favour and asked if I would lend him a hat to wear instead of his military cap. I gave him one which I found in a back room but, having tried it on, his uniform appeared under his greatcoat. I therefore offered him a black coat that was lying on a chair, and which I did not intend to take with me. He wrapped his uniform in a towel and departed in the coach I came in which, in my haste, I had forgotten to discharge.

No other person was seen by me at my house on Monday 21 February though possibly other officers may have called, and I certainly saw no person at my house in the dress described in the Stock Exchange's advertisement – Captain Berenger having arrived wearing a grey greatcoat, a green uniform and a military cap.

As for my investments, I held these openly, without prejudice to anyone and without the benefit of secret information. On 21 February I held £139,000 of Omnium, which I had bought from Mr Fearn at a premium of 28¼, on instructions that it was to be sold on a rise of one per cent. It was indeed sold at an average premium of 29½, although on the day of the fraud it could have been disposed of at 33½.

Shortly after Cochrane had issued his affidavit, the Lords of the Admiralty wrote to him saying that, having read both the report of the Stock Exchange Committee and his deposition, they considered further explanation was necessary. They had therefore decided to appoint an acting captain to superintend the fitting-out of the *Tonnant*. On 22 March Cochrane replied angrily to what amounted to a notice of suspension, again protesting his innocence and enclosing five further affidavits in support of his version of events, including three from his servants (Exhibit 8). These were later appended to a pamphlet attacking the Stock Exchange investigation, published on behalf of the investment syndicate.

The first supporting affidavit was that of Thomas Dewman, Cochrane's footman, who confirmed the details regarding the unexpected appearance of an officer at Green Street and the delivery of a note to Mr King's tin manufactory in Cock Lane. According to Dewman, the officer wore a grey regimental greatcoat, buttoned up, and a green collar underneath. Then Isaac Davis, a black servant, who was still at Cochrane's house in Green Street that morning although his service had just expired, testified that Captain de Berenger had called. He recognised him from visits de Berenger had made to his master's previous residence in Park Street, and on this occasion he was wearing a buttoned-up greatcoat with a green collar underneath. Mary Turpin, the kitchen maid, also swore that the officer she had seen in Cochrane's parlour when she went to make the fire had a grey greatcoat and an undercoat with a green collar. Finally, Mr King confirmed Cochrane's presence at his workshop between 10 a.m. and 11 a.m. that Monday, and a Mr Thomas swore that he had not sold foreign coins to Cochrane, as some of the papers had reported.

Without prejudging the issues raised at the trial, it is perhaps fair to point out the limitations of the affidavits produced by Cochrane. First, they were, like his own deposition, voluntary affidavits that carried no legal penalty if proved to be false; second, affidavits of servants in relation to matters affecting their master were, for obvious reasons, open to question, given the dependent nature of the master–servant relationship; and it was later revealed by Cochrane's solicitors that these particular affidavits were not prepared in the usual way by the solicitor from the servants themselves. Rather they were taken down in Cochrane's house by a solicitor's clerk to whom Cochrane dictated from papers, and without the witnesses being present. Subsequently the servants were taken to Mansion House to swear their statements. Finally, it is worth noting that, while the three servants agreed that the collar of the officer's undercoat was green, none of them went so far as to deny that the undercoat itself was red.

His own affidavit, together with the supporting statements that accompanied his letter to the Admiralty, represented Cochrane's attempt to clear his name ahead of any trial that might ensue. However, the Lords of the Admiralty remained impervious to his protestations, the Stock Exchange persisted in its investigations and press speculation remained rife. To make matters worse, certain unsavoury characters began to come out of the woodwork to challenge Cochrane's integrity.

One such was Mr James Le Marchant who wrote to Cochrane from the Gloucester Hotel, Piccadilly on 6 April (Exhibit 2). Le Marchant requested a meeting with Cochrane, whom he did not know, 'for the purpose of exploring a conversation I had with Mr de Berenger a few days prior to the hoax of February 21st last, and which must be of interest to you'. On receiving no immediate response, Le Marchant wrote again the next day saying that, in view of Cochrane's 'silent contempt', knowing as he did that Cochrane was at home when the letter was presented at the door, he proposed to make his information public. This blatant attempt at blackmail produced a surprisingly restrained response from Cochrane.

13 Green Street
April 8th, 1814

Sir,

I should have hoped, circumstanced as I am, and attacked by scoundrels of all descriptions, that a gentleman of your understanding might have discovered some better reason than that of 'silent contempt' to account for the delay of a few hours in answering a note; and more particularly as your note of the 6th led me to conclude, that the information offered to me was meant as a mark of civility and attention, and was not on a subject in which you felt any personal interest.

I am, Sir,
Your obedient servant,
Cochrane

Encouraged by this ambivalent reply Le Marchant immediately sent round another letter apologising for his impetuosity, assuring Cochrane that 'no power or consideration shall ever induce me to come forward as evidence against you' and requesting, as a reciprocal favour, a temporary loan from his lordship. Enclosed with the letter was a very full statement (see Exhibit 2) about the information he had been given by his acquaintance, de Berenger, whom he evidently used to meet quite regularly at the Gloucester Coffee House, Piccadilly.

According to Le Marchant's statement, de Berenger had said that he was on intimate terms with both Cochrane and Cochrane Johnstone, with whom he frequently dined, and that he had made drawings for Cochrane's lamp invention. On 16 February de Berenger had paid a late visit to Le Marchant after dining with his lordship and told him joyfully that his financial problems were over, Cochrane having arranged to give him a percentage of profits arising from de Berenger's stock-market suggestions. By recalling this conversation, which was carried on with the aid of Hollands (gin) and water until 2 a.m., Le Marchant had linked the stock-market hoax not only with de Berenger (whom he took to be du Bourg) but also with Cochrane. However, his accompanying letter promised that 'all I know on the subject shall be buried for ever in oblivion'.

Cochrane did not reply, and, the blackmail attempt having failed, Le Marchant promptly agreed to appear as a witness for the prosecution in the trial, although his evidence, unsurprisingly, appears to have counted for little. Indeed, Cochrane evidently felt that his exchanges with Le Marchant were more damaging to the credibility of the latter than to himself and, presumably anticipating that Le Marchant would go public with his story, decided to have the correspondence published in full as part of his pre-trial defence.

In order to corroborate his version of the circumstances in which the masquerading officer had visited his house on 21 February, Cochrane also published the following correspondence with de Berenger, who was now in prison:

13 Green Street,
April 27 1814

Sir, – Having, I trust, given ample time and opportunity to those who have endeavoured to asperse my character to learn from your own mouth the circumstances which induced you to call upon me on the 21st of February last, I feel it now due to myself no longer to delay this my earnest request, that you will afford me that explanation.

I am, Sir, your obedient Servant
(Signed)   COCHRANE
Baron de Berenger

De Berenger replied:

King Street, Westminster
April 27, 1814

My Lord, – I have the honour of acknowledging the receipt of your Lordship's favour, which has this moment been delivered.

27

Rest assured, my Lord, that nothing could exceed the pain I felt when I perceived how cruelly, how unfairly, my unfortunate visit of the 21st of February was interpreted (which, with its object, is so correctly detailed in your affidavit); but my agony is augmented, when I reflect that acts of generosity and goodness towards an unfortunate man have been, and continue to be, the accidental cause of much mortification to you: a fear of increasing the imaginary grounds of accusation caused me to refrain from addressing you.

I have the honour, etc.

CHAS. RANDOM DE BERENGER

Unknown to the outside world, however, de Berenger was at this time still hoping for favours from the Cochrane family and, while ostensibly supporting Cochrane's story, albeit in a somewhat oblique manner, he was also trying to use the situation to his advantage.

Cochrane Johnstone and Butt joined Cochrane in protesting their innocence and organising a campaign of self-vindication. Cochrane Johnstone solemnly declared his innocence from his seat in the House of Commons; he wrote a letter to the Stock Exchange purporting to demonstrate that the profits of the investment syndicate were significantly less than the Exchange had calculated; and he joined with Cochrane and Butt in publishing a lengthy attack on the Stock Exchange report in a best-selling pamphlet entitled *The Calumnious Aspersions contained in the Report of the Subcommittee of the Stock Exchange Exposed and Refuted*. This document sought to cast doubt on evidence published by the Stock Exchange, ridiculed the idea that du Bourg and de Berenger could possibly be one and the same person, and provided lengthy material on the investment syndicate's Stock Exchange transactions. Finally, the authors argued that the clearance sale of stock on 21 February was the result of earlier instructions given to their brokers to sell out whenever they could at a profit of 1 per cent.

Cochrane Johnstone was also involved in two rather curious incidents. First, he issued no fewer than 135 writs against individual members of the Stock Exchange, under a procedure which at that time allowed common informers to recover penalties imposed for certain breaches of statute. The law in question was Sir John Barnard's Act of 1734, which prohibited time bargains (forward contracts) – a provision that had been largely ignored by the investment community since its enactment. The prohibited contracts were indeed the very transactions that Cochrane Johnstone and his partners had entered into, since they allowed speculative positions to be built up without any initial capital outlay. In any event, the wave of litigation unleashed by Cochrane Johnstone disrupted the operations of the Stock Exchange and in one instance provoked a fist fight between his agent and a broker on whom the agent was trying to serve a writ.

Cochrane Johnstone was involved in an even more bizarre episode and one that establishes some kind of link between himself and M'Rae. Shortly after the arrest of de Berenger at Leith, Cochrane Johnstone wrote as follows to the Chairman of the Stock Exchange Committee investigating the fraud:

To the Chairman of the Committee, Stock Exchange,
No. 18 Great Cumberland Street

12th April 1814

Sir,
I have this moment received a letter, of which the enclosed is a copy, and lose no time in transmitting it to you for the information of the gentlemen composing the Stock Exchange Committee; from the bearer of the letter, I am given to understand, that Mr M'Rae is willing to disclose the names of the Principals concerned in the late hoax, on being paid the sum of £10,000 to be deposited in some banker's hands, in the names of two persons, to be nominated by himself, and to be paid to him on the conviction of the offenders.

I am happy to say, that there seems now a reasonable prospect of discovering the authors of the late hoax, and I cannot evince my anxious wish to promote such discovery, more than by assuring you that I am ready to contribute liberally towards the above sum of £10,000 and I rest assured, that you will eagerly avail yourselves of this opportunity, to effect the proposed discovery (an object you profess to have so much at heart) by concurring with me in such contribution.

I have the honour to be Sir,

Your obedient humble servant,

(signed) A. Cochrane Johnstone

Enclosed was the letter from M'Rae, which ran as follows:

April 12th

Sir,

I authorise the bearer of this note, to state to you that I am prepared to lay before the Public the names of the persons who planned and carried into effect the late hoax, practiced at the Stock Exchange the 21st February, provided you accede to the terms which my friend will lay before you.

I am, Sir,

Your obedient Servant,

A. M'Rae

Perhaps unsurprisingly the Stock Exchange Committee did not reply to this offer of information, and in a follow-up letter delivered by hand on 18 April Cochrane Johnstone declared that he, Lord Cochrane and Mr Butt were each willing to subscribe £1,000 towards the £10,000 required by Mr M'Rae as his price for revealing the names of the culprits (Cochrane later admitted that he had allowed his name to be included in his uncle's proposal). But the Stock Exchange, which was by now well advanced in its preparations for a trial, would not be drawn.

While on the run, de Berenger was not in a position to put his own case before the public. However, two witnesses came forward with evidence that, if true, would rule out the possibility that de Berenger was the masquerading du Bourg. De Berenger's long-standing servant, William Smith, and his wife, Anne, made voluntary affidavits on 24 March insisting that this was done for the vindication of their master's character and without any prompting by or collaboration with anyone else – although Smith did take the affidavits straight away to Mr Cochrane Johnstone so they could be published in the latter's pamphlet attacking the Stock Exchange Committee's findings. In his affidavit, William Smith said that de Berenger had slept at home on the night of Sunday 20 February. At around midday on the Monday he had gone into de Berenger's room and seen there a grey military greatcoat, his master's green drill dress and a black coat, which was not his master's, lying on a chair. Anne Smith's affidavit was along similar lines, saying that de Berenger's bed had been slept in on the Sunday night and that on the Monday he had come home at about noon in a hackney coach, wearing a black coat and carrying a bundle 'which by its appearance contained his grey military greatcoat and green uniform'. The Smiths' evidence was entirely consistent with Cochrane's own affidavit in suggesting that de Berenger had been wearing his green drill uniform but had returned in a borrowed black coat. However, it also went much further: if de Berenger had indeed slept at home on that Sunday night he could not have been knocking on the door of the Ship Inn, Dover, in the early hours of Monday.

By the time an indictment for conspiracy was presented before the Grand Jury for the City of London on 27 April the British public had been treated to a flood of sensational allegations and counter-allegations relating to the extraordinary events of 21 February. The intensity of the propaganda war conducted through posters, the press and pamphlets meant that most of the key issues to be determined in court had already been given a good airing in the run-up to the trial. The main elements of the prosecution and defence cases, as they appeared to the public, can be summarised as follows:

- The sub-plotters who had masqueraded as French officers in a coach and four had effectively owned up, although they denied any connection with the main plot involving Colonel du Bourg.
- The Stock Exchange Committee had found evidence, in the form of witness descriptions and identification, that du Bourg was de Berenger. However, the latter's servants had produced

affidavits that, if true, provided a cast-iron alibi for de Berenger.

- The Stock Exchange Committee had found circumstantial evidence linking du Bourg's fraud to Cochrane, Cochrane Johnstone and Butt. This was based on the allegation that de Berenger was du Bourg; the admitted fact that de Berenger had visited Cochrane on the Monday morning; the allegation that he had been wearing at that time the red uniform in which he had committed the fraud; the fact that money found on de Berenger had previously been in the possession of members of the investment syndicate; and the unusual pattern of Stock Exchange transactions, which had enabled the investment syndicate to profit handsomely from the temporary surge in prices in the morning of 21 February.

The investment syndicate's defence to these allegations was that du Bourg was not de Berenger, that the syndicate's investment activities were routine and easily explained and that the tracing of money into the possession of de Berenger also had an innocent explanation.

Cochrane's personal defence had been set out in his affidavit. Clearly, if du Bourg was not de Berenger, he had no case to answer, since de Berenger's visit to his house was the key factor linking him to the fraud. On the other hand, if it were proved that de Berenger was du Bourg, Cochrane had provided an innocent explanation for de Berenger's visit to his house as well as evidence suggesting that de Berenger had been wearing his green uniform rather than a red coat. Cochrane could therefore argue that he had no reason to suspect de Berenger of having committed the fraud even if it turned out that he was du Bourg. Furthermore, Cochrane claimed that he volunteered the information that de Berenger had come to his house, thereby giving the Stock Exchange the first intimation that du Bourg might be de Berenger. This information, it might be supposed, would not have been so freely provided if Cochrane was a co-conspirator. (However, Cochrane was mistaken on this last point: the Stock Exchange Committee had five days prior to the publication of his affidavit given a £250 reward to an unnamed gentleman for identifying du Bourg as de Berenger.) Cochrane could also take comfort in the fact that his version of events was supported not only by the affidavits of his own servants but also by the affidavits of de Berenger's servants. Against this background Cochrane claimed later that he felt entirely confident in a favourable outcome to the trial.

It was now left to the judicial process to determine a number of key questions. Was de Berenger really du Bourg, given the conflict of evidence? Was de Berenger wearing a red or green coat when interviewed by Cochrane at his house in Green Street? What investment policy lay behind the syndicate partners' suspicious Stock Exchange transactions? And how was it that de Berenger ended up in Leith with money that had previously been in the possession of members of the investment syndicate? The stage was set for the hearing of these issues in what was to become one of the most contentious and high-profile cases ever to come before an English court.

FIVE

The Case for the Prosecution

An indictment for conspiracy was presented on 27 April to the Grand Jury for the City of London at the Old Bailey against de Berenger, Lord Cochrane, Cochrane Johnstone and Butt, as well as those involved in the sub-plot led by Holloway. The charges having been accepted, the case was then removed to the Court of King's Bench for trial on 8 June. Under the procedures of the King's Bench the defendants were able to appear at the trial by attorney instead of in person, although de Berenger, who was already in custody on a charge under the Alien Acts, was present throughout the proceedings. Cochrane himself declined to attend even as a spectator, preferring to pursue his lamp patent. Because the case involved quite complex financial matters, a 'special' jury was selected from a list of merchants produced by the Sheriff of London. This was normal procedure, although Cochrane was later to suggest that the jury was 'packed'.

The trial, which was to be held at the Guildhall before Lord Ellenborough, Lord Chief Justice of the King's Bench, brought together a galaxy of legal talent that has seldom been equalled. Edward Law, first Baron Ellenborough, was the presiding judge. The son of a bishop, he had established a formidable reputation at the Bar, his advocacy having played a major part in the acquittal of Warren Hastings, Governor General of the East India Company, in the most famous state trial in English history. He had been appointed Lord Chief Justice in 1802 and was to hold that office for sixteen years, during which time he showed himself to be a man of unbending strength of character. He was no respecter of persons, had an irascible temper and was acknowledged, even by his detractors, to be incapable of a dishonest act.

The Stock Exchange, which was bringing the prosecution, entrusted its leading brief to Richard Gurney. Gurney, a member of a well-known Quaker family, already had a large criminal practice but it was the reputation he established in the handling of the Cochrane case that was to bring him to the forefront of his profession. Gurney was assisted by two other counsel, Bolland and Adolphus, both of whom had already established strong reputations at the Bar.

Cochrane, Cochrane Johnstone and Butt were represented by the same counsel, although different solicitors. Their leading counsel was William Best who had been appointed a King's Serjeant or Counsel in 1799. He was a dapper man of independent means whose considerable success at the Bar was attributable to an agile mind and a remarkable ability to cajole, charm and persuade juries. He later became a judge in the Court of King's Bench and then Chief Justice of the Common Pleas. Best was assisted by a trio of outstanding lawyers, Topping, Scarlett and Brougham, and together they constituted a formidable defence team.

The defendants were charged with unlawfully conspiring by false rumours and reports to induce others to believe that Napoleon Bonaparte was dead and that a peace would soon be made, thereby prompting a great rise in the price of government securities to the injury of those who, on 21 February 1814, were purchasers of stock. In opening the case for the prosecution, Gurney underlined the gravity of the offence: to circulate false news, still more to conspire to circulate false news, with intent to raise the price of any commodity was, by the Law of England, a crime. If the intent was to raise the price of government securities, the potential damage to the public and therefore the gravity of the offence was still higher. If the object of the conspiracy was not merely to abuse the public credulity, but to enable the conspirators to sell out of securities on terms favourable to themselves but disadvantageous to others, the offence assumed the character of cold-blooded fraud. It was then capable of but one further aggravation, and that was, if the conspirators endeavoured to poison the sources of official intelligence, and to make the officers of government the instruments of their fraud. It was this offence, in its most aggravated form, with which the defendants were charged.

Gurney recounted in detail the events of the morning of 21 February. He began with the appearance of the officer in red at the Ship Inn in Dover shortly after midnight, followed by the dispatch of a letter to Admiral Foley at Deal. He then described the officer's coach journey up to London and the spreading of news of a great victory, which prompted a surge in the price of government bonds after the Stock Exchange opened for business at 10 a.m. He alluded to the extraordinary coincidence of the Stock Exchange dealings of the defendants who sold out completely on that Monday morning with a profit of a little more than £10,000, noting that, 'if the telegraph had worked, that ten thousand would have been nearer a hundred thousand'.

Gurney then focused on the core defence provided by Cochrane in his own voluntary affidavit of 11 March. After criticising the use of such affidavits, on which no indictment for perjury could be maintained, Gurney challenged Cochrane's version of events in a scathing attack, the key passages of which are reproduced here in full:

Let us examine it: Lord Cochrane tells us that being at this manufactury of Mr King's he received a note, the name of the writer of which he cannot read, yet, that he hastens home directly; engaged as he is in supervising the making of a Lamp for which he had a patent – engaged too in this tremendous stock account, which is at this very moment, under the guardian care of Mr Cochrane Johnstone and Mr Butt, being liquidated, he instantly quits the City, and hastens home to see a person whose signature he cannot decypher, and when he comes there he finds Mr De Berenger to be the writer of the note, and he has all this extraordinary conversation with him about going on board the *Tonnant* to instruct the crew in sharp-shooting, and then when Mr De Berenger's application is refused at least for the present, Mr De Berenger tells him he '*cannot go to Lord Yarmouth or to any other of his friends in this dress*'. Why, I beg to know, cannot Mr De Berenger go to Lord Yarmouth or any other nobleman or gentleman in the dress in which he waits upon Lord Cochrane?

If he was dressed as Lord Cochrane describes, there could be no impropriety. As for the suggestion that his dress might excite suspicion on returning to his lodging, how could this be? *Coming out* of his lodging in this dress might excite suspicion, for persons who saw him might imagine that a gentleman thus dressed was going a little beyond the rules of the King's Bench, but how could his *return* excite suspicion? If he was returning to his lodgings why would he want any other dress unless he was afraid to return to his lodgings in that dress because it would afford the means of tracing and detecting him? According to Lord Cochrane de Berenger *requested the favour of borrowing a hat to wear instead of his military cap*. Then we are to suppose that De Berenger was satisfied; he had got rid of this cap with the gold border which might excite suspicion, and he was content to go. No says Lord Cochrane that will not do. '*Having tried the hat on, his uniform appeared under his great coat, I therefore offered him a black coat that was laying on a chair and which I did not intend to take with me.*' We are, I presume then, to understand that he put on the black coat, wrapped his uniform in a towel and shortly afterwards went away.

Gurney questioned the character of a person in Cochrane's eminent position who was prepared on his own admission to assist an undischarged debtor to escape the rules of the King's Bench:

Gentlemen, I am sorry to find that my Lord Cochrane, filling the high situation that he does, sees nothing wrong in assisting a person within the rules of King's Bench to abscond, for whose stay within those rules sureties have entered into a bond; either Lord Cochrane's mind has confounded all right and wrong, or what is more probable, he confesses this smaller delinquency to conceal the greater.

Gurney then drew particular attention to the colour of the military uniform which de Berenger was wearing when he arrived at 13 Green Street. Its crucial significance lay in the fact that if

Cochrane saw de Berenger in the red uniform of an aide-de-camp he would know he was an imposter, whereas the green uniform of Lord Yarmouth's sharpshooters would arouse no suspicion:

> Another part of this affidavit is very important, '*Captain Berenger wore a grey great coat, a green uniform, and a military cap.*' I will prove to you that the uniform was scarlet, that it was embroidered with gold, and that there was a star on the breast. I will prove that by many persons who saw it, and I will produce it to you today.

Having dealt savagely with Cochrane's affidavit, Gurney went on to address three specific issues: the pattern of securities sales by the investment syndicate; the identification of du Bourg with de Berenger; and the tracing of money from the investment syndicate into the hands of de Berenger.

Cochrane, Cochrane Johnstone and Butt had suggested in their pre-trial defence that their sales of stock on the early morning of Monday 21 February pointed to their innocence. This was because they sold well below the top of the market and at a relatively modest profit: had they waited to sell later that day they could have done much better. However, Gurney turned this argument on its head by suggesting that it was because the investment syndicate knew the good 'news' to be false that they took the earliest opportunity of unloading their securities, correctly anticipating that prices would fall as soon as the hoax was exposed:

> They have thought it a favorable circumstance for them that they sold out their stock early in the day at a small profit; in my mind it is one of the strongest circumstances against them. If they had believed the news would they have sold out early, and at that small profit? Why did they sell out? Because they knew that belief in the news would last but a very short time, and that they must take advantage of it without delay, for when I have stated that ten thousand five hundred pounds was the amount of their profit I have very much understated it: their profit vastly exceeded that,

their profit was all they had been saved from losing. In the language of the stock exchange, they were *Bulls* and, having raised prices by their purchases, they had gone on plunging deeper and deeper till they were completely out of their depth. They could not have got rid of their million of omnium and stock without an immense loss; and when they tell me they sold at once, I say yes, so you did, that is my argument against you: I say you did not wait half an hour when the news came, but as soon as prices rose Mr Fearn was set to work – he was ordered to sell, and he did sell by twenties, thirties, forties, and fifties of thousands, and in the hurry and confusion they were in, one sold ten thousand Consols less than he had, and the other twenty-four thousand Omnium more than he had; I think therefore this selling early, and selling at a small profit will not much avail them, but very much the contrary.

On the question of du Bourg's identity, it was obvious that if the officer in red could be shown to be de Berenger, the latter's meeting with Cochrane in Green Street became highly suspicious. If, on the other hand, du Bourg was not de Berenger, Cochrane had no case to answer. In dealing with this issue, Gurney attacked on two fronts. First, he questioned the veracity of the voluntary affidavits sworn by de Berenger's servants, which, if true, provided an alibi for de Berenger. Second, he referred to the various witnesses along the coach route to London who were able to identify the officer in red as the man now sitting before them in court.

As for the Smiths' affidavits, Gurney pointed out that an alibi is the best of all defences if a man is innocent, but if it turns out to be untrue, it is conclusive proof against those who resort to it. He noted that it was Cochrane, Cochrane Johnstone and Butt who arranged for the publication of the Smiths' affidavits, and that in form the affidavits were very similar to those used by Cochrane himself and his servants because (unusually) the signatory used the first rather than the third person ('I William Smith, servant to Baron de Berenger, do swear . . . '). The implication was that the Smiths' affidavits had been originated and even drafted by the investment syndicate themselves, assuming that de Berenger was by then safe out of the country, with no risk of contradiction from those who might identify him as du Bourg.

However, de Berenger was arrested in Leith on 8 April and on being brought to London was shown to various people who had seen du Bourg in the course of his journey from Dover to Green Street. Every one of these persons, according to Gurney, identified de Berenger as du Bourg and an identification was also made by a Mr Solomon, an army accoutrement maker, who was to be called as a prosecution witness (see p. 44). Gurney then turned to the jury:

> Gentlemen, what now becomes of these affidavits and of those who made them? What becomes of this alibi for Mr De Berenger? What becomes of the affidavits of his servants Smith and his wife? What becomes of Lord Cochrane swearing as he does to his green coat? Why do persons resort to falsehood, but because truth convicts them?

Having challenged Cochrane's story and cast doubt on the de Berenger alibi, Gurney drew attention to further evidence linking the Cochrane investment syndicate to de Berenger. This was in the form of bank notes found in the possession of de Berenger when he was arrested at Leith, and also notes found to have been used by him during his journey North via Hull and Sunderland. It was possible to trace the origins of such notes, first, because they were numbered by the issuing bank and second, because notes when transferred were often endorsed with the name of the transferee.

The most important single transaction (see Exhibit 3) was a cheque for £470 14s 4d drawn by Smallbone (one of the investment syndicate's brokers) on bankers Jones, Lloyd & Co. on 19 February and given to Cochrane. This cheque was cashed in the form of one £200 note, two £100 notes, one £50 note and some small notes and coins. On 24 February the £200 note was, on Butt's instructions, exchanged by a clerk at bankers Bond and Co. into two £100 notes which the same clerk then carried to the Bank of England and exchanged again – this time for 200 £1 notes. They were returned to

Butt who gave them to Cochrane Johnstone. Of these 200 £1 notes, several had been paid in Hull, where de Berenger was at the time. Others had been returned to the Bank, marked with de Berenger's name, and sixty-seven were found in de Berenger's writing desk at Leith. On the same day that the £200 note was exchanged (24 February), the two notes of £100 were taken to the Bank of England by another clerk and exchanged for a further 200 £1 notes which were given to Butt. Of these, forty-seven came back to the Bank with de Berenger's name on them and forty-nine more were found in de Berenger's writing desk at Leith.

These multiple transactions using different banks, varying note denominations and different clerks were suspicious to say the least, suggesting as they did a deliberate attempt to obscure the route by which some £540 encashed by members of the investment syndicate had ended up in the hands of the alleged chief perpetrator of the fraud. The implication was that de Berenger had received this sum for his masquerade, spending some of it on his travels North while attempting to flee the country.

Having established these financial links between the Cochrane investment syndicate and de Berenger, Gurney then referred contemptuously to the letter written by Cochrane Johnstone to the Stock Exchange Committee on 12 April. This had enclosed M'Rae's offer to disclose the names of the true perpetrators of the 'hoax' on payment of £10,000. Gurney objected to the use of the word 'hoax', and begged to know what word in Cochrane Johnstone's vocabulary would be found to express fraud. He suggested that the Stock Exchange Committee must be thought very gullible to pay any serious attention to such a letter, noting that undoubtedly the committee

> would have had no objection to the assistance of an accomplice, but it must not be an accomplice chosen by his associates . . . [for such] is not chosen to divulge but to suppress the truth. . . . Gentlemen, what men would have resorted to such a scheme but men who felt they were on the eve of detection, and who tried this desperate expedient to see whether they could ward it off?

In concluding his speech for the prosecution, Gurney characterised the Cochranes and Butt as the main beneficiaries and authors of the fraud, de Berenger as their principal agent and the others as subordinates – even though it could not be proved that the parties had met and conferred and assigned to each other their respective roles. He then asked the jury to return a verdict of guilty:

> It will show the world that as there is no man beneath the law, so there is no man above it. It will teach evil minded persons the absurdity of expecting that schemes of fraud can be so formed as to provide for all events. It will teach them that no caution can insure safety: that there is no contrivance, that there is no device, no stratagem, which can shield them from detection, from punishment, and from infamy.

The prosecution then called a number of witnesses from whose evidence it was possible to trace the movements of the officer in red from his first appearance at the Ship Inn in Dover to his arrival at Cochrane's house in Green Street, via staging posts at Canterbury, Sittingbourne, Rochester and Dartford. Several of these witnesses – including the innkeeper William Wright from Rochester, the postboy Thomas Shilling, who had ridden the last stage from Dartford, and hackney-coachman William Crane, who had taken du Bourg from the Marsh Gate to Green Street – positively identified du Bourg as de Berenger as he sat before them in court.

Shilling's examination revealed how nervous du Bourg had become when approaching the outskirts of London (Exhibit 4). On being told that the Bricklayers Arms was the first hackney coach stand, du Bourg had said it would not do since it was too public and somebody might 'cast some reflections'. He was then driven to the Three Stags in the Lambeth Road, but there was no hackney coach there so Shilling suggested that they drive on to the coach stand at Marsh Gate where 'I dared to say nobody would take any notice of him'. On reaching Marsh Gate, Shilling noticed that the officer had pulled up the side-blind of the coach as if to conceal himself. Shilling then drove him alongside the only coach at the stand and the officer, after stepping from one vehicle to the next without touching the ground, handed down to Shilling two Napoleon coins. Questioned about the officer's dress, Shilling said that he wore a red coat underneath his brownish outer-coat and when asked whether he could see the gentleman in court he pointed without hesitation to de Berenger.

While the evidence of Shilling and other eye-witnesses showed clearly that du Bourg's military uniform was red, there was to be much greater controversy over the colour of the uniform in which de Berenger presented himself to Cochrane in Green Street – an issue that had a direct bearing on whether Cochrane himself was implicated in the plot. As we know, Cochrane in his affidavit claimed that de Berenger's uniform was green, but Crane, the hackney coachman, stated in his cross-examination, 'this gentleman that I took from a post-chaise and four, when he got out at Green Street I saw that he had a red coat underneath his great coat'.

Crane's evidence was particularly important to the prosecution case (Exhibit 5), but it included one statement that, as it turned out, was helpful to the defence. Crane said that he was the driver of a hackney coach, licence number 890, and that he had taken a fare at Marsh Gate on the morning of 21 February from a gentleman who had come on a post-chaise and four from Dartford. He was directed to drive to Grosvenor Square and when he got there the gentleman put down the front glass and told him to go to 13 Green Street. On arriving at Green Street, the gentleman got out and asked for colonel or captain somebody (he did not know the name) and they said he was gone to breakfast in Cumberland Street. The gentleman then asked if he could write a note for him and he went into the parlour. According to Crane, before he went in 'the gentleman gave me four shillings and I said I hoped he would give me another shilling: he took out a bit of a portmanteau that he had, and a sword, and went in, and came out into the passage and gave me another shilling'. The portmanteau was a small black leather one but (and this curious description was to prove helpful to Cochrane) it was 'big enough to wrap a coat in'. Crane was then asked whether he saw the gentleman in court and he said, 'I think this is the gentleman here,' pointing at de Berenger.

During cross-examination it was suggested to Crane that he could not possibly recollect every person he carried in his hackney coach every day. This elicited the response that was so damaging to Cochrane's defence: 'No, but this gentleman that I took from a post chaise and four, when he got out in Green Street I saw that he had a red coat underneath his great coat.' If du Bourg was de Berenger and had arrived at Green Street in the red costume in which he had committed the fraud, it would be difficult to believe Cochrane's version of events – unless, that is, de Berenger had the opportunity to change into his green drill dress while at Green Street before Cochrane returned from the City.

Mr Simon Solomon, a military accoutrement maker, was then called as a prosecution witness. He had a shop at Charing Cross and another at New Street, Covent Garden. He confirmed that on Saturday 19 February he had sold to a gentleman at his Charing Cross shop a scarlet regimental coat described as the uniform of an aide-de-camp, with embroidered gold lace, a star and a badge. He had also sold to the same gentleman a military greatcoat and a foraging cap made of dark fur with a pale gold band. When it was suggested that the items might be taken on hire, the gentleman had said he would rather purchase them and he did so, paying for them in £1 notes and taking them away in a hackney coach. The gentleman had told Solomon that the items were wanted for someone who was to play the character of a foreign officer; they were to be sent into the country that evening. Solomon then identified the fragments dredged up from the Thames as the remnants of the red coat and the star and badge that he had sold. When Solomon had been taken to see de Berenger before the trial, he said he recognised him as the person who had bought the clothes but in court he was more guarded: he would only say that the person resembled de Berenger except that he had black whiskers.

Mr and Mrs Davidson were then called as witnesses. They had a house in the Asylum Buildings where de Berenger was their lodger. He and his servants occupied the four rooms on the upper floor, while the Davidsons occupied the two parlours downstairs. The Davidsons knew when de Berenger was in residence because he rang for his servants, paced about a lot and played the trumpet or violin in the early morning. According to their evidence, de Berenger left the house wearing a new greatcoat at around 11 a.m. on Sunday 20 February and they did not hear or see anything of him until the afternoon of the following day. Mrs Davidson also said that a gentleman, whom she later identified as Cochrane Johnstone, left a letter for de Berenger on the evening of Saturday 26 February, the day before de Berenger quit his lodgings. In her evidence Mrs Davidson also stated that de Berenger wore whiskers when he was her lodger (in court he was clean-shaven).

After dealing with the question of the identification of de Berenger as du Bourg and the former's alibi, the prosecution called witnesses to give evidence on the defendants' stock transactions. First to appear was Joseph Fearn, a stockbroker who acted for the investment syndicate, mainly (but not always) on the instructions of Butt. By a curious coincidence it transpired that on the very morning in question, 21 February, Fearn had moved his office from 86 Cornhill to 5 Shorters Court, close to the side door of the Stock Exchange. The office was one of a suite of three rooms, the others being occupied by Butt, Cochrane, Cochrane Johnstone and their clerk, Lance. Mr Fearn had removed a transparent blind with 'Fearn, Stock-Broker' imprinted on it in black lettering and put it in the window of his new office. A Mr Charles Addis who had responsibility for letting 5 Shorters Court, gave evidence that Cochrane Johnstone rented an office there on 15 February and then took the further rooms, one for Butt and one for Fearn, having left a rather curious letter for Mr Addis on 17 February. In part this read: 'I called again upon you to know if you have powers to sell the house, part of which I have taken, as I find there are several persons in the house at present, which is rather awkward, and makes it too public.'

Fearn said that between 12 and 19 February he traded actively for the investment syndicate and for this purpose met Butt daily, frequently in the company of Cochrane and Cochrane Johnstone. On the morning of 21 February he had sold all the stock in the names of his three principals, amounting in total to £413,000

Omnium and £268,000 Consols. The Omnium had been sold at prices ranging from 29¼ to 30½ and the Consols from 70⅝ to 72¼. Fearn had evidently dashed backwards and forwards between the Exchange and his office next door where Butt and Cochrane Johnstone (Cochrane was not there) gave him instructions as the market responded to the news of the military messenger from Dover.

Three other brokers were called – Robert Hitchins who had acted for Cochrane Johnstone, William Smallbone who had acted for Butt and Cochrane Johnstone, and Malcolm Richardson, a bookseller and part-time broker, who undertook business for Butt. It emerged that on the morning of 21 February the combined sales of all the brokers acting for the investment syndicate (including Fearn) amounted to £795,000 Omnium and £278,000 Consols. Of particular significance was the evidence of Richardson who said that on the morning of Saturday 19 February Butt asked him to purchase £150,000 Omnium but Richardson baulked at such a large order and only purchased £30,000. It would seem that the investment syndicate's stock purchases had stretched their credit to its limit.

On this last point, it should be pointed out that the bulk of the stock purchases appear to have been forward transactions or contracts 'for time'. Questions were asked in court as to whether the securities bought by the syndicate had been immediately paid for but Lord Ellenborough intervened to point out that no broker was obliged to incriminate himself by answering. Contracts 'for time' had long been prohibited under Barnard's Act and a broker who admitted to selling securities that his principal did not actually possess at the time of sale exposed himself to the risk of legal action. However, another witness, Mr Francis Bailey of the Stock Exchange, was under no such constraint and he gave his opinion that the size of the syndicate's transactions indicated they must be time bargains.

Among other witnesses called by the prosecution was Le Marchant, whose attempts to blackmail Cochrane have already been described. It was shown in cross-examination that his evidence relating to de Berenger's familiarity with Cochrane had only been given after Cochrane had refused him a loan. In his later summing up, Lord Ellenborough referred to Le Marchant in scathing terms and suggested that he was a person 'whom the Government might do very well in letting ride at anchor here without going abroad' (he was due to take up a government appointment overseas but this was later revoked).

One intriguing piece of evidence to emerge from the prosecution evidence relates to the documents found in de Berenger's writing case at Leith. An extract from a memorandum-book belonging to de Berenger read as follows:

> To C.J., by March 1st, 1814, £350–£4 to 5,000 – assign one share of patent and £1,000 worth of shares of Jn. De Baufain at Messrs H. to their care. – Believe from my informant £18,000 instead of £4,800 – suspicious that Mr B. does not account correctly to him as well as to me – Determined not to be duped. No restrictions as to secrecy – requesting early answer.

Gurney suggested that this was a note of a letter written by de Berenger to Cochrane Johnstone on 1 March. The first part is obscure but de Berenger then appears to express his concern that the combined investment gains of Butt ('Mr B') and Cochrane Johnstone were not £4,800 as they had reported to him but rather £18,000. (It is perhaps significant that in his letter to the Stock Exchange of 14 March Cochrane Johnstone had reported that the combined profits from his and Butt's sales of stock on 21 February was £4,800.) Since de Berenger was evidently remunerated on the basis of a percentage share of their profits, he was understandably anxious to clarify the matter. This, at any rate, was Gurney's interpretation of the note.

The prosecution finally called witnesses relating to the tracing of bank notes into de Berenger's hands. This involved detailed statements from bank clerks and others as to numbering of notes and the exchange of notes of different denominations. By the time this was completed it was around 10 p.m. and the court had been sitting since 9 a.m. After a session of thirteen hours, counsel were no doubt extremely tired, but Lord Ellenborough said that he would like to hear the opening speech for the defence and get into the defendants' case as far as he could since there were several public officials attending as witnesses who could not, without great inconvenience, appear the next day. The opening case for the defence was therefore presented by weary lawyers late that night and into the early hours of the following morning – a circumstance that attracted considerable criticism after the trial. In any event, conscious of the heavy responsibility that now lay upon him, Serjeant Best rose to address the jury at around 10.30 p.m.

SIX

The Case for the Defence

Serjeant Best began his speech for the defence by acknowledging the gravity of the offences charged, although he also noted that while certain innocent investors had no doubt been damaged by the so-called hoax, the great majority of those affected were stock-market gamblers for whom there could be little public sympathy.

Best then outlined his approach to the defence of his three clients. The question of whether du Bourg was or was not de Berenger was a matter to be addressed not by him but by de Berenger's own counsel, Park. However, since those he represented had no case to answer if du Bourg were not in fact de Berenger, he would present his defence as if this identity had already been proved (although he trusted that Park would be able to prove the contrary). He said he would present the case of each defendant in turn, following the order in which they appeared in the indictment, taking Cochrane first, then Cochrane Johnstone and finally Butt.

Best focused on three circumstances that allegedly linked Cochrane to the fraud: the notes found on de Berenger in Leith, Cochrane's Stock Exchange transactions and de Berenger's visit to Cochrane's house on 21 February.

Earlier testimony showed that one £200 note and two £100 notes had been received by Cochrane and that these had been changed into £1 notes which had been traced into the hands of de Berenger (see Exhibit 3). Best argued that since the two £100 notes received by Cochrane had been given by him to Butt and that it was on Butt's instructions that they were exchanged for £1 notes, there was nothing to link Cochrane directly to de Berenger. He would later provide an innocent explanation for Butt's transactions. However, no explanation was given by Best for the £200 note received by

Cochrane – a matter that Cochrane sought to clarify after the trial (see p. 88).

So far as Cochrane's Stock Exchange transactions were concerned, the defence focused on three points in his favour. First, contrary to the impression given by the Stock Exchange, Cochrane had been speculating actively in government bonds as far back as the previous November and counsel was therefore able to argue that his purchases of Omnium in the week prior to 21 February, far from being unusual, were merely the continuation of a pattern of heavy trading that had taken place over several months. Similarly, Cochrane's sale of £139,000 Omnium on that Monday could not be viewed as suspicious, given the scale of earlier transactions. Second, Best argued that the sale of Cochrane's stock on 21 February was the result of previous instructions given to his broker to sell whenever a profit of 1 per cent could be obtained. Furthermore, Cochrane was not himself present in the City that Monday and the stock was sold without any further instructions from him – indeed some sales evidently occurred before either Butt or Cochrane Johnstone arrived on the scene. Finally, Best made great play with the argument that if Cochrane had really been in the know as far as the fraud was concerned, he would have been aware that the Stock Exchange bubble that developed on the Monday morning would soon burst. Surely, then, he would have taken advantage of this knowledge not merely by selling the stock of which he was already possessed but also by engaging in time bargains or forward contracts for the sale of stock which he did not possess. Yet neither Cochrane, nor his partners, engaged in such forward transactions, thereby missing an opportunity to make their fortunes. The implication was that they were unaware of the fraud and believed the incoming news of Napoleon's death to be true.

There remained the crucial question of de Berenger's visit to Cochrane's house on that Monday morning. Here Best went through the version of events described in Cochrane's voluntary affidavit, and referred to corroborating evidence that would be provided by witnesses to be called for the defence. He argued that it was Cochrane's affidavit which had first supplied the name of de Berenger to the Stock Exchange – but for Cochrane's statement the Exchange would be entirely ignorant of de Berenger's existence. Was it the act of a guilty man knowingly to point out to the prosecution the identity of an individual who might link him directly to the fraud? (In fact Best was mistaken: as previously explained, the Stock Exchange had rewarded an informer for identifying de Berenger prior to the date of Cochrane's affidavit.)

Then, quite unexpectedly, in the midst of a robust defence of his client's conduct, Best appeared to make a damaging retraction of a key statement contained in Cochrane's affidavit. This concerned de Berenger's dress on his arrival at Green Street, a subject introduced by counsel almost as an afterthought.

> Gentlemen, it has been said that this affidavit is false in this; that it states that Mr de Berenger when he came to Lord Cochrane's had on a green coat, whereas it is proved by several witnesses that he had on a red one; but let me suppose that their account as to the colour of the coat is true, and that Lord Cochrane's account is incorrect. Gentlemen, I think I can account for the mistake; my Lord Cochrane made this affidavit a great many days, I think some weeks, after the transaction had taken place; Mr de Berenger belonged to a corps of riflemen in this country, commanded by Lord Yarmouth, and the proper dress of Mr de Berenger, as a member of that corps was a green uniform; my Lord Cochrane had often seen Mr de Berenger in this green uniform. His lordship, when he made his affidavit, recollected the circumstance of Mr De Berenger's being dressed in a military uniform, but there being nothing to fix on his lordship's mind the colour of the uniform, the sort of dress in which he had been accustomed to see Mr de Berenger presented itself to his lordship's mind as the dress de Berenger wore when his lordship saw him last.

The damaging admission made on behalf of Cochrane by his own counsel that de Berenger had appeared at 13 Green Street dressed in his incriminating red uniform, was later to become a matter of intense controversy. In the post-trial debate Cochrane insisted that de Berenger had appeared to him in green and accused Best of misrepresenting his case, a mistake due allegedly to his extreme exhaustion at that late hour. We will return to this contradiction between Cochrane and his legal advisers at a later point, but as far as the trial goes it was Best's version that was laid before the jury.

In concluding his defence of Cochrane, Best reminded the jury of Cochrane's eminent position in the life of the nation: 'Is a man so circumstanced likely to commit so sordid a crime as that with which he is charged? No prospect of gain could hold out any temptation to Lord Cochrane to put in hazard what he now possesses.'

Best then turned to the case of Cochrane Johnstone. Here, again, the defendant's Stock Exchange transactions had been presented in a false light, since he had traded actively on a large scale well before the events of 21 February and there was nothing to differentiate his actions on that day from his previous conduct. The taking of an office in Shorters Court could not be viewed as suspicious because no office was needed for a fraud that would be over in a single day. As for the letter allegedly left by Cochrane Johnstone at de Berenger's lodgings on 26 February, the day before the latter's flight North, he would not dispute the fact, but what was so suspicious about one close acquaintance leaving a note at the house of another? Finally, with regard to the notes found on de Berenger, some of which had passed through the hands of Cochrane Johnstone, there was a perfectly innocent explanation: de Berenger, who was a most ingenious draftsman, had prepared plans for a new Ranelagh, or pleasure gardens, to be called Vittoria, which Cochrane Johnstone was planning to develop near Alsop's Buildings in Paddington. Cochrane Johnstone, according to counsel, paid £200 to de Berenger on 25 or 26 February in respect of this work and lent him a further £200, being 'exceedingly desirous of relieving the distresses of Mr de Berenger'.

Moving on to the case of Butt, the defence argued along the same lines as for Cochrane Johnstone. Regarding the question of notes shown to have passed through the hands of Butt to de Berenger, a simple explanation could be offered: the £400 provided by

Cochrane Johnstone to de Berenger, in payment for his services as well as by way of loan, had been given first to Butt, who acted as Cochrane Johnstone's agent, and was then paid by Butt to de Berenger after the large denomination notes had been exchanged into £1 notes.

Having dealt with the three cases separately, Best suggested that it was hardly credible that there was a conspiracy since there was no evidence that the alleged conspirators (who included the sub-plotters Holloway, Lyte, Sanders and M'Rae) had been seen together or communicated with each other. Indeed, the seizure of de Berenger's papers had not yielded a single message written between the parties – and without communication there could be no conspiracy.

Finally, Serjeant Best appealed to the jury to consider the eminent position of the three defendants:

> They have all up to this moment been the best possible characters, two of them are persons of very high and distinguished situations in life, members of a very noble family; and with respect to one of them, he has reflected back on a long and noble line of ancestors more glory than he has received from them, and it would be the most painful moment of my life, if I should tonight find that that wreath of laurel which a life of danger and honour has planted round his brows, should in a moment be blasted by your verdict.

It was after midnight when Serjeant Best sat down and it was then left to Park, de Berenger's counsel, to put the case for his client. The task was unenviable because of the late hour and the fact that, as Park observed to the court, 'it is now sixteen hours and a half since I left my own dwelling'. It was also a daunting challenge because the only question at issue was de Berenger's identification as du Bourg – something that Park would have to dispute despite the numerous witnesses who had identified de Berenger as the officer in red.

De Berenger had managed to obtain witness statements from a number of individuals, including his servants, Mr and Mrs Smith, in order to support his alibi defence. However, unknown to the court, there had been a behind-the-scenes dispute between de Berenger and his lawyers over the advisability of calling these witnesses. In a pre-trial memorandum Park had warned that an alibi defence would not prevail against the evidence of the numerous witnesses who had identified du Bourg as de Berenger. Any witnesses called by de Berenger to support his alibi would probably end up being committed to Newgate and if de Berenger were found guilty, he would very likely have to face the pillory in addition to any punishment. Despite these strong misgivings on the part of his legal advisers, de Berenger insisted on going ahead with his alibi defence.

Park's reluctance to call witnesses in favour of his client was reflected in the unusually hesitant opening of his address to the jury:

Now gentlemen, upon the subject which I am about to address you I should not at this hour in the morning call evidence, but in a matter so highly penal as this is, (and where I am placed in so delicate a situation, and in which, thank God, I can very seldom be placed) I do not think it right to act on my own judgment. My client assures me that he is an innocent person, and is determined to have his witnesses called. He shall have those witnesses called and I shall prove to you most completely that which will dispose of the case, if it is believed.

After this inauspicious beginning, Park proceeded to explain the circumstances in which witnesses had come forward to support de Berenger's alibi. He accepted that de Berenger was in the habit of violating the Rules of the King's Bench, which restricted him to the vicinity of his Lambeth lodgings. In order to do that with safety he used to walk down an alley to the Thames instead of crossing Westminster Bridge, believing that on the bridge he would be more likely to meet officers, which could result in his losing the benefit of the rules. He was well known to the watermen plying there and two of these gentlemen were prepared to swear that on the Sunday morning, which was shortly after the Thames had been reopened after freezing over, de Berenger crossed at the ferry to go over to the Westminster side.

In fact, the watermen failed to appear in court and Gurney suggested caustically that perhaps the river had frozen over again that June morning. Nevertheless there were other witnesses prepared to testify that they had seen de Berenger in Chelsea on the day in question, their familiarity with him being due to the fact that he had lived in the area for some time prior to his confinement within the Rules of the King's Bench.

At around 2 a.m. Park sat down, having addressed the jury for some two hours in the most difficult circumstances. It was then the turn of Serjeant Pell, representing Lyte, Holloway and Sanders (M'Rae having absconded), to present some sort of case for his clients. The only defence that could be offered was that these self-confessed fraudsters were not party to the wider conspiracy involving the investment syndicate and de Berenger. In presenting his argument Pell had to try to persuade the jury that the fact of the two episodes occurring on the same day was a pure coincidence, and that there had been two quite separate plots, both as it happened involving 'military officers' proclaiming the death of Napoleon with the objective of raising the price of government stock.

In winding up his defence for the sub-plotters, Pell drew attention to 'the great misfortune to my learned friends, as well as myself, that we should have been called upon to make our defences, when both you and we are so much exhausted'. It was now 3 a.m. on Thursday and Lord Ellenborough, having allowed the proceedings to continue uninterrupted for eighteen hours, at long last decided that 'this would be the most convenient time for dividing the cause'. Accordingly, the court was adjourned until 10 a.m. – leaving only a few hours respite before battle was joined once more.

When the court reopened the defendants called their witnesses. On behalf of Cochrane statements were made by Lord Melville, Second Lord of the Admiralty, Colonel Torrens, Secretary to the Commander-in-Chief, and a Mr Coulbourne MP, Under-Secretary of State for the Colonial Department, each supporting Cochrane's assertion in his affidavit that application had been made by Sir Alexander Cochrane to allow de Berenger to serve with him on the North American station.

William King was called to confirm that Cochrane had visited his workshop at 1 Cock Lane, Snow Hill, on the morning of 21 February to supervise the manufacture of a new type of signal lamp for use in naval convoys. A clerk in the Adjutant General's office stated that Cochrane's brother, then serving in the south of France, had been placed on the sick list on 25 January, although he could not say when this information was received by him. Thomas Dewman, Cochrane's manservant, gave evidence that he had received a note from a military officer at Green Street and delivered it to Cochrane at King's workshop – although, significantly, he was not questioned by defence counsel as to the colour of the military officer's uniform.

A Mr Gabriel Tahourdin was then called on behalf of Cochrane Johnstone. Tahourdin was de Berenger's attorney and also a close acquaintance and agent of Cochrane Johnstone. He had acted in business dealings between the two defendants. Tahourdin's evidence purportedly went to show that Cochrane Johnstone owed money to de Berenger, thereby helping to explain the notes found in de Berenger's possession which had previously passed through Cochrane Johnstone's hands. Letters from Cochrane Johnstone to Tahourdin and from de Berenger to Cochrane Johnstone were produced and they appeared to show that de Berenger had charged the latter £250 (including a £50 downpayment) for the pleasure garden plans and had requested a further £200 by way of loan. However, the letters had been hand-delivered and therefore not post-marked, which led Lord Ellenborough to observe that such self-serving correspondence could have been written after its stated date.

Park then called Lord Yarmouth on behalf of de Berenger. There had been conflicting testimony given earlier as to whether the letter written by du Bourg in Dover was in de Berenger's handwriting. Lord Yarmouth was Lieutenant Colonel Commandant of the Duke of Cumberland's Sharpshooters and since de Berenger was a non-commissioned officer, acting as adjutant of the corps, there had been considerable correspondence between the two. Asked whether he believed the letter written by du Bourg in Dover was in de Berenger's hand, Lord Yarmouth replied 'Certainly not'. This response appeared to be strongly in de Berenger's favour, although Lord Ellenborough pointed out that if de Berenger was the author of the Dover letter he would hardly have written it in his own recognisable hand.

The questioning of Lord Yarmouth then moved on to the dress of his sharpshooters:

Park. What is the uniform of your corps?

Lord Yarmouth. The uniform is, the waistcoat green, with a crimson cape.

Q. A bottle green, is it not?

A. Some have got it a little darker than others, but it should be a deep bottle-green with a crimson collar; the great coat is a waistcoat with black fur round it, consequently no crimson collar.

Q. The body in your uniform is not red?

A. It is deep bottle green.

Juryman. A jacket or a coat?

A. It is a waistcoat, very like the light-horse uniform.

Lord Ellenborough. It is almost unnecessary to ask you, whether the members of your corps wear any decorations; a star or a cross?

A. When in uniform, some wear medals that they have gained as prizes given by the corps; they occasionally wear them hanging by a ribband.

Q. You wear no such decorations as this? *(showing the star to his lordship)*

A. No certainly not.

Q. Supposing a gentleman appeared before you in an aide-de camp's uniform, with that star upon his breast, and that other ornament appendant, should you consider that was a man exhibiting himself in the dress of your sharp-shooting corps?

A. Certainly not.

Q. If a sharp-shooter belonging to your corps presented himself to you in that dress, you would think it a very impertinent thing?

A. Certainly.

Juryman. If Colonel de Berenger had appeared before your
lordship in the uniform of his corps, would it have been any
thing extraordinary?

A. Nothing extraordinary; it would have been more military that
he should do so, thought I never exacted it.

This last observation was damaging to Cochrane, undermining as it
did the assertion in his affidavit that de Berenger could not have
gone to see Lord Yarmouth in his green drill uniform.

At this juncture de Berenger's alibi defence was brought into play.
The witness line-up began with Mr and Mrs Smith, de Berenger's
servants for the past three and a half years. Mr Smith said that he
knew de Berenger slept at home on the night of Sunday 20 February
because he had let him in at around 11 p.m. and later heard him
going upstairs to his bedroom. He did not see him again until 3 p.m.
on the Monday. Gurney's cross-examination on this last point
revealed that de Berenger was in the habit each morning of washing,
cleaning his teeth, shaving and powdering his hair without calling
for his manservant. The exchange also revealed that Smith had been
handsomely paid off by de Berenger with a £50 note on 27 February
– the day on which the latter disappeared.

Mrs Smith corroborated her husband's version of events but
became confused when cross-examined on the subject of a bundle
containing a grey coat which she said de Berenger had brought
home with him on Monday 21 February.

Lord Ellenborough. What did you see besides the grey coat in the
bundle?

A. I saw nothing but that.

Lord Ellenborough. Recollect yourself, because you have sworn
you saw a green uniform.

A. There might be a green uniform.

Q. Was there, or was there not?

A. Yes, there was a green uniform.

Q. Was it in the bundle or not?

A. Yes it was in the bundle.

Mr Bolland. Was there anything extraordinary in your master going out in his green drill dress?

A. No, not that I know of.

Q. Was he in the habit of going out in it?

A. Yes.

Q. And of returning in it?

A. Yes.

Q. Did you ever know him go out in his green drill dress, and come home in a black coat?

A. No.

Q. That morning he had his green drill dress in his bundle, with his great coat?

A. Yes.

Mrs Smith's agitation increased when she was asked whether her master wore whiskers.

Lord Ellenborough. Did Mr de Berenger ever wear whiskers?

A. Yes sometimes he used.

Q. How long before the 20th of February had you seen him wear whiskers?

A. I do not know; I was so little in the habit of seeing my master, that I do not know whether he had whiskers or not.

Q. You saw him come in at the door, did you not?

A. On the Monday morning.

Q. At times you used to see him?

A. Yes.

Q. You were so little acquainted with the countenance of the man in whose service you had lived two years and a half, that you did not know whether he was a whiskered man or an unwhiskered man?

A. I never attended the door when my husband was at home.

Q. You used to go backwards and forwards; just before you did not know whether there was a green coat in the bundle; and then when I put you in mind of what you had sworn, you say positively there was?

A. Yes there was.

Q. And now you mean to say, you saw so little of your master, that you do not know whether he had whiskers?

A. No I do not know.

In addition to her general state of confusion and the effect this had on her credibility, Mrs Smith had seriously undermined Cochrane's version of events by stating that it was quite usual for de Berenger to come and go in his green drill dress (Cochrane had referred in his affidavit to the suspicions de Berenger would excite if he returned to his lodgings in green uniform).

John McGuire, an ostler with Smith's livery stables at the Cross Keys Yard, Chelsea, was called. According to McGuire, de Berenger, whom he knew, had called at the Yard at around 6.15 p.m. on Sunday 20 February to ask whether the coach from London had gone. McGuire told him the 6 o'clock coach had left but there would be another in three-quarters of an hour. According to McGuire, de Berenger then turned on his heels and began to walk home – a distance of between 3½ and 4 miles via Buckingham Gate and Westminster Bridge. He clearly recalled the Sunday in question because he was surprised to see de Berenger outside the Rules of the King's Bench and mentioned this to his wife. When called to confirm this she said that the precise date was imprinted on her mind because that Sunday was her oldest child's birthday. However, the independence of the McGuires' evidence came into question when it transpired, under cross-examination, that they and de Berenger's servants, Mr and Mrs Smith, were on very familiar terms.

The next witness was Henry Tragear, a hat-maker whose business had failed. He and his wife were staying with Mrs Tragear's cousin, Mr Donithorne, a cabinet-maker, at his house in York Street, Westminster. Tragear claimed that de Berenger had visited Donithorne's house both on the morning and again in the evening of Sunday 20 February, the implication being that de Berenger had dropped in when returning from Chelsea to his lodgings situated about half a mile away on the other side of Westminster Bridge. However, Gurney's cross-examination of Tragear, which demonstrated his formidable forensic skills, totally destroyed this witness's credibility.

Gurney. Do you remember being struck with any alteration in [de Berenger's] appearance that night?

Tragear. No.

Q. How long before that time had he left off wearing the large whiskers he used to have?

A. I cannot say.

Q. He had not them on that night?

A. I cannot say that I saw any alteration.

Q. He had no whiskers on that night?

A. No.

Q. He had never been used to wear whiskers?

A. That I cannot say.

Q. You knew him well, and had seen him often?

A. Yes.

Q. And you mean to say, you do not remember whether he wore whiskers or not?

A. He might or might not, I do not look so particularly into a gentleman's face, as to see whether he has whiskers or not.

Q. I happen to look at your face, and I cannot help seeing that you have whiskers, and a man who has such, might look at those on another person's face; do you mean to say, that in viewing the countenance of a gentleman you were acquainted with, you did not look so as to see whether he had whiskers?

A. Not unless a person spoke to me about them.

Q. Unless a person said 'whiskers', you would not look at them?

A. No.

Q. Mr de Berenger had not whiskers that night, however?

A. No.

Q. You were a hatter, in business at one time, and are not now?

A. Yes, I sell a great many hats now, though I have no house.

Q. Perhaps though you do not take notice of a man's whiskers you take notice of his coat; what coat had he on?

A. A black coat.

Q. That you did take notice of?

A. Yes.

Q. It was so remarkable he should wear a black coat, you took notice of that?

A. No; I do not know that it is remarkable, but I know he had a black coat.

Q. Was his head powdered?

A. I cannot say, I did not see his hat off.

Q. He staid half an hour with his hat on?

A. He went into the back part of the house.

Q. Do you mean to say, he staid half an hour in the house with his hat on?

A. I do not mean to say, he stopped the whole time in the house; he went into the garden.

Q. On the 20th February he went into the garden?

A. Yes.

Lord Ellenborough. Did he stand ankle deep in the garden, or how?

A. I cannot say, indeed.

Gurney. Was not there a good deal of snow at that time on the ground?

A. I cannot say, indeed.

Q. At what time was this?

A. Between eight and nine in the evening.

Q. And they took a walk in the garden?

A. Yes; it was in consequence of some alteration they were going to make in the premises.

Q. So that they went at ten o'clock at night to survey this alteration in the premises?

A. No; it was between eight and nine.

Q. It is just as dark then as it is at ten o'clock; they went to make a survey in the morning, did they not?

A. They had made a survey in the morning, I saw them pacing the garden.

Q. You told me they went out in the evening, to make a survey of the premises?

A. I cannot say what they went for, but I know they were there.

A note to the transcript of the trial tells us that the witness, at the beginning of the examination, had affected not to hear, but that Gurney gradually lowered his voice and at last spoke very softly, the witness nevertheless responding to his questions.

Gurney concluded his cross-examination by congratulating Tragear on the cure of his deafness. Lord Ellenborough was clearly less than impressed with Tragear as a witness, particularly after it had emerged that the failed hatter had twice acted as bail in recent months, despite his reduced financial circumstances. The judge dismissed him with a warning: 'You may go away, but let me advise you not to be either a bail or a witness again.'

Mr Isaac Donithorne, with whom the Tragears lived, confirmed that de Berenger had visited him between 8 and 9 p.m. on the Sunday. This was in connection with a plan to convert the front part of his house into an inn, and the main part into pleasure grounds. But he contradicted the previous witnesses' statements when he insisted that at no stage did he and de Berenger go into his garden that evening. Further doubts were cast on his evidence when it emerged that Tahourdin was his attorney and that Cochrane Johnstone was a close business associate.

The alibi witnesses having been heard, Gurney asked to be allowed to call a Mr Murray to contradict certain evidence given by Smith. Lord Ellenborough's response showed what he thought of the alibi witnesses presented by Park: 'If that question occasions a reply that will throw us into the night. If you think this case of alibi requires a serious answer, you will of course give it, but I think you would disparage the jury by doing so.'

Reassured by the great judge's openly expressed contempt for de Berenger's alibi defence, Gurney said he would not trouble to call Mr Murray. Instead, he turned to the jury and began to deliver his formal reply to the case for the defence which they had just heard. Although much briefer than his opening address, Gurney's concluding speech was equally savage in its treatment of the defendants' evidence. He began by saying that he took no pleasure in his present duty for he, like every honest Englishman, must feel degraded by the disgrace of a man whose name was so closely associated with the naval glories of his country.

Gurney first dismissed the idea that there were two conspiracies on the same day, since to believe it was to accept that miracles had not ceased. It was not necessary in a conspiracy that every party should know every other party, but in this case M'Rae provided a clear link between the two plots, his conversation with Vinn at the Carolina Coffee House on 15 February indicating that he was aware of the whole plan. As far as the defendants' stock transactions were concerned, yes, there had been previous large-scale dealings as the defence had pointed out. But the purchases had been much larger than sales, and the total balance of their government stock on the morning of 21 February amounted to £1.6 million and would have been larger if all their purchase orders had been implemented. This meant that every ⅛ fluctuation in price would result in a gain or loss of £2,000 pounds to the syndicate:

> Recollect, gentlemen, that just one month afterwards came the news of the rupture of the [peace] negotiation at Chantillon, when the premium on Omnium fell from 28 to 12 per cent; if that news had come instead of this false news, on the morning of the 21st of February, the loss of these three defendants would have been upwards of one hundred and sixty thousand pounds.

On the central issue of the identity of de Berenger with du Bourg, Gurney said that 'we have had, for the last two hours, evidence which has nauseated every man in court', a succession of witness statements characterised by self-contradiction, inconsistencies and confusion. More to the point, the prosecution case could not be defeated by an alibi defence:

> I take up de Berenger at Dover as I would a bale of goods – I have delivered him from hand to hand from Dover to London – I have delivered him into the house of Lord Cochrane – and I have Lord Cochrane's receipt acknowledging the delivery. You have, at the

Ship at Dover, the person pretending to be Colonel du Bourg, the aide de camp, in a grey military great coat, in a scarlet uniform embroidered with gold lace, and he has a star and a medallion. You have him traced from stage to stage, identified by the Napoleons with which he is rewarding his postillions; the first postillion delivers him to the second, the second to the third, and so on till he is landed in the house of Lord Cochrane. Who went into the house of Lord Cochrane? Ask Lord Cochrane. It was Mr de Berenger, and it is not pretended that any other person entered that house in that dress, or any thing resembling it; and therefore even if I had no witness to speak to the identity of the countenance of Mr de Berenger, I have proved a case that no alibi can shake.

Gurney then turned his fire on the defence evidence relating to Cochrane's affidavit:

My learned friends were properly anxious not to leave Lord Cochrane's affidavit to stand unsupported; they were desirous of giving it some confirmation, and they exhausted two or three precious hours this morning in calling witnesses to confirm it; but those witnesses were called to confirm the only part of the affidavit which wanted no confirmation; they were called to give Lord Cochrane confirmation about applications to the Admiralty, and applications to the War Office, and applications to the Colonial Office, by Sir Alexander Cochrane for de Berenger; and after they had called witness after witness to give confirmation on this insignificant and trifling point, they leave him without confirmation upon that important, that vital part of Lord Cochrane's case, namely the dress which Mr de Berenger wore at the time he came to that house, and had the interview with him. Lord Cochrane puts him in a grey military great coat, a *green* uniform and a fur cap. I have proved that the uniform he wore was *red*. My learned friend, Mr Serjeant Best, felt the strength of the evidence for the prosecution upon that, and he endeavoured to answer it by a very strange observation. 'Why,' says he, 'consider,

Lord Cochrane had been accustomed to see Mr de Berenger in *green*; he did not make his affidavit until nearly three weeks afterwards; and how very easily he might confound the *green*, in which he ordinarily saw him, with the *red*, in which he saw him on that day, and on that day only.' Now, if I wanted to show how it was impossible for a man to make a mistake as to the colour of the coat in which he had seen another, I should select the one instance in which he had seen that other in a peculiar dress.

Finally, Gurney derided Cochrane's statement that he had lent de Berenger a black coat because de Berenger could not visit Lord Yarmouth in his green uniform. He reminded the jury that this same green uniform was, according to Lord Yarmouth, the most correct dress in which to wait upon his lordship.

Gurney noted that defence counsel had not dared to ask Cochrane's own servant, though called as a witness, the colour of de Berenger's uniform; that another servant, Davis, had been allowed to go abroad, suggesting 'his absence was more wanted than his presence'; and that the maidservant at Green Street, who also saw de Berenger, had not been called.

Lastly, Gurney came to the evidence of the bank notes and the defendants' explanations for their discovery in de Berenger's letter-case. He ridiculed the correspondence relating to the debt allegedly owed by Cochrane Johnstone to de Berenger concerning the development of an acre of ground behind the house in Alsop's Buildings.

Oh, gentlemen, when does this fit of money-paying and money-taking seize these two persons? On the 22nd of February! The day speaks volumes. Added to all the extraordinary coincidences, which the defendants wish you to believe were coincidental, we now have the acknowledged payments by Mr Cochrane Johnstone to de Berenger on the day after [the fraud].

As for Cochrane himself, Gurney hoped and believed that he would until recently have been incapable of deliberately engaging in anything so wicked as the fraud:

but you must see in what circumstances men are placed, when they do these things; Lord Cochrane had first found his way to the Stock Exchange, he had dealt heavily in these speculations . . . he had involved himself so deeply, that there was no way, but by this fraud, of getting out of them; he had then got out of them in this way, and then he found, as guilty people always do, that he was involved still deeper.

Gurney concluded by saying that the case was clear. De Berenger was du Bourg and the rest followed from that. He was the agent of others and the stream of perjury to which the court had been subjected that day merely served to make conviction more certain.

Lord Ellenborough then delivered his summing up. This went over the ground already covered but the great judge's tone and critical treatment of parts of the evidence was later criticised by Cochrane and his supporters as being calculated to prejudice the jury against him. On the question of du Bourg's identity with de Berenger, the judge left no room for doubt: referring to the various witnesses who had recognised de Berenger in court, he said, 'so multiplied a quantity of testimony, so clear, and so consistent, was, I think hardly ever presented in the course of a criminal trial'. On the finding of the remnants of the officer's red coat in the Thames, he commented memorably, 'you have before had the animal hunted home and now you have his skin'.

Lord Ellenborough also cast doubt on Cochrane's assertion that he had immediately returned home on the morning of 21 February because he thought the officer who had sent for him was bringing news of his sick brother. The judge said it did not appear that Cochrane had received at that time any communication about his brother's illness in Spain (as he claimed) since the relevant letter had not been produced.

But the judge's most damaging comments directed at Cochrane were reserved for de Berenger's visit to 13 Green Street. Again and again he returned to the colour of the uniform in which de Berenger had appeared. De Berenger must have been wearing the dress, whatever it was, that he had worn in the coach which delivered him, since he had no means of 'shifting himself'. If he had appeared in the red uniform which witnesses had described, 'he must have appeared to any rational person, fully blazoned in the costume of that or some other crime'. More particularly:

> if he had on an aide-de-camp's uniform with a star, and so presented himself to Lord Cochrane, how could Lord Cochrane reconcile it to the duties he owed to society and to Government, and to his character as a gentleman and an officer, to give him the means of exchanging it? It must be put on for some dishonest purpose; this red coat and star and all this equipment must have appeared most extraordinary, and must have struck Lord Cochrane most forcibly if he was not aware of the purpose for which it was used. . . . If de Berenger put that uniform in a towel he must have pulled it off his back, for it was on his back before, and then Lord Cochrane, one would think, must have seen him do it.

On the other hand, if de Berenger had been wearing his green sharpshooter's uniform, it was, according to the judge, difficult to see why this should excite suspicion and why it should be considered necessary to change into another dress. Indeed, according to Lord Yarmouth, it was the very dress he should have worn to attend on his lordship. Why, then, would Cochrane offer him his black coat?

As the trial reached its conclusion it was clear that the defence had been breached at several points. De Berenger's alibi had been undermined by a succession of suspect witnesses and by the ease with which other, more credible, witnesses had identified de Berenger as du Bourg. This meant that Cochrane's first line of defence – based on du Bourg not being de Berenger – had been blown. More worrying for Cochrane was the assault that had been made on his second line of defence. This relied on an innocent explanation for his meeting with de Berenger at 13 Green Street on the morning of 21 February. But the damaging evidence relating to the colour of de Berenger's uniform when he stepped out of his hackney coach challenged Cochrane's version of events.

Cochrane meanwhile had been communicating with his solicitors on the handling of his case and urging them to call his servants as witnesses. The day before the trial he had asked for part of Mary Turpin's deposition to be expunged from the defence brief (Exhibit 6), and on the first day of the trial he sent his servants over with another note: 'I have now sent Thomas Dewman and Mary Turpin in case their evidence should be required in addition to that of Elizabeth [*sic*] Barnes and Sarah Cotton. I beg that you will have the goodness to call some person to show them where to go.'

The unexpected appearance of Barnes and Cotton outside the court, evidently arriving in a separate coach from that carrying Dewman and Turpin, seems to have caused some consternation. A scribbled note from a clerk reads 'Lord C. has sent Miss Barnes and Cotton in case of their evidence being wanted and they are at present waiting in a coach at the door – what should be done with them?' On the second day of the trial, 9 June, Cochrane wrote that he was again sending over his servants whom 'I submit ought to be examined in order to prove the appearance of de Berenger'. This note, however, was received after the defence case had closed and the servants were never called.

Cochrane's pleas to his defence lawyers therefore went unheeded and while Lord Ellenborough was concluding his summing up Cochrane's solicitors sent round one of their clerks to 13 Green Street. The clerk carried a message from Brougham warning Cochrane that in view of the judge's damaging remarks 'the very worst result may be apprehended'. But, even though forewarned, Cochrane was not fully prepared for the denouement that was to follow.

SEVEN

Downfall

By the time Lord Ellenborough had completed his lengthy summing up it was past 6 p.m. The jury then retired and deliberated for around two and a half hours. On their return they delivered a verdict of guilty against all the defendants.

Five days later, on 14 June, Cochrane appeared in person before the full Court of King's Bench, consisting of Lord Ellenborough and Justices Le Blanc, Bayley and Dampier. Cochrane said he wished to submit new evidence to the court with a view to applying for a retrial. He was told, however, that under the rules of the court any such application had to be made on behalf of and in the presence of all the defendants, which was clearly not possible since first M'Rae and now Cochrane Johnstone had absconded.

Cochrane was, however, able to tell the court that in one crucial respect his case had been misrepresented. He said that he had not read over his counsel's brief before the trial but on doing so now he found a gross error with regard to the dress in which de Berenger had appeared at his house. In the brief his servant, Thomas Dewman, was represented as having observed that de Berenger was dressed in a red coat, but this was incorrect: 'The fact was, that being questioned as to the colour of the coat, he stated that he appeared to be an army officer, to which he very naturally attached the idea of a red coat, for the servants did not see it.' Cochrane's brief statement before the court once again focused attention on the single most important issue in the trial – the colour of the coat worn by the visitor to 13 Green Street on the morning of 21 February.

On Monday 20 June the Court of King's Bench was reconvened in order to pass sentence after hearing pleas for mitigation from the defendants. Cochrane used the opportunity to make further application for a retrial, and for this purpose he read a very full statement addressing the various points raised at the trial against his version of events. This submission showed Cochrane at his very best: the arguments were skilfully presented, the language restrained and the tone defiant rather than bitter – in marked contrast to the vitriolic outpourings that were to characterise his later attempt at self-vindication in Parliament. Cochrane's presentation to the court (Exhibit 7) was accompanied by a sworn statement that repeated on oath the account previously given in his voluntary affidavit. The main arguments laid before the court can be summarised as follows.

As far as de Berenger was concerned, Cochrane knew him hardly at all, had never asked him to his house and had no knowledge of his character. It would, however, have been an easy matter for de Berenger to find out Cochrane's new address (which had been left at his old address) and he might very well have come to Green Street in order to facilitate his escape – that is in the hope of immediately going on board the *Tonnant*, with the prospect of obtaining employment in America.

The fact that Cochrane had left Mr King's tin workshop in such haste after receiving de Berenger's note was easily explained. He had no idea that the note was written by de Berenger, whose signature he could not read and whose handwriting was not familiar to him. On being told by his servant that the messenger was an officer, he had believed there might be grave news respecting his brother who was serving in France at the time and from whom he had received a letter just three days before saying that he was dangerously ill. To back up this statement Cochrane produced his brother's affidavit to the effect that he, William Cochrane, had written to his brother in early February regarding his illness, together with a surgeon's certificate dated 12 February providing medical details.

If Cochrane had been part of the conspiracy he would hardly have arranged for de Berenger to come to his house in broad daylight, which would have invited detection and ruin: 'The pretended du Bourg, if I had chosen him for my instrument, instead of making me his convenience, should have terminated his expedition and have found a change of dress elsewhere.'

Furthermore, if he, Cochrane, were guilty he surely would not have volunteered the potentially damaging information that de Berenger had visited his house that Monday morning – the name of de Berenger having been mentioned by no one up to that point. Still less would he have divulged that he had helped de Berenger to change his clothes at Green Street, a circumstance that might be expected to arouse suspicion and that would never have come to light but for Cochrane's voluntary statement.

As for de Berenger's dress, prosecution witnesses had stated that he arrived in town wearing a red coat, while Cochrane was now prepared to swear on oath that he appeared before him in a green coat. But could de Berenger not have changed his clothes in the coach on his way to Green Street? The portmanteau which he carried with him could have furnished him with his green dress and might then have been used to dispose of his discarded red uniform. (The coachman, Crane, had said very helpfully in his evidence that de Berenger's portmanteau was 'big enough to wrap a coat in'.)

It had been suggested in court that the uniform in which de Berenger appeared could not have been the green dress of Lord Yarmouth's corps because he had been reluctant to appear before that noble lord in the clothes he was wearing (Lord Yarmouth having testified that it would be entirely appropriate to appear before him in uniform). Yet surely no volunteer officer makes morning calls dressed up in his regimentals? Furthermore, it was he, Cochrane, who had suggested that de Berenger go to Lord Yarmouth and that he should for this purpose change into Cochrane's own black coat.

Cochrane repeated that in the knowledge of his own innocence and confident of his acquittal he had not taken the trouble to read his own counsel's brief, which contained a crucial error regarding the colour of de Berenger's dress. He was now able to clear up the matter by producing the affidavits of his three servants which corroborated his assertion that de Berenger appeared at his house wearing a green uniform under his grey greatcoat. A fourth affidavit from his former servant, Isaac Davis, would have been submitted in his favour had Davis not already sailed for Gibraltar in the service of Admiral Flemming. Cochrane's three servants had attended the trial for the very purpose of testifying but due to an oversight by his lawyers, which he found difficult to explain (he himself not being in court), the servants were never called upon to give evidence on this crucial matter of de Berenger's dress.

Cochrane concluded his statement with a dignified appeal for justice:

> The artifices which have been used to excite so much prejudice against me I despise. I know it must subside and I look forward to justice being rendered my character sooner or later: it will come most speedily, as well as most gratefully, if I shall receive it at your Lordships' hands. I am not unused to injury; of late I have known persecution: the indignity of compassion I am not yet able to bear. . . . I cannot feel disgraced while I know I am guiltless. Under the influence of this sentiment I persist in the defence of my character. I have often been in situations where I had an opportunity of showing it. This is the first time, thank God, that I was ever called upon to defend it.

Cochrane's sworn deposition largely repeated the material contained in his original voluntary affidavit but added a pointed comment regarding Lord Ellenborough's handling of the trial:

> this deponent believes that the jury who tried the said indictment, and the counsel for the defence, were so completely exhausted and worn out by extreme fatigue, owing to the Court having continued the trial without intermission for many hours beyond that time which nature is capable of sustaining herself without reflection and repose, that justice could not be done.

Among those who attended the court hearing on 20 June and listened to Cochrane's statement was Henry Crabb Robinson, the observant diarist, fellow radical and man of letters who was also at that time a practising barrister. He noted in his diary:

Lord Cochrane in a long speech asserted his innocence. To a skeptical man strong asseverations of innocence will excite doubt when opposed to circumstantial evidence only, but I have very little doubt in this case. I learned afterwards that, as de Berenger left the Court and passed Lord Cochrane, he said to him loud enough to be heard by Newman: 'Coward! Scoundrel: and Liar. You know you are as guilty as any of us.' So I heard from Belsham who had it from Gurney. Cochrane's endeavour to account for his lending a black coat to de Berenger because he could not appear before Lord Yarmouth, in the uniform in which Lord Yarmouth said he ought to appear before him, because it was early in the morning, was most unsatisfactory – yet his earnest manner had all the appearance of truth.

After making his statement and submitting his sworn affidavit to the court, Cochrane offered the affidavits of his three servants. However, Lord Ellenborough and his fellow judges explained that these could not be considered because it was a settled rule not to allow the affidavits of persons who might have been called upon at the trial, nor could the court hear the reason for keeping back their testimony.

The prosecution was then allowed to respond to the pleas for clemency. Gurney commented that Cochrane's counsel had not dared to call his servants to testify on the colour of de Berenger's coat because in the context of all the other evidence, if they had said it was green, no man alive would have believed them. He concluded with a scathing reference to Cochrane's naval achievements, which had been pressed upon the jury by Serjeant Best. These services had neither been forgotten nor unrewarded by his sovereign or his country. In return he had engaged in a conspiracy to perpetrate a fraud by artificially raising the price of government securities. For an officer on actual service and on full pay, in command of a line-of-battle ship, in time of war, to attempt to deceive his own Admiralty by propagating false war news was a dishonour to the profession of which he was a member.

Here, then, is the essence of a controversy that has raged down the years. Was Cochrane at heart a rogue capable of resorting to any subterfuge in order to make a fast shilling? Or was this undoubted naval hero brought down by his own ingenuous disclosures, a biased judge and a disgraceful judicial proceeding that denied him the opportunity to prove his innocence? Opposing interpretations of the events that took place on that fateful Monday morning in February 1814 have divided the legal profession, naval commentators, historians and, above all, the two families most intimately involved: the Cochranes on the one hand and the descendants of Lord Ellenborough on the other.

Whatever the judgement of history, the trial verdict was clear: Cochrane's renewed application for a retrial was unanimously rejected and punishment followed swiftly. On Tuesday 21 June sentence was pronounced by Mr Justice Le Blanc. All six defendants present in court were to be incarcerated in the King's Bench prison for twelve months and during that period Cochrane, de Berenger and Butt were to be placed in the pillory opposite the Royal Exchange in the city of London for one hour. Cochrane and Butt were also fined £1,000 each and were to be detained in prison until their fines were paid.

Crabb Robinson was again in court to hear the sentencing and his diary records the occasion:

> The sentence of the pillory was passed against Lord Cochrane, de Berenger and Butt. The severity of this sentence has turned public opinion in favour of his Lordship and they who first commiserated him afterwards began to think him innocent. His appearance today was certainly pitiable. When the sentence was passed he stood without colour in his face, his eyes staring and without expression and it was with difficulty he left the court like a man stupefied.

Further humiliations were heaped on Cochrane. The Admiralty lost no time in dismissing him from the Royal Navy and on 5 July he was released from prison to enable him to take his place in the House of Commons to face a motion for his expulsion from the chamber (Cochrane Johnstone was also summoned before the

House but information was given that he had last been seen in Calais on 21 June).

Before Cochrane's case was heard there was a brief discussion in the House of a petition from Alexander M'Rae who, though a fugitive from justice, had managed to contact his parliamentary representative and persuade him to present a statement on his behalf. In his petition M'Rae asserted that he was anxious to rescue Lord Cochrane who, though unhappily included in the verdict, had been unjustly convicted of participation in a plot of which he knew nothing. The House refused to receive the petition from a convicted prisoner who had already made the preposterous offer to tell all he knew for £10,000 and who had turned informer at this late hour.

After this preliminary, Cochrane took his seat in the House and was asked by the Speaker to state what he had to say in his defence. Cochrane began to read from a prepared script but it soon became clear that he had abandoned any attempt at a reasoned defence and was instead laying about him in all directions. Indeed, the extravagance of his language and the wildness of his allegations suggest that he had been pushed beyond breaking point and that paranoia had taken over. The Speaker intervened at one point to say that the House could not be expected to listen to mere invective; Lord Castelreagh, as government spokesman, warned reporters afterwards that if they printed the libelous allegations they had just heard they would do so at their own peril; and the leader of the opposition, George Ponsonby, while opposing the motion for expulsion, observed that Cochrane had inflicted more damage on himself through his intemperate remarks than his worst enemy could have done.

The allegations made by Cochrane targeted just about every person and every institution involved in any way with the trial. The government had allegedly colluded with the Stock Exchange in initiating legal proceedings, apparently with a view to getting him expelled from Parliament, where his radical views had upset those in high places; the special jury had been deliberately 'packed' with government supporters; his solicitors had ignored his instructions by joining his defence with the other accused when his own stated preference was to be defended separately; they had also failed to draw his attention to an inconsistency in the brief regarding the colour of de Berenger's coat; his counsel had made gross errors in presenting his defence, notably by representing the coat as red to the jury and by refusing to examine his servants on this point despite repeated requests on his behalf that this should be done; the Admiralty had been in collusion with the Lord Chief Justice who had urged that Cochrane's naval command be suspended; and, above all, Lord Ellenborough's handling of the trial had made a mockery of the judicial process. Cochrane's criticisms of the Lord Chief Justice were later to be elaborated but he used this occasion to accuse the distinguished judge of being an agent of the government, of demonstrating gross bias in his summing up and directions to the jury, and of deliberately disadvantaging the defence by adjourning when he did, thereby separating the evidence from the argument and requiring exhausted counsel to begin upon the defence after midnight while reserving the strength of prosecuting counsel for the close.

Having delivered his broadsides against the government, the Admiralty, the Stock Exchange, the judge, the jury and his own solicitors and counsel, Cochrane concluded his statement to the House with a sworn declaration of his innocence: 'I solemnly declare before Almighty God that I am ignorant of the whole transaction and uniformly I have heard Mr Cochrane Johnstone deny it also.' After a brief debate, the House of Commons reached a different view. The motion for Cochrane's expulsion was upheld by a majority of 144 to 44, while a separate motion against Cochrane Johnstone was passed unopposed. Writs for new elections were then ordered for the constituencies of Westminster and Grampound.

There was, however, some consolation for Cochrane. First, Lord Castlereagh, on behalf of the government, announced to the House of Commons that the Crown had interposed to exempt both Cochrane and his co-defendants from the pillory. There had been unease in the House and outrage among some elements of the population at the indignity of such a punishment, which exposed the victim to the abuse and missiles of the mob. For a naval hero, even a fallen hero, to be humiliated in this way seemed to many unnecessarily vindictive. The government itself was evidently worried that there might be civil disturbances if the pillory were to go ahead, although the official reason given for the act of clemency was that the conviction and sentence, though not fully implemented, would deter others from repeating this unusual crime. Cochrane himself remained aloof. 'If I am guilty,' he said, 'I richly merit the whole of the sentence which has been passed upon me. If innocent, one penalty cannot be inflicted with more justice than another.'

Cochrane's second consolation was that the electors of Westminster remained strongly supportive, influenced no doubt by his powerful but belated post-trial defence before the Court of King's Bench. Acceptance of his expulsion would be tantamount to accepting his guilt, and this they were not prepared to do. On 11 July a mass meeting of 5,000 constituents endorsed his candidacy after listening approvingly to attacks on Lord Ellenborough and Cochrane's defence lawyers from Sir Francis Burdett, the sitting member for Westminster (which returned two representatives) and a close friend of Cochrane. The two other would-be candidates for the seat – Henry Brougham and Richard Brinsley Sheridan – withdrew to give Cochrane a clear run and he was duly re-elected without opposition on 16 July.

There was, however, a portent of things to come. Brougham, who had been one of Cochrane's counsel at the trial, wrote to a friend about the Westminster election. Referring to Burdett's address to the Westminster electors he gave a prophetic warning: 'I fear the extreme folly of attacking Lord Cochrane's attorneys etc will lead to such a defence on their part as will damage both Cochrane and Burdett. I fairly warned them of the danger. Lord Cochrane partly listened; Burdett would not.'

Despite his election triumph Cochrane's fortunes remained at a low ebb. He was delisted from the Navy, his parliamentary career was over and the prospects of resuming any kind of career after release from prison at the age of 40 were problematic, to say the least.

Yet the final humiliation was yet to come. On 11 August, by order of the Secretary of State, Cochrane's banner as Knight Commander of the Bath was taken down from its fixing on the wall in King Henry VII's chapel at Westminster. His coat of arms, his helmet and sword were similarly torn from their place, and all these emblems of nobility were then ceremonially kicked out of the chapel and down the steps into the dust. At the same time an anonymous individual stood proxy for him while the spurs of knighthood were hacked from his boot heels with a butcher's cleaver. The hero of Basque Roads may have been spared the pillory but he had been stripped of all honour.

EIGHT

Counter-Attack

Cochrane was now confined in the King's Bench prison, although it may be said that his accommodation was more spacious than the cramped living quarters he was used to at sea. At that time prisons were privately run, the warden buying his position as an investment and obtaining a return on the capital sum by charging inmates for lodging and food. Cochrane paid for two rooms on the upper floor of a superior wing of the prison known as State House and here he lost no time in channelling his prodigious energies into various projects. He continued his work on perfecting a new lamp and adapting it to civilian use, and during the third month of his confinement he had the satisfaction of learning that oil lamps of his design were to be installed in the parish of St Anne's, Westminster. However, his hope that this invention would rescue him from financial worries was to be disappointed, since oil lamps were soon to be replaced by gas.

ATTACK ON THE LAWYERS

Cochrane's main preoccupation while in prison was the vigorous pursuit of his campaign to clear his name. On 25 July he wrote to his solicitors, Farrers, demanding answers to numerous detailed questions relating to their conduct of his defence. A number of these questions concerned the evidence of his servants regarding de Berenger's dress on his arrival at Green Street:

> Did you not particularly question Thomas Dewman and Mary Turpin as to the colour of the under coat? Did you not expressly ask them whether it was a red coat? And whether

they could swear that it was not a red coat? Which they could not, because it was worn under a great coat which was buttoned up.

Was it not in consequence of repeated questions that they were induced to admit that the under coat might be red? Did either of my servants admit that any part which he or she saw of the under coat was red?

Did you not, in consequence of the examination of my servants, insert in the brief that the under coat worn by de Berenger was a red coat with a green collar?

Did you ever call my attention to that part of the brief by word or letter? And do you really believe that I was privy and consenting to the fact of my Counsel being authorised by the brief to admit that coat to be red, which I uniformly declared to you was green, and which I had sworn to be green?

Farrers declined to be drawn and instead presented Cochrane with their bill of costs, in which, they said, 'you will find most of the facts to which your questions relate as they occurred'. The bill of costs was never published by Cochrane (and has not been published to this day) but Farrers had earlier issued a statement defending their handling of his case in response to his attack on them in the House of Commons on 5 July. Cochrane having forfeited the normal rules of client confidentiality, his solicitors focused on three key areas of contention: (1) Cochrane's familiarity with the brief they had drafted for him; (2) the contradiction between the servants' affidavits organised and published by Cochrane himself (where de Berenger's undercoat was described as having a green collar) and their later evidence given to the solicitors (where the undercoat was described as red with a green collar); and (3) the decision not to call the servants to testify on this issue.

The statement by Farrers reads as follows:

Lord Cochrane having, in a statement prepared for the purpose of being read by him in the House of Commons on Tuesday next (a copy of which is herewith left), charged us with irregularity and neglect of duty in preparing the brief, and taking the examination of witnesses for the late trial, we feel ourselves compelled, with the greatest regret, to submit the following facts and make the following declarations in justification of our conduct, as far as relates to the different matters charged against us by his lordship:–

1st. With regard to the irregular manner in which Lord Cochrane alleges the brief to have been drawn up by us as his solicitors, we beg to observe that the whole of the statement contained in it (except the pleadings, the Stock Exchange Committee's report, his lordship's affidavit and the proofs) was drawn up in his lordship's presence, and afterwards read over to and approved of by him.

2nd. With regard to the affidavits made by Thomas Dewman and Mary Turpin on the 21st of March, and which his lordship states to have been sworn at the Mansion House, in the presence of one of our clerks, we have to make the following declaration, viz.:–
That on the morning of Sunday, 20th of March, Lord Cochrane called in Lincoln's Inn Fields, and requested we would immediately send a stationer's man or a clerk to write for him in Green Street. That, agreeable to his lordship's request, one of our clerks, waited upon him in Green Street about half-past two o'clock, and was employed there from that time till a quarter before six on that day, in writing by his lordship's dictation from some minutes or papers he had before him (but not in the presence of the witnesses), four affidavits, to be sworn by Thomas Dewman, Mary Turpin, Isaac Davis, and Sarah Cotton, his servants, and afterwards making copies of the affidavits for his lordship. That when the affidavits and copies were finished, Lord Cochrane kept the copies, but ordered the clerk to take the affidavits home with him, and desired that either he or some other person would attend the witnesses to the Mansion House for the purpose of getting them sworn. That on Monday morning, the 21st of March, Thomas Dewman, Mary Turpin, and Isaac Davis [but not Sarah Cotton] called in Lincoln's Inn Fields, and the same clerk who attended his lordship the day before sent them to the Mansion House, and afterwards followed

them there and got the affidavits sworn, Davis having previously read over his own affidavit, and the clerks having read over to Thomas Dewman and Mary Turpin their affidavits; and that the three affidavits, when sworn, were sent to Lord Cochrane, and afterwards published by him.

3rd. With regard to the examinations of Thomas Dewman and Mary Turpin, as taken by us on the 11th of May, and stated in the brief, being different from the affidavits sworn on the 21st of March, we declare that those examinations were taken from the witnesses separately, and in the usual manner, by requiring them to state fully and correctly, and as they would be able to prove on oath at the trial, all they knew or recollected respecting de Berenger's coming to Lord Cochrane's house in Green Street, and the dress he appeared in there on the 21st of February, and by taking down every circumstance as they stated it; but certainly without pointing out or referring them either to Lord Cochrane's affidavit or their own affidavits sworn the 21st of March. That the examinations were afterwards read over to the witnesses separately and approved of by them. And we further declare that the examinations so taken were afterwards read over to Lord Cochrane, who made no objections to any part thereof, except to one part of Dewman's examination which alluded to another officer who had been at his lordship's house in Green Street, not on the 21st, but on some other day, and in consequence of his lordship's objection that part of the examination was expunged, and not inserted in the brief delivered to Counsel.

4th. With regard to what Lord Cochrane states, that Dewman and Turpin, upon being subsequently asked how they came to state to us, as his lordship's solicitors, that the under coat was red, they replied they never had said so; we must positively assert that when that question was put to Thomas Dewman after the trial, on his being sent by Lord Cochrane to make a further affidavit for the purpose of applying for a new trial, his answer was, not that he never told us that De Berenger came to Green Street in a red coat,

83

but that, when he was before examined by us, he must have concluded the under coat was red, because de Berenger appeared to be a military officer.

After explaining why they had attached Cochrane's own affidavit to counsel's brief but not the affidavits of his servants, Farrers went on:

5th . . . as both his lordship's affidavit and the testimony of Thomas Dewman and Mary Turpin, as taken down by us, were copied, the difference between the two, as far as related to the colour of De Berenger's under-coat, was apparent upon the face of the brief although we admit we never distinctly called his lordship's attention, or that of his Counsel, to that point *by letter*; and we further beg to state that in the affidavits sworn to by Dewman and Turpin, on the 21st of March, they did not state what the colour of De Berenger's under coat was, but only that the collar of it was green, which was not contradictory to what they stated to us on their examination.

Lastly, with regard to the orders Lord Cochrane states to have given to us for the examination of Dewman and Turpin, we beg to state that every direction we received from his lordship on this subject was communicated and submitted to Counsel, and particularly his lordship's letter of the 9th of June, received in Court during the trial.

In fact Cochrane had written a letter to Parkinson of Farrers the day before the trial (7 June), which showed he was fully aware that the colour of de Berenger's coat had been described in counsel's brief as red (see Exhibit 6). Indeed, he specifically asked for Mary Turpin's description of the coat as red to be expunged from the brief, which discredits his later claim that he was completely ignorant of his servants' inconsistent statements on this point.

Cochrane refused to accept the explanations given by Farrers. On 10 August he circulated a statement to the electors of Westminster reiterating that he had no idea that de Berenger's coat, which he had sworn to be green, was in any part of the brief described as red 'because it is impossible, unless I had been absolutely insane, that I should . . . have been satisfied with a brief which authorised my counsel to contradict my own affidavit'. He went on:

> To come now to the manner in which the errors in the brief originated, I have no hesitation in acknowledging that I am at issue with my solicitors on that point. Their account is that two of my servants, whom I had sent to their office to be examined as to the evidence they could give on the trial, admitted that de Berenger wore a *red* coat with a green collar. My servants, on the contrary, assure me that they did not, and could not admit that it was a red coat, because when they saw de Berenger he wore a great coat buttoned up, and they saw neither the body nor the skirts of the under coat, but the collar and so much of the breast as they saw was green; but they admit that on being questioned by my solicitors whether they could swear that it was not a red coat, they confessed that they could not, and admitted that it might be red, and that the green which they saw might be green facings to a military coat; but they have constantly declared that no part which they saw was red, and they deny that they ever admitted that they saw any red.

There is, then, a direct conflict of evidence here regarding the manner in which the defence brief was drawn up and the extent of Cochrane's involvement in the process. Did Cochrane, as he himself insists, really neglect the presentation of his case, so confident was he in a favourable outcome to the trial? Or was he, perhaps, seeking now to establish an alternative defence after his trial, which would require him to distance himself from the original brief drawn up by his solicitors?

ATTACK ON LORD ELLENBOROUGH

Besides confronting his solicitors, Cochrane spent much of the first six months of his imprisonment preparing a lengthy and carefully argued treatise, with numerous supporting appendices, seeking to rebut the charges against him. This attempt at self-vindication was published as a pamphlet in early 1815 under the title *A Letter to Lord Ellenborough*. Here Cochrane, having recovered his composure after the débâcle of his House of Commons address, displayed his considerable forensic abilities. Much of the material went over ground that is by now familiar but *The Letter* also developed some new arguments and introduced additional evidence.

A good deal of attention was given to the opportunities presented to de Berenger to change his masquerade dress *before* he appeared before Cochrane. In his statement to the Court of King's Bench Cochrane had already suggested that de Berenger might have changed his uniform while driving in the hackney coach to Green Street. Justice Le Blanc, however, had observed that de Berenger would have been pressed for time to do this on such a short journey. Cochrane now pointed to an alternative possibility. Yes, he acknowledged, it would take some time for de Berenger to change out of his red uniform into his green one. But Cochrane's servant, Dewman, had said in evidence that he had to go from Green Street to Great Cumberland Street and back, which would have taken at least a quarter of an hour – surely sufficient time for de Berenger to change his clothes in Cochrane's own house. And if that were not long enough, then Dewman had gone on to Snow Hill, a distance of more than 5 miles, which would involve a return journey of an hour and a quarter. Certainly, de Berenger had the opportunity to change before Cochrane arrived back at Green Street.

There was yet a third possibility and this was the one favoured by Cochrane. Shilling, the postboy who drove the post-chaise on its last stage from Dartmouth, had testified at the trial that de Berenger had pulled up the blind as he came round the corner between the coach stand at The Three Stags, Lambeth Road, and the stand at Marsh Gate. Cochrane suggested that this was done in order to conceal de Berenger while he changed his clothes in the coach. In support of this idea Cochrane now produced voluntary affidavits sworn by two men, described as 'respectable tradesmen', residing in the neighbourhood of Marsh Gate (Exhibit 9). One man, named Miller, said that on 21 February he saw the supposed messenger get out of a chaise into a hackney coach, that he was dressed in green with a grey coat, and that there was no red on any part of his dress. The second man, named Raiment, said that he also saw the supposed messenger get out of the chaise into the hackney coach, and on stepping out, his great coat parted to enable the witness to see the undercoat which appeared to be dark green 'like that of the Sharp Shooters'. These affidavits were apparently unsolicited, the two tradesmen going before the Lord Mayor to make their statements.

Lord Ellenborough, in his summing up at the trial, had suggested that de Berenger could not have changed his clothes prior to appearing before Cochrane because he had no means of 'shifting himself'. Cochrane now accused the judge of failing to draw the jury's attention to the possibility that de Berenger could have removed his red uniform, particularly bearing in mind the portmanteau he carried, which was, according to Crane's evidence, 'big enough to wrap a coat in'.

Further buttressing his argument that de Berenger had arrived at Green Street wearing green, Cochrane pointed out that only one witness, the hackney coach driver Crane, had testified that de Berenger arrived in red. And Crane, according to Cochrane, was a most unreliable witness. In the first place he had been convicted of cruelty to his horses shortly before the trial – a particularly shocking case according to the Commissioners of the Hackney Coach Office. (That he was a thoroughly bad lot is further suggested by the fact that twelve years later he was sentenced to transportation for theft.) Cochrane now appended to his *Letter to Lord Ellenborough* five affidavits by people who knew Crane and testified as to his bad character. One deponent had heard him say in relation to the evidence he gave at the trial that 'he would swear black was white, or anything else if he was paid for it'. Crane had allegedly told this same witness that 'he did not see de Berenger's under-dress as his coat was closely buttoned up'. Two of the five affidavits, however, put an entirely new gloss on Crane's evidence. The deponents asserted that Crane had first identified the 'messenger' he drove from Marsh Gate as Lord Cochrane himself and had given this information to the Stock Exchange Committee. Shortly afterwards

Crane was said to have boasted that he had received a part of the reward offered by the committee and expected more.

In his autobiography, written towards the end of his life, Cochrane claims that he was deliberately framed by the prosecution: first, through the false evidence of Crane to the effect that the person he drove to Green Street on 21 February was none other than Cochrane, who by implication was du Bourg; and then, when Cochrane had publicly identified the visitor to his house as de Berenger, by having Crane resort to the false evidence of a red coat, which would link Cochrane indirectly to the fraud. In other words Crane was the paid instrument of sinister elements who were determined to bring Cochrane down through trumped up charges and perjured evidence. Was this interpretation of events the result of Cochrane's paranoia, the mischievous invention of a fraudster or a genuine belief based on the evidence?

Apart from dealing with de Berenger's visit to Green Street, Cochrane produced new evidence in *The Letter* regarding his money transactions. A £200 note had been paid by Cochrane to Butt, the proceeds of which had then found their way into the hands of de Berenger: this item had not been accounted for at the trial and the omission was a weakness in the defence case. Cochrane now explained that the £200 note was paid to Butt in part discharge of a wine bill:

It was not till very shortly before the trial that I had the least intimation or idea that the produce of that note had also been traced to De Berenger, *and it was not even attempted to be accounted for at the trial*, because it was not till after my arrival at this place that I could call to mind in what manner that note passed into the hands of Mr Butt. I am indebted to my uncle, the Hon Basil Cochrane, for urging my recollection on this subject, and particularly putting the question whether I had not at any period subsequent to the 19th February deposited in Mr Butt's hands any money for the payment of my ship bills. And I was then 'struck as by electricity' with the recollection of the fact of having paid into his hands a thousand pound note and a *two hundred pound note* for that express purpose. By documents tendered to the House of Commons, and which are now annexed to this letter, it is proved that Mr Butt did accordingly, on the 8th of March, pay to Messrs Wilkinson and Crossthwaite nearly seven hundred pounds for wines shipped on my account on board His Majesty's ship *Tonnant*.

Cochrane also had an explanation for the fact that the £200 note he had given to Butt was changed by the latter, first into two £100 notes and then into the £1 notes that were found on de Berenger. Apparently this double transaction was due to the mistake of a clerk who was told to get 'ones' and instead got 'one hundreds'.

In support of his explanation for this payment of £200 to Butt, Cochrane produced a letter signed by Mr James Hullock of Messrs Wilkinson and Crosthwaite (Exhibit 10). This testified to the fact that Cochrane had visited the wine merchant in Fenchurch Street with Butt 'on or about the 19th of February last' and, having occupied himself with tasting wines for two hours or more, then ordered a large stock for his ship, later paid for by Butt. There are, however, three rather curious aspects to this evidence. First, Hullock could only say that the relevant date was 'on or about' 19 February when one would have thought that the precise date of such a very large order would have been entered in the company's books and therefore easily verified. Second, Cochrane adds his own postscript to his letter saying that it is important to fix the day of the relevant transaction which he suggests must indeed be 19 February because Butt, who paid his own wine bill on the same day, had preserved a receipt bearing that date. Finally, Farrers received a pre-trial memorandum including the statement that Cochrane had visited his wine merchant on the afternoon of 21 February – a little odd if he really had spent so much time with them just two days before.

But why should it be so important to fix the date as Saturday 19 February? And why was Cochrane so keen to show that he was engaged with his wine merchant for a considerable time? Perhaps he was anxious to establish an alibi for that day which happened to be the very day on which, according to de Berenger's later account (see

Chapter 10), the investment syndicate had planned together the execution of the Stock Exchange fraud. If that is the case, why would an innocent man try to establish an alibi against charges which had not yet been made?

Having savaged the Lord Chief Justice in his lengthy pamphlet, Cochrane was still not finished with the noble judge. Once he had identified his enemy, Cochrane was not one to let go and he was shortly to initiate impeachment proceedings against Lord Ellenborough in the House of Commons. But before that could happen, another episode highlighted the extraordinary impulsiveness of this remarkable man.

With only three months to run before his release from prison Cochrane decided that he had had enough. On 6 March 1815, with the aid of a rope smuggled in by his servant, he scaled the roof of State House, threw a noose over the spikes that topped the outer wall and made his way hand over hand to the prison perimeter. From there he used the rope to drop down on the other side, and after falling the last 20 feet, he managed to crawl, in a severely concussed state, to the house of a former servant. His strength recovered, Cochrane then travelled down to his Hampshire residence, Holly Hill, and from there returned to London to take his seat in the House of Commons on 21 March. The House could not countenance such brazen behaviour and, after some altercation with the Speaker, there was an unseemly physical struggle as Cochrane was removed forcibly from the chamber by Bow Street runners.

Following this apparently pointless escapade, Cochrane was returned to the King's Bench prison but not to the relative comfort of State House. Instead, he was incarcerated for three weeks in the prison's 'Strong Room', a damp, windowless cell 14 feet square with no ventilation or heating. When doctors certified that the prisoner was becoming ill from this close confinement he was moved again to other secure accommodation. On 20 June 1815, as London celebrated the news of Napoleon's defeat at Waterloo, Cochrane's prison term expired but his release was delayed until he had paid the £1,000 fine to the Marshal of the King's Bench. For two weeks he refused but, after his show of defiance, a note for this sum was eventually paid over bearing the following endorsement: 'My health having suffered by long and close confinement, and my oppressors being resolved to deprive me of property or life, I submit to robbery to protect myself from murder, in the hope that I shall live to bring the delinquents to justice.'

Cochrane was now able to take his seat in the House of Commons unchallenged and on 6 July he gave notice that in the next parliamentary session he would move for the impeachment of Lord Ellenborough. Accordingly, on 5 March 1816 he set out a number of charges against the Lord Chief Justice (Exhibit 11). In the debate that followed the solicitor general, Sir Samuel Sheppard, noted that Cochrane was condemning the judge's conduct of the trial on the basis of evidence that had never been brought before the jury and that was supported by mere voluntary affidavits produced after the trial. Furthermore the judge had every right to assume that the defendant's counsel had said everything that could be said on behalf of their client – the judge could not be expected to remedy any alleged deficiencies in the defence case as presented to the jury. The Attorney General, Sir William Garrow, commented on the abuse which had been heaped on the character of Crane, the hackney coachman, and asked pointedly why in the two years that had elapsed, Cochrane had not brought a private prosecution against Crane if he really believed he could prove the coachman had given false evidence. Sheppard and Garrow, along with George Ponsonby, the leader of the Opposition, also dismissed the idea that the defence case had been disadvantaged by the timing of the adjournment during the trial. And on one further point there was general agreement: there was hardly an individual at the Bar or on the Bench less likely to be influenced by corrupt motives or improper partisanship than Lord Ellenborough. That view was reflected in the vote on the motion for impeachment which was defeated by eighty-nine votes to nil.

ATTACK ON THE STOCK EXCHANGE COMMITTEE

While Cochrane's *Letter to Lord Ellenborough* was being printed, the Stock Exchange Committee appointed to enquire into the fraud sprang into action once more. The committee had earlier been criticised in Parliament by Cochrane for allegedly acting in collaboration with the government, and questions had been raised in the press by Cochrane's supporters as to the motivation of the Stock Exchange in bringing legal proceedings against him. The committee issued a response at the end of January 1815. It dealt first with the general issue by emphasising the Exchange's duty to protect the interests of investors in government securities. The prosecution was necessary to maintain the integrity of financial markets, although the committee 'lamented that a character which had hitherto shone with so much luster in the naval annals of this country should appear to have been so implicated in this affair as to render it imperative on them to include his name in the indictment for the conspiracy . . .'.

However, the committee then went on to address specific points that had been raised during and after the trial. These declarations, which were signed by each of the ten committee members, throw a very important light on the investigation that preceded the trial and the weight of evidence against Cochrane. The most important declarations are reproduced below:

1. That William Crane, the hackney coachman, was the first person examined by them in their inquiry respecting the pretended Colonel Du Bourg, and that at his first examination (prior to its having been ascertained that Lord Cochrane resided in Green Street) he stated that the pretended Colonel du Bourg wore a *red* coat under his great coat, when he got out of the coach and entered the house.

2. That Thomas Shilling, the Dartford post-boy, afterwards confirmed the fact of the pretended Colonel du Bourg having worn a *red* coat, without his having previously had any communication with Crane, and prior likewise to its having been ascertained that Lord Cochrane resided in the house to which the pretended Colonel was driven.

3. That William Crane never asserted before them, nor ever gave them any reason to believe that the person whom he took in

his coach from the Marsh Gate to Green Street was Lord Cochrane himself.

4. That neither William Crane nor any other witness at the trial received any portion of the reward which was offered for the apprehension of the pretended Colonel du Bourg.

5. That William Crane was not paid higher than the other witnesses in his station of life; which was at the rate of ten shillings per day. And that the whole sum paid to him did not exceed 17/-, which included sundry expenses that he had incurred, and the hire of his coach for part of the time when he was in attendance on the sub-Committee.

6. That Lord Cochrane was not the first person who pointed out to the Sub-Committee that De Berenger was the pretended Colonel du Bourg, since the gentleman to whom the whole of the reward of 250 guineas has since been given for that important service, as well as some other gentlemen, whose names it is unnecessary here to mention, had pointed him out to the sub-Committee *five* days prior to the publication of his lordship's affidavit of the 11ᵗʰ of March, and a warrant had actually been previously obtained against him.'

Cochrane had attacked on three fronts with mixed results. His criticisms of his solicitors had met with a vigorous rebuttal, the Parliamentary assault on Lord Ellenborough's integrity had badly misfired, but the *Letter to Lord Ellenborough* with its supporting affidavits appears to have gained considerable public support. Finally, the attacks on the Stock Exchange Committee, while eliciting a strong response, may have left a question mark in the public mind about the role of the government in the affair.

THE DAVIDSON TRIAL

Cochrane, however, had a fourth target in his sights. On 20 July 1816 he brought a private prosecution for perjury against Davidson, one of the prosecution's witnesses at the original trial. It will be recalled that Davidson was de Berenger's landlord and had given evidence that he had seen de Berenger leave his lodgings at 11 a.m. on Sunday 20 February 1814 – the day before the Stock Exchange fraud. This was not possible because other evidence, as well as de Berenger's subsequent confession, showed that de Berenger had by that time arrived in Dover. Clearly Davidson in his evidence had either deliberately misled the court (perhaps to protect his tenant) or else had made a mistake about the day in question. Cochrane's purpose in bringing the proceedings was apparently to undermine the credibility of the prosecution case, even though the evidence given by Davidson was in favour of the defence. After all, if Cochrane could demonstrate that the prosecution had called one false witness, admittedly on a question irrelevant to his guilt, could they not have employed other false witnesses, such as Crane, to secure his conviction?

In the event, the jury delivered a verdict of not guilty because there was no evidence that Davidson had uttered a deliberate falsehood, the presumption being that he had made a genuine mistake. But the Davidson trial was revealing in several important ways. First, the defence counsel, who happened to be Gurney, drew attention to a curious aspect of the case. Here was a prosecution for perjury brought by Cochrane on a point of evidence irrelevant to the merits of the case in the original trial. If Cochrane had not been party to the conspiracy, why on earth had he not indicted for perjury the witnesses who had in that trial sworn that he was? According to Gurney, the defence in the original trial, if true, furnished material for two or three prosecutions not only for perjury but for the more profligate crime of subornation.

While Gurney baited Cochrane for failing to indict Crane and other prosecution witnesses, the Davidson trial yielded some interesting new evidence bearing on the original trial. To show that de Berenger could not have left his lodgings at the time stated by Davidson, the prosecution called two witnesses who testified that de Berenger had arrived at the Royal Oak Inn, Dover, in the early morning of Sunday 20 February. David Bangham, the waiter at the Royal Oak, and Henry McCrow, the landlord, both confirmed this fact and Bangham further said that de Berenger had arrived dressed in a dark bottle-green coat with a pepper-and-salt coat on his arm. He wore boots, had a travelling cap on his head and carried a sword in a green bag, as well as a leather portmanteau. De Berenger came and went during the day and finally left at about 11 p.m. but he did not take away his portmanteau which remained at the inn for several months.

Part of this evidence might be viewed as favourable to Cochrane in so far as it suggested that de Berenger was in possession of a green coat when he arrived at Dover. On the other hand the testimony also indicated that de Berenger had left at the Royal Oak the portmanteau he was carrying his change of clothes in and did not have it with him on his return to London. What, then, becomes of the portmanteau brought by de Berenger to Green Street which, according to Crane's testimony, was 'big enough to wrap a coat in'? That is a mystery to which we shall return.

By the summer of 1816 Londoners had been treated to a stream of sensational material relating to the Stock Exchange fraud. There were the pre-trial pamphlets and press coverage; the headline treatment of the trial itself; the post-trial pamphleteering and parliamentary debates; the furious correspondence between Cochrane and his solicitors, made available to the public; the declarations of the Stock Exchange Committee; and now the publicity associated with the Davidson trial. The only omission here is the detailed confession by de Berenger published as a book in early 1816 under the ironic title *The Noble Stockjobber*. But before de Berenger's version of events is presented it is necessary to form a judgement as to whether Cochrane was a participant in the fraud.

NINE

Was he Guilty?

How could Cochrane, a brilliant naval officer honoured by his sovereign, a scion of an ancient family, a radical member of Parliament, a man with dazzling prospects ahead of him, have become caught up in a Stock Exchange fraud? Was there something in his complex character that could have tempted him into such a venture? Or was Serjeant Best, his counsel, correct when he said it was inconceivable that a man of such illustrious reputation, with so much to lose, could have resorted to a sordid crime of this kind for the sake of a few thousand pounds profit?

THE MAN

Of Cochrane's brilliant and heroic qualities as Britain's greatest naval commander second only to Nelson, little need be said here. He was a man who combined fearlessness and extraordinary inventiveness with an ability to judge and take risks – but never at the expense of his men's lives. Not having the opportunity to be fully tested as a fleet commander, he proved most formidable in single ship-on-ship combat and in masterminding lightning raids on the enemy's coastline. He was, however, viewed with caution by the British naval high command because of his tendency to insubordination and his willingness to take on the Admiralty in arguments over anything ranging from naval tactics to pay, prize money, pensions and seamen's working conditions.

It was in the context of such misgivings that Lord St Vincent, First Lord of the Admiralty, referred disparagingly to Cochrane and his uncle, Sir Alexander Cochrane: 'The Cochranes are not to be trusted out of sight. They are all mad, romantic, money-getting and not truth telling.' He might have added that they were exceptionally able seamen who served their country well.

However, the money-getting accusation was undoubtedly well founded. Cochrane's reduced family circumstances, and particularly the forced sale of the Dundonalds' Culross Abbey estate in 1793 to satisfy his father's creditors, had instilled in him a steely determination to do well for himself financially. He openly acknowledged that his marauding naval operations were motivated in part by the desire for booty, he campaigned for a higher proportion of prize money to be allocated to ship captains so as to incentivise commanders like himself, and he was in constant dispute with the Admiralty prize courts over court fees and the distribution of prize proceeds. But Cochrane's entrepreneurial approach to naval command was not particularly unusual for the period and there was no suggestion of anything underhand in his financial dealings prior to the events of February 1814.

One aspect of Cochrane's character that had a direct bearing on the Stock Exchange episode was his tendency to apply the techniques and rules of war to civilian life. When his close friend and radical political ally, Sir Frances Burdett, was threatened with arrest for breach of parliamentary privilege, Cochrane brought a barrel of gunpowder to Burdett's town house at 78 Piccadilly to deter constables and soldiers from making a forced entry. He was evidently ready to blow up those who had come to enforce the law and prepared to reduce part of Piccadilly to rubble. As Donald Thomas, his biographer, says of this incident: 'It was an essential feature of [Cochrane's] conduct that he believed in politics as a war to be fought.'

A not dissimilar episode occurred in the spring of 1817. After his election for Honiton in 1806 Cochrane had refused to pay £1,200 for a banquet for his supporters and now, more than ten years later, his creditors obtained a court order against his house at Holly Hill in Hampshire. When the sheriff of Hampshire and twenty-five constables laid siege to his property he posted notices stating that 'explosion-bags are set in the lower embrasures, and all the garrison is under arms'. In fact, the explosion bags contained nothing more than powdered charcoal and the confrontation was eventually resolved peaceably. But for Cochrane absolute victory was required in any dispute – and that could mean war.

Cochrane, then, had some difficulty in identifying the boundary between warfare and the ordinary responsibilities of civilian life. Furthermore, one of his favourite techniques when engaged in naval conflict was to dupe the enemy. This might involve sailing under false colours, elaborately disguising his ship, setting up decoy lights at night for the enemy to follow, or using misleading signals. Cochrane was, indeed, a master of deception and this remained a key element of his naval tactics during the South American campaigns of his later seafaring days.

It should also be said that Cochrane enjoyed a prank. His escape from prison and sudden appearance in the House of Commons in 1816 was but one example. The way he treated the electors in Honiton was another. When standing as a parliamentary candidate for that constituency in 1805, he refused to offer any bribes and consequently lost to his opponent, who had offered £5 to anyone who would vote for him (the ballot not being secret). However, after the result had been declared, Cochrane announced that anyone who had voted for him could collect 10 guineas from his agent. Believing that Cochrane would repeat this exercise, the constituents of Honiton voted him in at the next general election but found, to their dismay, that he was prepared to give them nothing. He had secured the seat at no cost. Even his military exploits showed his love of a good prank. In the words of Donald Thomas: 'He was a swashbuckling commander whose triumphs were half the result of tactical genius and half the outcome of a practical joke played on his enemies.'

Finally, Cochrane seemed to relish a fight with the powers that be. In the aftermath of the Basque Roads triumph he had accused Admiral Lord Gambier, his commander-in-chief, of failing to follow up the assault by sending fireships in an immediate attack on the French fleet while it was in a state of complete disarray. When a vote of thanks was to be proposed to Gambier in the House of Commons, Cochrane made known his intention of opposing the motion, with the result that Gambier felt obliged to call for a court martial to enquire into his conduct and clear his name – which it did. Previously, when Cochrane applied for the promotion of one of his lieutenants who had played an important part in the *Speedy*'s capture of the Spanish warship *Gamo*, the First Sea Lord, Lord St Vincent, unwisely suggested that 'the small number of killed on board the *Speedy* does not warrant the application'. Cochrane replied furiously and insultingly that the rejection of the application on these grounds was

> in opposition to his Lordship's promotion to an earldom, as well as that of his flag captain to a knighthood, and to his other officers to increased rank and honours: for in the battle from which his Lordship derived his title [Cape St Vincent], there was only one man killed on board his own flagship, so that there were more casualties in my sloop than in his line-of-battle ship.

What do we learn from all this? Cochrane was very keen to make money, he recognised few constraints when pursuing his interests, in civilian life as in war deception was his master weapon, he enjoyed a prank, and he liked to upset the establishment. These might be viewed as the characteristics of someone who was prepared to engage in a Stock Exchange 'hoax' which involved impersonating officers, duping the Admiralty and making a mockery of the financial establishment.

THE INVESTORS AND THE MONEY

Cochrane was on very familiar terms with his rogue uncle, Cochrane Johnstone. Although he stated before the Court of King's Bench that 'with Mr Cochrane Johnstone I had the intercourse natural between close relatives', the ties were in fact much more intimate. They had campaigned for each other when seeking election to the House of Commons; Cochrane had lodged with his uncle in Harley Street when fighting his seat at Westminster; the two men had apparently had business dealings in connection with the investment of

Cochrane's prize money; Cochrane was a regular visitor to his uncle's house at 18 Great Cumberland Street; and now they were involved together in a common investment strategy on the Stock Exchange, using the same investment adviser, Butt, and the same broker, Fearn. In the days preceding the Stock Exchange fraud, Cochrane, his uncle and Butt had all taken long positions in 'the funds' and they all sold out on the day of the fraud. Furthermore, on the morning of the fraud these three were closeted together for approximately one and a half hours, first having breakfast at Great Cumberland Street and then travelling to the City in a hackney coach. Surely, if Butt and Cochrane Johnstone were the sole originators of the plot, they would have found some reason to be rid of Cochrane's company at this critical juncture.

Is it conceivable, then, that Cochrane was not let in on his uncle's planned Stock Exchange coup? Lord Brougham, who was one of Cochrane's counsel at the trial, insisted later that the trial verdict was wrong but he also implied that Cochrane might have been aware of his uncle's activities: 'If Lord Cochrane was at all aware of his uncle Mr Cochrane Johnstone's proceedings, it was the whole extent of his privity to the fact.'

But if Cochrane *was* aware of his uncle's planned hoax, is it possible that he would not himself have become more directly involved, given his mastery of military deceptions and the fact that he stood to gain from the success of the project? In his own defence Cochrane suggested that the £2,470 profit he made from selling his stock on the morning of the fraud was hardly sufficient to have induced him to risk his future career by engaging in a fraudulent conspiracy. But it is clear from his subsequent statements that Cochrane did not view the 'hoax' on the Exchange as a serious offence. Furthermore, the profit he made would no doubt have been much greater if the telegraph had worked that day, and if all the stock that Butt had tried to acquire on the previous Saturday had in fact been bought (it will be recollected that a Mr Richardson was given an order to purchase £150,000 worth of stock but was only prepared to commit to £30,000). Finally, as to the sum involved, it may be noted that later in life Cochrane was very persistent in pursuing his navy back-pay, amounting to between £4,000 and £5,000. If this sum was of such interest to him, then so would be the prospect of several thousand pounds profit from the Stock Exchange hoax, not to mention the avoidance of several thousand pounds of losses if his stock holdings had to be sold in an unreceptive market.

It should be added that Cochrane's account with Coutts, his bankers, shows a marked deterioration in his income relative to expenditure in the years 1809–14. His prize money had come to an end, he was on half-pay, and he was spending heavily on his family, his property (having bought Holly Hill, a 200-acre estate in Hampshire) and his inventions. Cochrane was not as financially distressed as his uncle and de Berenger were, and he still had good prospects now that he was appointed to the *Tonnant*. Nevertheless, money was becoming a worry.

In the close relationship between Cochrane, Butt and Cochrane Johnstone, one further circumstance is of interest. Dewman, Cochrane's manservant, in a statement to Farrers contained in the defence brief, revealed that Butt had visited 13 Green Street at 8.30 a.m. on Sunday 20 February, the day prior to the fraud. Cochrane was not up at this hour and Dewman sent Butt away, but one may ask what urgent matter would have impelled Butt to make such an early call – unless it was to report that he had failed to obtain all the stock he had tried to buy the previous afternoon. After all, one does not normally expect to receive an early Sunday morning visit from an investment adviser: something very out of the ordinary must have been on Butt's mind and he wished to communicate it to his distinguished client. (It seems likely that it was this reference to Butt visiting his house on Sunday morning that Cochrane wished to have expunged from the defence brief – see p. 83.)

It will be recalled that on 19 February Cochrane cashed a cheque from his broker for just over £470. The proceeds included one £200 note and two £100 notes. These were given to Butt who, on 24 February, instructed his clerks to change them into £1 notes. It seems, according to de Berenger's later account, that Butt then gave the 400 £1 notes to Cochrane Johnstone who handed them that same evening to de Berenger. In order to account for these highly suspicious transactions Cochrane Johnstone tried to show that he was owed money by Butt and at the same time owed money to de Berenger, while Cochrane sought to demonstrate that he had bona fide debts justifying his £400 payment to Butt. According to Cochrane's trial evidence Butt had lent him £200 in connection with a Stock Exchange transaction. Having failed at the trial to account for the other £200, Cochrane had later been 'struck as by electricity' with the recollection of paying Butt for settling his ship's wine bill.

That the precise amount paid by Cochrane to Butt should (after being exchanged for smaller notes) end up on the same day in the hands of de Berenger is, of course, strongly suggestive – the more so as the relevant transactions occurred just after the day of the fraud. On the other hand, there is one piece of evidence concerning the financial dealings between de Berenger and his co-conspirators that appears to be in Cochrane's favour. The memorandum found on de Berenger at Leith, which refers to a letter written by him to Cochrane Johnstone on 1 March, included the statement: 'Believe from my informant £18,000 instead of £4,800. Suspicious that Mr B. [presumably Butt] does not account correctly to him as well as me.' The figure of £4,800 coincides with Cochrane Johnstone's estimate of his and Butt's combined profits, which he presented to the Stock Exchange on 14 March. If indeed de Berenger is referring to the same estimate, it is interesting that Cochrane's profit (calculated by Cochrane Johnstone to be £1,700) is not mentioned in the memorandum. This omission might suggest that de Berenger's 'cut' was calculated only on the basis of Butt's and Cochrane Johnstone's stock market gains. On the other hand, the true meaning of de Berenger's figure is obscure; and if Cochrane were a party to the fraud, he might have wished to avoid having any direct financial obligations to de Berenger, preferring to deal only with Butt and/or his uncle who was, after all, de Berenger's patron and paymaster.

COCHRANE'S AFFIDAVIT

The voluntary affidavit sworn by Cochrane on 11 March sought to explain the circumstances in which de Berenger had visited his house in Green Street. However, this account is highly implausible for a number of reasons.

If Cochrane was not a party to the fraud, why would de Berenger go to his house? He was muddied, unshaven and dishevelled from his journey, which would surely arouse suspicions even if, as Cochrane insists, he was wearing a green uniform. Furthermore, why would he turn up at Green Street without an appointment on the off-chance that Cochrane was there and on the further off-chance that, if there, Cochrane would immediately allow him to go on board the *Tonnant*? It is surely even more improbable that someone in de Berenger's humble position would send the servant of a noble lord to go and fetch his lordship from his business so that he could ask him a very great personal favour. More to the point, if de Berenger really had managed to change into an 'innocent' green uniform in the coach, there was nothing whatever to stop him returning immediately to his lodgings since, as his servant's wife admitted, he routinely went in and out of the Asylum Buildings in his green sharpshooter's uniform.

Cochrane's explanation for his own behaviour in offering de Berenger a change of clothes is also implausible. He must have been struck by de Berenger's dishevelled appearance as well as the fact that he had turned up without an appointment, requesting to come immediately on board the *Tonnant* carrying with him only a black dispatch case and a sword. Furthermore, it was surely quite extraordinary for Cochrane to suggest to de Berenger that he change out of his sharpshooter's uniform so that he could visit Lord Yarmouth, bearing in mind that Lord Yarmouth said at the trial that to appear before him in uniform would have been quite correct and normal. Of course, at the time Cochrane made his affidavit he and his co-defendants were still arguing that de Berenger was not du Bourg, so he might have been reluctant to suggest that de Berenger had asked to borrow a coat lest it appear that de Berenger had something to hide. In any event, it is difficult to accept that de Berenger would have visited Lord Yarmouth in an unkempt and unshaven state, wearing a broad-brimmed hat and borrowed black coat that was far too long for him (Cochrane being 6 inches taller).

Later, when making charges against his solicitors, Cochrane offered a rather different explanation for lending his coat to de Berenger. He suggested that he did so out of concern that de Berenger's creditors might 'come upon him' should they discover that he had broken the rules of the King's Bench. Evidently Cochrane was aware that the explanation provided in his affidavit for giving de Berenger a change of clothes was one of the weakest points in his defence.

In addition to the implausibility of the circumstances described by Cochrane, there are some interesting points of detail here. Did Cochrane really 'forget' to discharge his hackney coach or did he deliberately keep it waiting outside while he bundled de Berenger out of the house? Why did he return from the City without his manservant, Dewman, unless it was to prevent Dewman from witnessing an embarrassing transformation in his visitor's appearance? And why, if the servants' testimony is to be believed, did Cochrane not have the courtesy to ring the bell for his maidservant to help de Berenger out of his house carrying a large bundle of clothes?

Beyond these questions there is also the issue of Cochrane's brother, William, who was serving in France and who, it will be recalled, provided the alleged reason for Cochrane's hurried return from the City. In his affidavit Cochrane said he feared that the officer who had arrived at Green Street might be bringing news of an 'accident' to his brother, which was why he returned home so promptly. In support of this explanation Cochrane later produced an affidavit from his brother stating that he had written to Cochrane early in February to tell him that he had been seriously ill. A medical certificate providing details of the illness was also submitted. However, when it was pointed out in court that his brother's original letter was not affixed to the affidavit, Cochrane's reply was that 'I had no idea of bringing the letter of my brother before a Court of Justice'. So there was no proof that Cochrane was in possession of the letter prior to the morning of the Stock Exchange fraud. It is curious that Cochrane, normally so assiduous in his production of supporting documents, never made public the letter from his brother. He later explained that he had sent it to another relative in Ireland, but since the matter was so important why did his brother William not testify at the trial (he was back in England by then, although admittedly unwell)?

In his *Letter to Lord Ellenborough* Cochrane elaborated on the note he had received from de Berenger which he had allegedly misunderstood to be referring to an 'accident' to his brother. According to Cochrane, the writer said that 'he had something to communicate which would affect my feeling mind' or words to that effect. But is that how an officer would communicate the fact that he was bringing bad news about a near relative? And would someone in de Berenger's position write an obscure note appealing to Cochrane's 'feeling mind' without any mention of what his mission was about? But, of course, if Cochrane was guilty he would have to come up with a form of words that could be interpreted either as a note from an officer bringing news about his brother or as an appeal from de Berenger for help in his distressed circumstances. Hence, perhaps, the rather tortuous explanation offered.

If Cochrane was indeed a participant in the fraud, there remains the puzzle as to why the final stage of the otherwise carefully planned deception should go so disastrously wrong. If it was prearranged that de Berenger was to terminate his mission at Green Street, why was Cochrane not there to meet him? And who was supposed to be responsible for providing a change of clothes for de Berenger? These questions remain unanswered but some light is thrown on the matter in de Berenger's own version of events presented in the next chapter.

RED OR GREEN?

The colour of de Berenger's coat when he appeared before Lord Cochrane on the morning of 21 February is the critical issue in the case. If the coat was red, Cochrane was certainly guilty; if it was green then very probably he was not. It will be recollected that successive witnesses testified to seeing du Bourg travelling in a red coat all the way from Dover to Green Street, while Cochrane himself insisted that de Berenger appeared before him wearing green, and his servants provided inconsistent evidence in their statements to Farrers (red) and their voluntary affidavits (green collar). Since we know that de Berenger was wearing red for most of his journey to London (there are too many witnesses to think otherwise), he must have changed his clothes from red to green towards the end of his coach ride, or at any rate before he saw Cochrane, if Cochrane's story is to be believed.

In order to untangle the evidence on this crucial point it is necessary to ask two questions: first, did de Berenger have the opportunity to change out of his uniform; and second, did he have the means to do so – was he carrying with him an alternative set of clothes? There are also the various contradictory witness statements to be considered, as well as the plausibility of the story told by Cochrane as to the circumstances of de Berenger's borrowing his coat and hat.

As far as opportunity goes, de Berenger would have had time to change at Green Street while waiting some two hours for Cochrane to return from the City. However, it is hardly credible that he could have arrived in his incriminating red uniform in the expectation that Cochrane, who was on leave, would be away from home; assuming that Cochrane was not party to the hoax, de Berenger would know that appearing before him as an aide-de-camp would be fatal. Furthermore, even if he gambled on Cochrane not being at home, finding a room to change in would present a problem: a parlour is open to the toings and froings of servants and any casual visitors, and one cannot invite oneself into a secure changing room. Therefore we must reject Cochrane's suggestion that de Berenger might have changed while waiting for him to return home (see also The Missing Witness, p. 115).

Could de Berenger have changed clothes in the hackney coach while driving from Marsh Gate to Grosvenor Square? Almost certainly not. This was a journey of little more than a mile and a half and would have taken, perhaps, fifteen minutes, bearing in mind that, according to the witness, Barwick, the coach was travelling fast. Furthermore, Barwick, the bank clerk, was in a position to observe de Berenger as he followed the messenger over Westminster Bridge to the Haymarket. Nor is there any mention of blinds being pulled up to protect de Berenger's privacy. But to understand the sheer physical impossibility of changing uniforms in a jolting coach over such a short journey, it is only necessary to quote Cochrane himself in *A Letter to Lord Ellenborough*:

And certainly there were so many things to do before a change of coats could be thoroughly performed that it would unquestionably have been a work of time. De Berenger would have had to take off his grey greatcoat, to open his portmanteau, to take out his green coat, to take off his scarlet coat, to put on his green coat and his grey great coat, to replace his scarlet coat in the portmanteau, and strap it up before the operation could be fully effected.

What about the third possibility, that de Berenger changed his clothes during the final stage of the post-chaise journey between Dartford and Marsh Gate? The difficulties of changing in a jolting carriage have already been referred to but more importantly, from Shilling's evidence it is clear that de Berenger was engaged in conversation with the postboys for much of the journey and this must have happened through an open window. Cochrane makes much of the statement by Shilling to the effect that de Berenger pulled up the side coach blind (but not the front blind) as they came to Marsh Gate, Cochrane's view being that de Berenger probably changed his clothes at this point. However, the facts point to the opposite conclusion. If de Berenger wanted to pull up the blind to give himself privacy while he changed, he would have done so well before the end of the coach stage: to do so between the coach stands at The Three Stags at Lambeth and Marsh Gate (a distance of a few hundred yards) would leave nothing like enough time to switch uniforms. It is much more likely that de Berenger was anxious not to be recognised as he approached the neighbourhood of his lodgings. There is also, of course, the statement from the waterman at Marsh Gate that the messenger who changed coaches there wore a scarlet uniform. (In his *Letter to Lord Ellenborough* Cochrane makes the rather tortuous argument that the waterman could not have seen de Berenger's coat because he was very short and would not have been able to see over the top of the carriage door which he would have opened towards him!) Finally, the driver, Shilling, would surely have noticed if de Berenger had stepped off his coach in different clothes to those he wore when he got in.

It would appear then that de Berenger had little if any opportunity to change out of red and into green prior to appearing before Cochrane on that Monday morning. More conclusive, however, is the evidence that he did not have the means with him to effect such a change. De Berenger's own statement that he carried a yellow portmanteau containing his red uniform down to Dover and left it there is corroborated by the evidence given at the Davidson trial. That portmanteau was indeed later found abandoned at the Royal Oak. No witness mentions the existence of a portmanteau carried by de Berenger on his journey from Dover to London, other than Crane who does say that the officer he took to Green Street had with him 'a bit of a portmanteau' which, curiously, he describes as 'big enough to wrap a coat in'. However, the only 'portmanteau' that de Berenger could have carried was his small black leather dispatch case, which was seen by numerous witnesses, but which most certainly was not big enough to hold a change of uniform. Crane himself says that the 'bit of a portmanteau' was black, so presumably he is referring to the same dispatch case, and it must be concluded that the gratuitous description 'big enough to wrap a coat in' was either a careless mistake or, as has been suggested, a deliberately misleading insertion.

The conclusion from all this is that de Berenger appears to have had neither the opportunity nor the means to change out of his aide-de-camp's uniform while travelling from Dover to London nor, indeed, while at Green Street itself.

THE WITNESSES

A remarkable feature of the trial was the apparent ease with which witnesses could be induced to give false evidence. De Berenger had evidently suborned each of his six alibi witnesses, whose statements about his whereabouts on Sunday 20 February were demonstrably false. If witnesses were so readily available to give false statements on oath and in court, one can imagine how easy it would be to find witnesses from the poorer classes to provide voluntary affidavits, without risk of penalty, to support whatever version of events was required. Clearly, voluntary witness statements that could not be tested under cross-examination in court were, to say the least, unreliable.

The statements of Cochrane's servants need to be viewed in this light. Thomas Dewman (footman), Isaac Davis (former black servant) and Mary Turpin (maidservant) had each made voluntary affidavits which had been prepared by Cochrane himself. However, Mr Parkinson of Farrers spent the whole morning of 11 May examining the servants separately after warning them that they would be answerable in court for what they said and that they must be able to support their statements on oath and under cross-examination. Indeed, that Farrers were unhappy about the manner in which the servants' earlier voluntary affidavits had been drawn up is clear from their response to Cochrane's attack on them (see p. 81) and from the following extract from their bills of costs: 'March 19: Attending your lordship on the drafts of certain affidavits which you had prepared to be sworn by your servants and conference thereon when *we recommended that no further affidavits should be published for the present*' (emphasis added). Having just published his somewhat incautious affidavit of 11 March, Cochrane proceeded to ignore his solicitors' advice by enclosing his servants' affidavits in his letter to the Admiralty of 22 March and subsequently publishing them.

The evidence of each of Cochrane's five servants needs to be considered separately. It should be borne in mind that there were three occasions when they had the opportunity to provide statements: first, when Cochrane prepared voluntary affidavits for them to swear on 21 March; second, when they were examined by Parkinson of Farrers on 11 May (these statements being included in the defence brief); and finally, when further affidavits were presented in support of Cochrane's application for a retrial on 20 June (the affidavits being sworn on 13/14 June).

As far as the three affidavits sworn on 21 March are concerned (Exhibit 8), little need be said other than that Dewman, Davis and Turpin all described the officer as wearing a greatcoat with a green collar underneath it – without mentioning the colour of the undercoat or even the fact that they could not see it (if this was indeed the case). Each of the servants testified that the collar of de Berenger's coat was green, which would rule out the uniform of Lord Yarmouth's sharpshooters, whose collar was stated by Lord Yarmouth himself to be red. On the other hand, the collar of de Berenger's aide-de-camp's uniform was a very dark blue (see back cover), which could quite easily be mistaken for bottle green. The depositions given to Farrers are more revealing.

Thomas Dewman stated to Parkinson that 'the officer wore a dark fur cap, a rough grey greatcoat such as the guards wear. He had a red military coat under it with a green collar . . . the officer had no portmanteau that the deponent saw.' His affidavit of 14 June went a little further than that of 21 March, saying that such part of the officer's undercoat as he could see was green. But he added that the officer carried 'a small leather clothes bag or portmanteau which deponent believes might have had a change of clothes'. This last statement was in flat contradiction of his deposition to Farrers and was surely inserted to meet the point made by Lord Ellenborough at the trial to the effect that de Berenger did not appear to have the means to 'shift himself'.

Isaac Davis was not examined by Farrers and played no further part in the proceedings because he had sailed to Gibraltar with Admiral Flemming on 1 May, having (it is suggested) collected £250 from the Stock Exchange as a reward for identifying de Berenger.

Mary Turpin stated to Parkinson that she had seen the officer get out of the coach (a fact omitted from her voluntary affidavit) and again later when she was putting coal on the fire. 'He wore a grey greatcoat with a red coat underneath it with a green collar.' He had a sword and a 'small portmanteau', and she did not see the officer leave. In a direct contradiction of this last statement, and in a new version inconsistent with her two affidavits given on 21 March and 14 June, Cochrane later claimed that Mary Turpin had opened the door to let de Berenger out of the house and had carried the 'portmanteau and bundle into the coach'. He added this information when making charges against his solicitors and said furthermore that she could have testified to this had she been called as a witness which, in his view, she should have been. This, surely, is one of Cochrane's more flagrant misrepresentations of his servants' evidence.

Eleanor Barnes, the housekeeper, was not a key witness because she was out when the officer arrived, and although she returned to the house between 11 a.m. and midday when the officer was with Cochrane in the drawing room, she did not see him herself.

Sarah Busk (or Cotton) appears to have been a reluctant witness. She did not provide a voluntary affidavit for Cochrane as the other servants did on 21 March, although one was prepared for her, and she was not examined by Farrers before the trial. She had been dismissed from Cochrane's service on the very day of the fraud for reasons about which there can only be speculation. Her departure may have been linked to the fact that Isaac Davis, Cochrane's former black servant, was in the kitchen at 13 Green Street on the morning of 21 February, even though his notice had just expired. If Cochrane was guilty and therefore knew that de Berenger would be turning up at his house that morning, he certainly would not have wanted Davis to be there, because de Berenger was known to Davis and would very likely be recognised. Why then was Davis in the kitchen? Perhaps Sarah Busk had illicitly invited him to the house, which would explain Cochrane's later furious description of her as an 'infernal faggot' and her immediate dismissal from his service on the day of the fraud when he discovered that Davis had witnessed de Berenger's arrival. The affidavit she eventually swore to on

13 June, while stating that such part of the officer's undercoat as she could see was green, omitted very sensitive matters that she had included in her original draft affidavit (see p. 115).

There are, then, important differences between what the servants swore to in each other's presence on 21 March, what they said individually and privately to Parkinson on 11 May, what they swore to on 13/14 June, and what Cochrane later claimed they meant to say or would have said had they been asked. Of these various versions there can surely be little doubt that the most reliable were the depositions taken by Farrers on the basis of best practice procedures. This evidence must be preferred over other inconsistent statements which would have been subject to Cochrane's interventions or influence. Clearly Farrers themselves took this view and that is why de Berenger's dress is described as red in their brief and why Cochrane's counsel, Serjeant Best, felt obliged to admit this in court. It is also entirely understandable that Cochrane's legal advisers declined to call his servants as witnesses, since they might not have been able to support his version in court. As Lord Brougham, one of Cochrane's counsel, said when responding to criticisms of the decision not to call the servants: 'We had too good reasons for not calling them, and were I tomorrow to conduct it, I should . . . still refuse to call any of them, and so would all the profession.'

It is also worth drawing attention to Cochrane's own contradictory explanations for Dewman's inconsistent statements. In his submission to the Court of King's Bench on 14 June, Cochrane said that in the brief Dewman was represented as observing that de Berenger was dressed in a red coat, but his servant's recollection was incorrect: 'The fact was that, being questioned as to the colour of the coat, he stated that he [de Berenger] appeared to be an army officer, to which he very naturally attached the idea of a red coat, for the servants did not see it.' Having both acknowledged that Dewman told Farrers that the coat was red, and provided a rather lame explanation for this alleged error, Cochrane subsequently denied that Dewman had ever described the coat as red.

In his letter to Lord Ellenborough, Cochrane also made an assertion that was at odds with the affidavits he produced on behalf of his servants. These affidavits, it will be recalled, testified to the fact that de Berenger's great coat was buttoned up and that the collar of his undercoat was green – the implication being that the breast and the skirts of the uniform worn underneath were not visible. Yet Cochrane says that when de Berenger appeared before him, and borrowed his hat, he then 'on trying on the hat and buttoning up the great-coat at the looking-glass' remarked that 'my uniform appears'. It was in response to this that Cochrane allegedly offered to lend de Berenger his black coat. But if de Berenger's uniform appeared so obviously under his buttoned up greatcoat, it is surely inconceivable that Cochrane's servants did not see it. And if they did see it but chose, under Cochrane's persuasion, not to mention its colour, it may reasonably be assumed that the uniform was the incriminating scarlet of an aide-de-camp.

We now come to the key witness, Crane. The Stock Exchange Committee in its second report said he was the first person to come forward in response to its enquiries. He told it that the gentleman he delivered to Green Street was wearing a red coat. (If the coat had been green, Crane would surely not have responded to an advertisement describing du Bourg as wearing red.) However, Crane was not given the Stock Exchange's £250 reward, presumably because he was unable to identify the officer in red as de Berenger, whom, of course, he did not know. The committee said that the gentleman who did receive the reward 'did not testify at the trial', which suggests strongly that the successful claimant for the reward was Cochrane's former black servant, Isaac Davis, who could not be called at the trial because he had gone overseas. Crucially, the Stock Exchange Committee went on to state the following:

That Lord Cochrane was not the first person who pointed out to the sub-Committee that de Berenger was the pretended Colonel du Bourg, since the gentleman to whom the whole of the reward of 250 guineas has since been given for that important service, as well as some other gentlemen, whose names it is unnecessary here to mention, had pointed him out to the sub-Committee *five* days prior to the publication of his lordship's affidavit of the 11th of March, and a warrant had actually been previously obtained against him.

This statement shows that there were at least two other 'gentlemen' who had identified de Berenger as du Bourg in response to the committee's advertised reward. These gentlemen may also have observed de Berenger in the red uniform, which raises the question of who they could possibly have been if not Cochrane's own servants. One of the gentlemen might have been the would-be blackmailer, Le Marchant, who evidently tried to claim the reward on the basis of de Berenger's imprudent conversation with him (see p. 25). In any event, the existence of so many witnesses identifying du Bourg as de Berenger removes one of Cochrane's main defences – namely that he was the first and indeed only person to name his visitor as de Berenger and that if he were guilty, he would not have dared to volunteer this connection with the perpetrator of the fraud.

There remains the question of the two 'respectable tradesmen' who came forward after the trial on behalf of Cochrane to swear that they had seen an officer in *green* changing coaches at Marsh Gate on that Monday morning (Exhibit 9). The value of such voluntary affidavits has already been questioned, but what are we to make of the statement sworn by Joseph Rayment? Rayment, who was described as a fishmonger, said that he saw a chaise and four pass his house, near Marsh Gate. Being informed that it brought intelligence that the French army was cut to pieces and Bonaparte killed, he went out to learn more when he saw the post-chaise draw up alongside a hackney coach. A person got out of the post-chaise and as he was transferring to the hackney coach his greatcoat partly opened, enabling the deponent to see the coat underneath, which appeared to be dark green 'like the sharpshooters'. How Rayment could have learned of the military news is baffling, as is his suggestion that he had time after seeing the post-chaise speed past his door and after hearing the news, to go out, catch up with the coach and witness the scene he described.

Thomas Cochrane as a captain. Cochrane had established a brilliant reputation as a fearless and resourceful naval commander who, with limited means, had inflicted great damage on enemy ships and communications.

WRIGHT'S HOTEL AND SHIP INN,
DOVOR,

The Ship Inn, Dover. Colonel du Bourg arrived at the Ship on a cold winter's night to reveal sensational news of the Allies' final victory and Napoleon's death at the hands of the Cossacks.

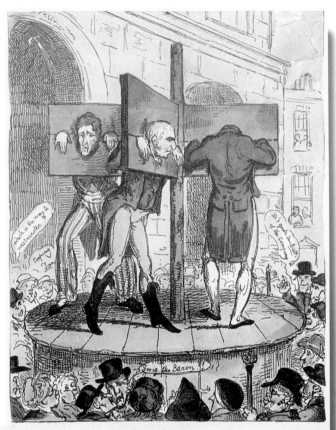

THE SEVERE

SENTENCE

ON

LORD COCHRANE & OTHERS,

TO

STAND IN THE PILLORY,

IN THE FRONT OF THE

Royal=Exchange,

FOR

A CONSPIRACY,

TO RAISE, BY FALSE REPORTS, THE PRICE OF THE PUBLIC FUNDS;

As pronounced by Sir Simon Le Blanc,

IN THE COURT OF KING'S-BENCH,

ON TUESDAY, the 21st of JUNE, 1814.

Broadsheet announcing the sentencing of Cochrane. Cochrane and his co-defendants were sentenced to the pillory but this punishment was later remitted amid concern that such humiliation of a popular hero might provoke public disorder.

Representation of y.e Gull Trap — & y.e principal Actors in y.e New Farce call'd y.e Hoax? — lately perform'd with great Eclat on y.e S — k X — ge.

Cruikshank's cartoon showing Cochrane in the stocks, still fighting. The Stock Exchange fraud was portrayed in numerous cartoons. Here Cochrane blasts away at Napoleon from the stocks, and a coach and four, heading for Green Street, heralds the death of the French tyrant.

Above: Bricklayers Arms, Old Kent Road. De Berenger took a coach from the Bricklayers Arms to travel down to Dover, but on his return trip to London he considered the inn to be too public a place to change coaches.

Right: The new Stock Exchange, Capel Court. The Stock Exchange had recently moved into its august new premises at Capel Court and was in the process of improving its public image with the introduction of stricter trading rules.

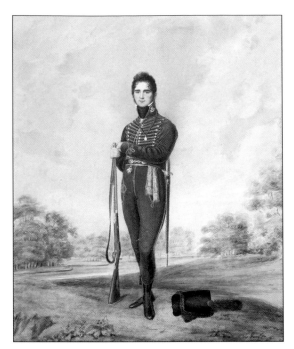

Left: A Duke of Cumberland's Sharpshooter. When de Berenger arrived at Cochrane's house in Green Street, was he wearing the bottle-green uniform of the Duke of Cumberland's Sharpshooters, or was he dressed in the incriminating red garb of an aide-de-camp?

Below: Court of King's Bench, Guildhall. Cochrane was tried in the Court of King's Bench by the Lord Chief Justice, Lord Ellenborough, who controversially allowed the proceedings on the first day to continue far into the night.

King's Bench Prison, Southwark. Cochrane managed to escape over the perimeter wall, but after he was recaptured, he was kept in a secure unit until his release.

The Chelsea Stadium at Cremorne House, opened by 'Baron de Beaufain' (de Berenger) in 1831. The sports festivals held here were a forerunner of the modern Olympic Games.

Cochrane in old age. Although pardoned and reinstated with all his honours, in his last years Cochrane was tormented by his conviction for the Stock Exchange fraud.

THE MISSING WITNESS

Cochrane had secretly married Katherine Barnes in Scotland eighteen months before the Stock Exchange fraud (the couple were later to remarry in an Anglican Church in 1818). Yet there is no mention of Lady Cochrane in any of the trial-related statements published by Cochrane, his servants or indeed anyone else. She becomes a non-person as far as the events of 21 February 1814 are concerned, suggesting that she might have been residing at Holly Hill while Cochrane was in London. However, evidence that has now come to light demonstrates beyond doubt that Lady Cochrane was not only at 13 Green Street when de Berenger called but also entertained him to breakfast while he awaited Cochrane's return from the City. The information is revealed in a note from Cochrane to Parkinson, his solicitor at Farrers, dated 31 March 1814. It reads as follows:

I am exceedingly anxious not to bring forward the name of a young friend who is living here with me and with whom Captain de Berenger sat until my return from the City. Can I avoid doing so if I prosecute the Committee? She can say nothing more than the others have deposed.

Yours very sincerely,
COCHRANE
PS. Destroy this

In case it should be thought that Cochrane's 'young friend' was his mistress, it should be recalled that his marriage at this time had not been openly acknowledged. Confirmation that the lady who entertained de Berenger was indeed Cochrane's wife is to be found in a draft affidavit by the servant Sarah Busk (or Cotton), prepared for the purpose of supporting Cochrane's application for a retrial. The draft reads as follows:

This deponent took up the water for breakfast to Mrs Cochrane in the Drawing Room and Mrs C. said that she understood an

115

officer was waiting for Lord Cochrane in the Parlour and requested deponent to ask him if he would like some breakfast which this deponent did but the officer declined saying he had breakfasted and upon this deponent making Mrs Cochrane acquainted with this Mrs C. requested this deponent to go to him again and ask if he wanted to take a dish of tea upon which he repeated he had breakfasted but then asked deponent for a little water to wash his hands which deponent took him and after he had wished his hands this deponent showed him into the drawing room.

In the final affidavit all mention of 'Mrs Cochrane' is expunged, and it is clear from this that the servant's evidence was edited to avoid any reference to her being at Green Street. (She was presumably known to her staff as 'Mrs Cochrane' because of her then unofficial position.) Interestingly, there is evidence in the trial papers that the prosecution's solicitors, Crowder, Lavie and Garth, at one point sought to have Lady Cochrane called as a witness but Farrers were successful in resisting this.

Cochrane may have been acting protectively towards his wife who at the time of the fraud was a girl of only 18 and heavily pregnant with her first child, a boy, born just two months later on 18 April. But he may also have been embarrassed by the possible disclosure of the fact that the military imposter had been welcomed with such intimate hospitality into his own home on the day of the crime. In any event, the evidence that Lady Cochrane entertained de Berenger at Green Street is very significant on several counts. First, the draft affidavit of Sarah Busk confirms almost precisely de Berenger's account of what took place there (see Chapter 10 and Exhibit 13), further strengthening the credibility of his version of events. Second, it demonstrates how vulnerable Cochrane's servants were to having their evidence suppressed or manipulated. Third, Lady Cochrane would have had a better opportunity than any of the servants to see the colour of de Berenger's uniform and could have been a powerful witness in her husband's favour *if* she were able to say that the undercoat was green. Fourth, it is rather surprising that a dishevelled casual caller and complete stranger, albeit an officer, should be invited to have breakfast with her ladyship – unless perhaps she had some forewarning of his arrival. Fifth, it demonstrates a certain audacity on the part of Cochrane in later suggesting, as he did, that de Berenger changed his clothes at Green Street, knowing full well that his servants and his wife had closely attended de Berenger while awaiting his return. Finally, the presence of Lady Cochrane during de Berenger's visit helps to explain why Cochrane's legal advisers were so reluctant to call his servants as witnesses: under cross-examination it could well have come out that Lady Cochrane was there and had entertained the unexpected guest, a revelation that would have been highly damaging to the defence.

THE BLACKMAILER

It will be recalled that Cochrane was approached by Le Marchant who claimed to have had a conversation with de Berenger that implicated him. Although it might be tempting to pass over the evidence of Le Marchant, coming as it did from a would-be blackmailer, the detailed statement he sent to Cochrane is nevertheless of some interest. This is because it shows familiarity with de Berenger's aspirations and his connections with the Cochranes, evidently revealed when he was the worse for drink, and also because it ties in with the evidence given at the trial by the Honourable Alexander Murray. Murray was a former military officer who, having fallen on hard times, was living as an undischarged debtor within the rules of the King's Bench. Therefore, like de Berenger, he was required to reside close by the prison. Murray had become friendly with his near neighbour and testified that he was visited by de Berenger one Sunday at the end of January or beginning of February. At some point in the conversation de Berenger revealed that he was involved in a plan with Cochrane Johnstone and Lord Cochrane that would put many thousands of pounds in these two gentlemen's pockets. Murray also testified to the intimacy between Cochrane Johnstone and de Berenger but he understood Lord Cochrane to be a more recent acquaintance.

It appears that de Berenger could be quite indiscreet, particularly when under the influence of drink, and that in his excitement he intimated to both Le Marchant and Murray that he was involved in something with the Cochranes that could make a lot of money for all concerned. It seems unlikely that two very similar stories about de Berenger's revelations, from persons unknown to each other, would be fabricated.

It is also significant that Cochrane and/or his solicitors appear to have been sufficiently concerned about what Le Marchant may have known to arrange for a Mr Palfreman to meet with him on 11 May at the Burton Ale House in Pontin Street, Haymarket. Palfreman made a note of their conversation, which was given to Farrers, and according to this le Marchant said that at the earliest opportunity he had communicated his knowledge of de Berenger to the Stock Exchange Committee along with supporting affidavits from two military officers. It would appear therefore that Le Marchant was seeking the advertised reward from the Stock Exchange while at the same time trying to extort money from Cochrane on the basis of 'not telling'. In any event, Cochrane would have been made aware of this conversation, which shows that his claim to have been the first (and only) person to identify de Berenger was mere bluster.

THE TRIAL AND ITS AFTERMATH

Cochrane alleged that the trial procedures and the behaviour of Lord Ellenborough as presiding judge contributed to the jury's unjust verdict against him. To begin with, the removal of the case from the Old Bailey to the Court of King's Bench meant that a 'special' jury was selected from men of commercial standing. Cochrane knew that he would have stood a better chance with a jury drawn from the general populace for whom he remained a great national hero. However, to suggest as he did that the jury was 'packed' was absurd.

Then there was the issue of the joint defence. Cochrane claimed that by insisting on linking his case to that of Butt and Cochrane

Johnstone, his legal advisers acted against his interest and played a major part in his downfall. However, Cochrane had himself conducted a pre-trial joint defence through the pamphlet war launched against the Stock Exchange and, as one of his own counsel later explained, the prima facie case against Cochrane was at least as strong as that against his co-defendants given that it was to his house that Colonel du Bourg had resorted at the end of his journey.

Cochrane also castigated Lord Ellenborough for allowing the first day's hearing to continue late into the night, to the alleged disadvantage of the defence. Today, such extended sittings would be totally unacceptable, but it is worth noting that some judges at this time adopted the practice of sitting out the trial, however long, whether for felony or misdemeanour, and never adjourning. It is also unlikely that the admitted tiredness of Cochrane's legal team affected their line of defence in a material way.

Cochrane was on much stronger ground when he criticised Lord Ellenborough for revealing only too clearly to the jury his own view of the guilt of the accused. Henry Cecil, himself a former judge, while convinced that Cochrane was guilty, acknowledged in his book *A Matter of Speculation* that Lord Ellenborough did not conduct this case dispassionately, was clearly convinced of the co-defendants' guilt and on a number of key issues offered his own opinion rather than leaving matters to the jury. The contemporary observer and diarist, Crabb Robinson, evidently had a similar impression of the great judge's conduct during the second day of the trial:

> I was in court soon after 10 to hear the exculpatory evidence of the defendants. It was most unsatisfactory. De Berenger called 5 or 6 witnesses to prove an alibi. Lord Ellenborough considered them as perjured. I am not so clearly impressed with a conviction of their guilt and thought his Lordship strained some points against them. Lord Ellenborough is very acute as well as judicious. And I have no doubt he is right in his impression 99 times out of a hundred. But he forms an opinion very soon and is

not easily shaken from an opinion once formed. Were I a defendant I should dread his first impression exceedingly.

Lord Ellenborough's controversial conduct of the Cochrane trial became a *cause célèbre* in itself but the undoubted bias he displayed, while it may have affected the jury's verdict, has no bearing on the question of Cochrane's guilt. Even so, Cochrane was later able to make great play with the argument that he, an innocent man, had been brought down by the unbridled prejudice of a judge who abhorred his radical politics.

Finally, Cochrane complained bitterly that his application to the court for a new trial was turned down by Lord Ellenborough who had invoked a technical rule requiring all the co-defendants to be present before the court, which clearly they could not be because Cochrane Johnstone and M'Rae had absconded. To many this looked like a flagrant denial of justice and Cochrane, again, made great play with it in his subsequent campaign of self-vindication. However, he and his supporters conveniently overlooked the fact that the rule applied only to the court hearing on 14 June. In the subsequent hearing on 20 June, before sentence was pronounced, Cochrane was permitted to make his case for a new trial. This was refused, but not by Lord Ellenborough sitting alone. The decision was made unanimously by the four judges of the Court of King's Bench. On 24 June the Attorney General, Sir William Garrow, made a statement in the House of Commons in which he pointed out that the court, in considering Cochrane's application for a retrial, had not entrenched itself behind technical rules but had considered the case on its merits after giving Cochrane a fair hearing. Cochrane deliberately misled the public when he later claimed repeatedly that a retrial was denied 'because all the persons tried were not present to concur in it, though the law gave me no power to compel their attendance'.

In the context of the question addressed here – the guilt or innocence of Cochrane – the attacks on Lord Ellenborough, the judicial procedures and the handling of the defence must be viewed as an irrelevant sideshow. Cochrane's fulmination on these matters was a deliberate diversion designed to excite sympathy for his cause.

Cochrane's conduct following the trial and his failed application for a retrial provide further insights into his involvement in the fraud. In the first place he made a number of statements which are demonstrably false or self-contradictory. In his address before the House of Commons he claimed that 'he took no care to prepare his defence being so conscious of his innocence, that he never read his brief, gave instructions or attended a consultation'. This statement was repeated on several occasions and also in *The Autobiography of a Seaman* where he says that 'conscious of my innocence, I took no personal steps for my defence, beyond forwarding a general statement of a few lines to my solicitors. . . . I never even read the completed brief which they drew up for the guidance of my counsel'. In February 1861, following publication of *The Autobiography*, Farrers refuted the implied criticism of their professionalism by releasing extracts from their bill of costs. These showed that they had met with Cochrane on five occasions between 9 May and 7 June 1814, going through all the evidence with him, drafting the brief in his presence and reading it over to him for his final approval. Any suggestion that Cochrane neglected his own defence is therefore quite wrong.

Another statement repeated by Cochrane on many occasions was that since he had volunteered the information that the visitor to his house was de Berenger, this should be taken as proof of his innocence for it was hardly the act of a guilty man to disclose such potentially damaging intelligence. Yet this assertion was untrue. At least three individuals had identified du Bourg as de Berenger five days prior to Cochrane's disclosure, according to the Stock Exchange Committee's second report. (The committee's reports were intended for its members only, but their contents seem to have been widely leaked – no doubt because the committee was anxious to protect its reputation in the eyes of the investing public.) Furthermore, Cochrane would almost certainly have known that his own former servant, Isaac Davis, had recognised de Berenger as he arrived at Green Street: servants talk to each other and Cochrane's faithful retainer, Dewman, would have reported the matter to his master. There can be little doubt that Cochrane publicly disclosed de Berenger's visit to his house and the fact that he had given de Berenger a change of clothes because he anticipated these circumstances were about to be made public. His subsequent claim that he was the only person to draw the Stock Exchange's attention to de Berenger was made in bad faith: he knew perfectly well that Le Marchant had communicated his information about de Berenger to the Stock Exchange Committee because this fact had been reported to his solicitors.

Cochrane also suggested after the trial that he had been framed for political reasons. In support of this interpretation of events he claimed that Crane, the prosecution witness, had at one stage told the Stock Exchange Committee that the person he drove to Green Street was none other than Cochrane himself. The committee in its second report dismissed this allegation as a fabrication, and the implication is that the affidavit produced to support Cochrane's allegation was also false. Similarly, the claim by the same witness to the effect that Crane had boasted of receiving part of the £250 reward for identifying du Bourg is refuted by the Stock Exchange Committee's statement that Crane had received no part of the money. These contradictions confirm that voluntary affidavits, though much favoured by Cochrane and his co-defendants, could be manufactured almost at will.

Cochrane's cavalier approach to questions of fact is further illustrated by the complaint made in *The Autobiography* against the Stock Exchange's prosecuting counsel, Gurney. Here he said he consulted Gurney on the preparation of his pre-trial voluntary affidavit and was then shocked to find that a man to whom he had confided so much personal information should become his prosecutor at the trial. But in the affidavit he presented to the Court of King's Bench when applying for a retrial he swore that his earlier affidavit was prepared 'on the impulse of the moment' and 'without any communication whatsoever with any other person, and without any assistance'.

Another glaring inconsistency emerges in Cochrane's treatment of the evidence provided by his servant, Dewman. Appearing before the Court of King's Bench on 14 June, Cochrane sought to explain the fact that in his brief Dewman had described de Berenger's coat as red: this was because de Berenger appeared to be an army officer 'to which he very naturally attached the idea of a red coat'. This lame explanation was later abandoned and instead Cochrane denied altogether that Dewman had ever told his solicitors that the coat was red.

However, far more important than any of the contradictions and inconsistencies is Cochrane's behaviour after the trial in relation to Crane's evidence against him. Time and again Cochrane attacked Crane as a liar, and, as we have seen, went so far as to obtain affidavits testifying to his bad character and improper motives. Cochrane also insisted that had his servants been called at the trial as they should have been, they would have contradicted Crane's assertion that de Berenger's coat was red and confirmed that it was green. If Cochrane was so confident of those assertions, why did he not clear his name by bringing proceedings against Crane for perjury and producing his servants and other witnesses to give evidence on his behalf? Cochrane complained bitterly that he was denied a retrial despite the new evidence he had produced, yet the solution lay in his own hands. After all, he had brought proceedings for perjury against one prosecution witness, Davidson, in order *indirectly* to undermine the prosecution case – even though Davidson's evidence had no bearing on Cochrane's own defence. Why then did he not bring proceedings against Crane in order to refute directly the charges against him? There can surely be only one answer: Cochrane confined himself to verbal assaults on Crane because he knew very well that if he brought proceedings against the key prosecution witness he could not rely on the evidence of his own servants, or that of other witnesses whose affidavits he had obtained, to stand up in court under cross-examination.

In May 1816 Cochrane published a pamphlet entitled *De Berenger Detected*, which was intended to refute de Berenger's account of the Stock Exchange fraud. However, the contents of this pamphlet are highly damaging to Cochrane's case because they are based on a letter from de Berenger to his solicitor,

Tahourdin, the date of which (ostensibly 17 February 1814) is clearly forged.* Whether the forgery was undertaken by Cochrane Johnstone, who had somehow obtained the document and sent it to his nephew, or by Cochrane himself, no one can say, but both de Berenger's letter and the circumstances of its publication are very significant.

The letter itself is written in a cryptic style, evidently because of the extreme sensitivity of the subject matter. It was clearly composed while de Berenger was in prison awaiting trial since it says 'should the trial go against me (and the law is gloriously uncertain), my fate is not bounded by disgrace and punishment only, for the doors of a prison will close upon me for life'. What de Berenger had in mind here is that once he was in prison, his creditors were in a position to keep him there, even after his sentence had come to an end. The gist of the letter is that faced with this appalling prospect de Berenger wanted unnamed parties to fulfil their stated promise to compensate him properly for his role in the fraud: 'services ought not to be appreciated by the gain alone, but by the prevention of serious loss, and next, by the injury such service entails on the person rendering it.' He wanted his solicitor to extract a legally binding agreement from those concerned: 'done it really must be, and regularly too, each party bearing his separate portion.' There is a strong indication here that de Berenger was using his negotiating position ahead of the trial to obtain a legally enforceable financial package from his partners in the fraud. The unspoken threat was that if they failed to cooperate, he might implicate them in the fraud, which was

---

* Douglas Cochrane (1965), in defending his ancestor, suggests that the misdating of de Berenger's letter was the result of Tahourdin's allegedly sloppy approach to dating his correspondence, i.e. the letter was inadvertently dated prior to the date of receipt. However, it is surely implausible that Tahourdin, a man of business, would have carelessly put a date of 17 February on a letter whose actual date of receipt must have been later than 21 June when de Berenger was sentenced, bearing in mind, too, that the letter was a highly sensitive document considered by Tahourdin to be so important that he passed it on to a third party.

presumably why de Berenger's solicitor handed the letter to his client and business partner, Cochrane Johnstone.

Cochrane, in his typically robust manner, turned de Berenger's letter on its head. He claimed that the subject matter was not the fraud that had just taken place but rather the fraud '*then about to be committed* through de Berenger's agency' (emphasis in original). He says that if the investment trio really were involved in the plot, de Berenger would have produced the bond implementing the proposed financial arrangements, presumably knowing full well that the other guilty parties had declined to offer such support. As with Le Marchant's blackmailing communication, Cochrane regarded publication as the most effective counter-attack – although here he appears also to have knowingly relied on a misdated letter to prove his point without realising that any casual reader could see that the date was a forgery.

There is one final aspect of Cochrane's conduct after the trial that is at least consistent with his direct involvement in the fraud. As the criminal investigation proceeded, one conspirator after another was 'given up' to the authorities. First it was M'Rae who was to become the scapegoat, as is apparent from Cochrane Johnstone's letter to the Stock Exchange enclosing M'Rae's proposed £10,000 reward for identifying the fraudster(s). In a pamphlet published after the trial M'Rae stated that if this outrageous scheme had been accepted by the Stock Exchange and the money paid, the conspirators, comprising Cochrane, Cochrane Johnstone and Butt, had agreed to pay him £5,000 in instalments for taking the blame. The next to be given up was de Berenger. Once he had been identified as Colonel du Bourg it became necessary to get him out of the way so as not to endanger the others. Hence de Berenger's flight to Scotland, with the inducement of an up-front cash payment as well as further promises from the other conspirators. Finally, Cochrane Johnstone in effect gave himself up when, in the face of the overwhelming trial evidence against him, he fled abroad, thereby acknowledging his guilt.

This left Butt as the remaining lead conspirator. Of course, were Cochrane innocent, it would be understandable if he expressed bitterness at being dragged down by his co-defendants, Butt and

Cochrane Johnstone. On the other hand, if he were guilty, he would have to handle Butt in particular very carefully since Butt would have information that could be used to implicate Cochrane. Interestingly, after the trial Cochrane was assiduous in his praise of Butt and seems to have taken every opportunity to express his belief in Butt's innocence. In his defence before the House of Commons he said he had witnessed many generous and disinterested acts by Mr Butt, and he thought him incapable of a dishonourable action. In his *Letter to Lord Ellenborough*, too, Cochrane devoted several pages to seeking to exculpate Butt even at the expense of his uncle. Luckily for Cochrane, Butt continued to protest his innocence and was not tempted to tell his story as de Berenger had done. However, some sixteen years after the trial, when Butt was a debtor in the Fleet prison, there is evidence that he tried to blackmail Cochrane. Certainly he made requests for money and there is a revealing entry for 1 November 1831 in the diary of William Jackson, Cochrane's secretary and personal assistant: 'Lord Dundonald [Cochrane] called. . . . Showed me letters from Butt accusing him of participating in the fraud! and of seeing him with de Berenger on the Saturday before at his office!!'

Butt's allegations corroborated de Berenger's version of events, which is recounted in the next chapter, although he could of course have concocted his claims on the basis of de Berenger's published book, *The Noble Stockjobber*. Jackson's diary entry continues: 'Believe I have a letter from Butt indignantly denying ever seeing de Berenger at his office in his life.' So Cochrane had evidently taken care to cover himself against any future attempt by Butt to support de Berenger's version of events.

THE CRIME

There can be little doubt that the perpetrators of the 'hoax' were taken aback by both the public outcry that followed and the determination with which the Stock Exchange pursued its investigation. Financial regulation barely existed at this time, the concept of insider trading was unknown and the planting of rumours was no doubt rife, particularly when so much depended on the outcome of great continental battles. Yet the Stock Exchange, now established in grandiose new premises at Capel Court, was beginning to regulate its affairs more rigorously, having in 1812 produced its first codified and printed rulebook. When the London press expressed outrage at the losses inflicted on ordinary investors by the masquerading aide-de-camp, the Exchange was prompted for the first time in its history to take action against those whose deception had created a false market in government securities.

The public's response to the hoax may have been aggravated by another factor. A contemporary pamphlet suggested that sophisticated speculators were aware that the great financiers of the day had their own communications link with the Continent based on signals flashed via fishing boats from the French coast, relays of horses and carrier pigeons. These investors therefore believed that any sensational news, such as the death of Bonaparte, would be first brought to London via these private networks rather than through an official messenger (as indeed occurred a year later when Rothschild was first with the news of Waterloo). When the officer in red spread the news it was the ordinary investing public who allegedly rushed to buy, while the experienced speculators stood aloof. The public outcry was accordingly all the greater.

Whatever the truth of this observation, the conspirators themselves were evidently confident that their deception would not be the subject of a full-blown investigation and prosecution. It may be recalled that M'Rae, when talking to Vinn at the Carolina Coffee House, explained that 'what is contemplated is practiced daily by men of the first consequence. It involves nothing more than biting the biters or, in other words, a hoax upon the Stock Exchange.' De Berenger, using the language of a soldier, referred to the hoax as a 'ruse de guerre'. Cochrane Johnstone, according to de Berenger, justified the proposed hoax on the basis that it was part of 'a war of cunning in the money market'. And it is interesting to note that Cochrane himself took a similar view. In *The Autobiography* he described the offence with which he was charged as 'the dissemination of groundless news to the prejudice of the Stock

Exchange speculators, one of those common deceptions which, I am told, were then, as now, practiced by parties connected with the transactions of the Stock Exchange'. At a later stage in *The Autobiography* he gave his opinion on the gravity of the offence:

Of the subject of the prosecution itself, I will here say one word. It was that of one set of stock-jobbers and their confederates trying – by means of false intelligence – to raise the price of '*time bargains*' at the expense of another set of stock-jobbers, the losers being naturally indignant at the successful hoax. The wrong was not then, and still is not, on the statute book. Such a case had never been tried before, nor has it since – and was termed a 'conspiracy'; or rather, by charging the several defendants – of most of whom I had never before heard – in one indictment, it was brought under the designation of a 'conspiracy'. The 'conspiracy' – such as it was – was nevertheless one, which, as competent persons inform me, has been the practice in all countries ever since stock-jobbing began, and is in the present day constantly practiced, but I never heard mention of the energy of the Stock Exchange even to detect the practice.

Would it be stretching the point to say that Cochrane believed the Stock Exchange, which in his mind consisted of little more than speculators trying to out-trick each other, to be fair game? And was this another example of Cochrane applying the rules of war to civilian life and employing a military deception to defeat an imagined enemy? The only problem in this case was that the enemy turned out to be the ordinary investing public.

CONCLUSION

It is clear that the circumstantial evidence against Cochrane is very strong. The character of this complex man suggests that he was well capable of planning the deception that took place on the morning of 21 February 1814; he was involved with his rogue uncle, an intimate friend, in a common investment strategy that stood to benefit from the fraud; the proceeds of a cheque that he cashed ended up in the hands of the perpetrator of the fraud; the account of his own conduct on the morning of the fraud is implausible; the evidence of witnesses, including his own servants, suggests that the masquerading aide-de-camp appeared before Cochrane in his incriminating scarlet uniform; Cochrane's behaviour after the trial suggests that, for very good reasons, he did not wish to have a rehearing of his case – despite protestations to the contrary; and the most damaging evidence of all, which has only now come to light, is that Cochrane suppressed the fact that his wife had entertained de Berenger to breakfast on the fateful day. Finally, it seems likely that Cochrane was genuinely unaware of the gravity of the offence that the deception involved and the consequences that would ensue: to him it was a question only of duping the speculators or 'biting the biters'. The inescapable conclusion is that Cochrane was very probably guilty as a co-conspirator in the Stock Exchange fraud. As one contemporary pamphlet put it: 'If Lord Cochrane is to be believed he is the most unfortunate man that ever lived; instead of being a conspirator himself, all the world must have conspired against him.'

In making this assessment, no account has been taken of another very important piece of evidence – the detailed account of the fraud given in de Berenger's book *The Noble Stockjobber*, published in 1816. This work directly implicates Cochrane in both the planning of the fraud and the subsequent attempted cover-up, but because de Berenger committed perjury and suborned witnesses at the trial it would be unsafe to rely on his version of events to determine Cochrane's guilt. Nevertheless, once it is established by other evidence that Cochrane very probably was directly involved, de Berenger's account becomes hugely significant. De Berenger, after all, had no obvious incentive to misrepresent Cochrane's role once he had confessed to his own part in the plot. Furthermore, where his story is open to corroboration, it appears to be accurate. The details of his overnight stay in Dover prior to the fraud were, for instance, confirmed by the evidence that came out in the Davidson trial; and his account of his visit to Green Street prior to Cochrane's return from the City is confirmed by the new evidence that Lady Cochrane played hostess to him over breakfast. It is significant, too, that Cochrane's attempt to discredit de Berenger's account in his pamphlet *De Berenger Detected* (also published in 1816) relies almost entirely on correspondence sent by de Berenger to his solicitors, the date of which either Cochrane or his uncle had forged. In other words Cochrane failed to offer any effective refutation of de Berenger's allegations against him.

It has to be said that *The Noble Stockjobber* is appallingly written, full of rambling diversions and philosophical musings and interspersed with scurrilous personal attacks on the Cochranes. In addition, in some points of detail the account cannot be relied upon, particularly where de Berenger's own professional competence is in question. He is clearly conscious of the fact that his disguise proved to be inadequate and his claim that he wore a black bandage or handkerchief over one eye when travelling from Dover to London – which no other witness remarked on – must be seen in this context. He is further embarrassed by his obvious tendency to talk too much, particularly when under the influence of drink. Therefore, in his public confession he disputed Shilling's evidence that he said the Bricklayers Arms was too public a place to get a hackney coach; he similarly contested Le Marchant's account of his very indiscreet conversation at the Gloucester Coffee House. It is presumably for these reasons that contemporary opinion, like modern historians and commentators, tended to ignore an account of the fraud which, when stripped of its emotional excesses and pretentious diversions, is in fact highly persuasive. The reconstruction of the events leading up to and including the fraud that appears in the next chapter is therefore based on de Berenger's story as recounted in *The Noble Stockjobber*.

TEN

How it Happened

In June 1813 de Berenger and Cochrane Johnstone were introduced to each other by Mr Gabriel Tahourdin, a solicitor in the Temple, who acted for them both. Thereafter Cochrane Johnstone consulted de Berenger on his idea for a new pleasure garden and the two men were soon on easy social terms, with de Berenger dining fairly regularly at Cochrane Johnstone's house in Great Cumberland Street. It was not long before de Berenger was introduced to other members of the Cochrane family, including Lord Cochrane, and the extent of his familiarity with them is shown by his social engagements for January 1814 (Exhibit 12). De Berenger met with Lord Cochrane no fewer than eight times in sixteen days.

In conversations at Great Cumberland Street, Butt was frequently mentioned as someone who provided invaluable advice to Cochrane Johnstone and his nephew on their stock market investments. It astonished de Berenger how sums varying from £300 to as many thousands could apparently be made daily without spending a shilling, simply by driving into the City to give instructions to buy or sell. Then, about the beginning of February, there was great excitement in the financial markets as investors awaited the news of an expected battle. According to *The Noble Stockjobber*:

> some false intelligence from abroad, perhaps emanating from the Stock Exchange itself, caused favourable opportunities for buying, and I understood that this induced this triumvirate to buy very largely, but the real periods of their large purchase I have no positive knowledge of. Good news! Great news! was wanted to make a rapid profit; perhaps even then to prevent an immense loss; great news of Buonaparte's defeat was generally expected,

and accordingly these speculators had bought largely, and, I
believe, at daring prices; I say, believe; for not understanding any
thing of these transactions, I can only surmise it from the *extreme
anxiety* which they manifested.

It was at this time that Cochrane Johnstone began to explore the
idea of a Stock Exchange hoax, saying how easy it would be to
arrange for a messenger to travel to London and to have a cossack
drive victoriously through the city: his beard and pike alone would
be sufficient to corroborate the news of Bonaparte's death. He began
to develop the idea on two fronts, presumably assisted by Cochrane,
who was after all the most brilliant exponent of military deception.
M'Rae was asked to look at the practicality of impersonating French
officers, which eventually resulted in his meeting with Vinn at the
Carolina Coffee House on 15 February. At the same time Cochrane,
Johnstone pressed de Berenger to take on the role of the messenger,
explaining that there would be little risk since such a hoax was not
punishable at law. De Berenger, however, pointed out that if he
should be discovered, it would probably ruin his prospects of
military preferment and his chance of going to America. Cochrane
Johnstone showed his displeasure at this response and said severely:
'Then you hesitate and even decline to serve those who have
tirelessly worked for your interests for fear of jeopardising a
preferment which you owe to their exertions alone.'
Shortly after this conversation, Cochrane Johnstone informed
de Berenger that he had tried to prevail upon a senior naval officer
to clear the way for de Berenger to be taken on board his ship and
accorded the rank of lieutenant-colonel but the Commander-in-
Chief's office had vetoed any such appointment. The message
seemed to be clear: serve the Cochranes and you will be rewarded;
otherwise, do not expect any favours. De Berenger did at any rate go
so far as to prepare a detailed plan, showing how an individual
could be conveyed to Dover and there impersonate a British aide-
de-camp carrying dispatches to be taken to London.
Meanwhile, Cochrane Johnstone had introduced de Berenger to
his investment manager, Butt, who said that he and Cochrane

Johnstone had as a favour bought £20,000 of Omnium for him at a price of 28⅞. When de Berenger expressed misgivings about possible losses which he would be unable to meet he was assured that a profit was guaranteed. Butt added: 'Baron, you must come and see us at our office in the city, where you will find us hard at it, buying and selling at a great rate, and pocketing the profits.'

At the invitation of Butt and Cochrane Johnstone, de Berenger went round to their office in Sweetings Alley on Saturday 19 February for what proved to be a fateful meeting with the investment syndicate. He had some intimation of what the meeting might be about because he brought with him the plan he had prepared for impersonating an aide-de-camp. He arrived at about 1 p.m. and passed through a shop at ground level before climbing a narrow staircase to the office on the first floor. There he found Cochrane and Cochrane Johnstone seated at a writing table in front of the window which looked onto the Bank of England. They were joined by Butt who paced about the room. The atmosphere was gloomy and the reason soon became apparent: there had been heavy losses on the investment account and the Omnium that had been bought for de Berenger himself was down 2 per cent or £400. It transpired, too, that Wednesday 23 February was settlement day and that all those present would then have to meet their losses or face the consequences. At this point Cochrane Johnstone asked de Berenger to produce his plan. Cochrane Johnstone read it carefully before passing it to Cochrane, explaining that 'there are no secrets among us, we are all as one in this business; you need not be uneasy either on Lord Cochrane's or Butt's account'.

Now that the plan was out in the open everyone present engaged in a vigorous discussion about how best to implement it. Since Wednesday was settlement day it was agreed that the false news would have to be planted on the Monday, which meant that preparations for the Dover charade would have to be made immediately. After some negotiation of financial terms, de Berenger agreed to perform the role of the aide-de-camp which would require him to go down to Dover that very night. There was some disagreement about the precise timing of the aide-de-camp's appearance in Dover, both Cochrane and Cochrane Johnstone favouring 3 or 4 a.m. which would bring the news to the Stock Exchange while trading was in full swing. De Berenger, however, wanted to avoid passing by daylight through towns where there was a military presence, since this could result in officers crowding round his chaise while horses were changed and asking awkward questions about friends and relations in France. The appearance of the aide-de-camp in Dover was therefore timed at between 1 and 2 a.m., de Berenger undertaking to slow the horses as necessary when approaching London.

At one point Cochrane suggested that de Berenger should wake up the commander at Dover, which de Berenger objected to on the grounds that this would risk discovery. Cochrane also suggested that de Berenger drive from Dover to Deal 'to knock up old Foley, the port-admiral' so that he could send the news by telegraph to the Admiralty. According to Cochrane, the effect on the markets of news transmitted in this way would be 'incalculable'. De Berenger again resisted and after some heated discussion a compromise was reached under which it was agreed that de Berenger would write a letter to the admiral from Dover.

Another question to be considered in all the rush and hurry of the meeting was how de Berenger was to end his journey from Dover to London and dispose of his aide-de-camp's uniform. Cochrane gave definite but brief instructions: 'Come to my house but change the hackney coach on the way.' He then gave de Berenger his new address in Green Street and added that de Berenger should send his servant over that very evening with a hat and coat to be there ready for him to change into on the Monday. However, de Berenger later had second thoughts about exposing himself to his servants' suspicions about such a curious errand and deliberately disobeyed the instruction. It was in this crucial stage of the planning, so cursorily dealt with in the feverish excitement of the moment, that the entire project was to founder.

On one further point there was disagreement. Cochrane Johnstone was insistent that de Berenger should spread the news 'everywhere'. De Berenger objected on the grounds that this would be out of character with the part he had to play, official messengers being subject to strict confidentiality. To be overly communicative would inevitably raise suspicions. Cochrane supported de Berenger on this and suggested that he disclose the news 'as if by accident, and unwillingly', and if by any chance the telegraph failed to work due to hazy weather, de Berenger could easily drop more information as he approached London.

De Berenger had made an estimate of the expenses that would be incurred – getting to Dover and driving back in a chaise, an overnight stay in Dover, the purchase of an aide-de-camp's uniform, etc. – and these came to £51. Cochrane immediately said: 'Say £60, that is twenty each – here is my share.' There was some caution, however, about the use of large notes and a stockbroker's clerk (Thomas Christmas) was therefore sent out to procure £1 notes: fifty of these, and the remaining cash, were then given to de Berenger.

As soon as the arrangements for de Berenger's masquerade had been agreed, Butt dashed off, saying that he must immediately buy all the stock that could be got, otherwise it would be too late. As he was leaving Cochrane called him back, saying, 'Take care, Butt, how you give instructions to the brokers; it's late in the day and from that and the prices they may suspect us.'

While Butt was putting in buy orders – including one for £150,000 from a Mr Richardson – the others settled some final practical matters. By now it was approaching 4 p.m. The three of them left the office in Sweetings Alley at the same time, but Cochrane Johnstone said that they should not be seen together. De Berenger had little time to buy his paraphernalia for Dover, so he left the others and hurried to Holywell Street where he had seen regimentals displayed for sale.

The shops, however, being Jewish owned, were all shut because of the Sabbath. De Berenger, now in some alarm, hastened to Russell Court in the theatre district, hoping to find a shop selling costumes. He was again disappointed here but someone told him that a Mr Solomon in New Street, Covent Garden, had a good assortment of military garments and kept his shop open on

Saturdays. On the way to Solomon's, de Berenger bought a wig in Tavistock Street as a partial disguise. Mr Soloman turned out to be very helpful, particularly when he learned that de Berenger wanted to buy rather than hire the articles he listed – the purchaser's explanation being that they were required for private theatricals that very evening.

While waiting for Solomon to select from his stock de Berenger took the opportunity to drop in on a close and discreet friend whom he prevailed upon to write the letter to Admiral Foley. It was much safer to take down to Dover a letter already written in the hand of another than to attempt to write the letter himself in a hand that would not be recognised (though he would, of course, appear to write the letter).

Returning to Mr Solomon's in New Street, de Berenger selected and purchased an aide-de-camp's uniform consisting of a scarlet coat with blue cuffs and collar and embroidered gold button holes, as well as a hat and a silver medallion. These items were sent on to Mr Solomon's other shop in Charing Cross where de Berenger was told he could pick up the remaining articles he required. Before doing so he purchased at a trunk-maker's a fair-sized portmanteau of yellow leather to carry his clothes in, a shop-soiled black leather brief-case with a lock (measuring about 10 inches by 6 inches and 1½ inches thick) and some white ribbon.

At Solomon's shop in Charing Cross de Berenger selected a plain grey military greatcoat with covered buttons, a dark brown fur foraging cap with a gold band and a list case to put his sword in while travelling to Dover. He packed everything he had bought into the portmanteau, paid the bill, and took a coach from the Strand which drove him to his lodgings in the Asylum Buildings.

On arrival at his lodgings de Berenger sent his servant on an errand some distance away to ensure his privacy. He shaved off his whiskers, changed into the clothes he intended to wear on his journey to Dover, left the Asylum Buildings unobserved and took a hackney coach to the Bricklayers Arms to await the last coach to Dover. The fateful journey that was to transform not only de Berenger's life but that of his three co-conspirators had begun.

When he arrived at the Bricklayers Arms de Berenger was clothed for the cold winter's weather in nondescript outerwear that was intended to avoid the attention of his fellow travellers. He wore drab Kerseymere breeches, an old blue coat, a black silk waistcoat, a grey military greatcoat, jockey boots and a round hat. He also wore a yellow silk handkerchief tied loosely over a white cravat in order to conceal the lower part of his face, and he carried a brass-mounted cavalry sabre in its list case. Packed into the large yellow portmanteau were the following items: the scarlet aide-de-camp's uniform, the star and the silver medallion, the dark brown foraging cap, a red silk sash, a sword belt of black leather, a pair of dark bottle-green overalls (as undergarments), a black silk neckkerchief, a black leather briefcase and a brown wig.

While waiting for the Dover coach, de Berenger felt faint, partly because he had not eaten since breakfast and partly, no doubt, because of the natural anxiety that would affect anyone setting out on such a mission as his. He therefore asked a man to secure him a seat in the coach when it arrived and went to buy a sandwich, some cold meat and a pint of port wine. When the coach arrived, de Berenger took his seat and was most concerned to ensure that his portmanteau was stored *inside* the coach to avoid any possibility of loss. The coach then proceeded on its way to Rochester. The effects of the port wine having taken hold, de Berenger was barely conscious of his fellow passengers as they jolted along and after a brief stop-over and change of horses the coach moved on towards Dover. De Berenger asked the coachman to stop at any respectable inn just outside Dover (since he did not wish to be seen in the town) but when nothing suitable could be seen, he was dropped off in Dover itself at the Royal Oak Inn, just off the London Road and opposite a church. Here he asked for a room and after ordering his dinner he lay down and slept for a couple of hours.

When he awoke de Berenger locked his bedroom door and began to unpack his portmanteau. He was alarmed to find that the aide-de-camp's uniform was bright scarlet and brand new, which had not been evident in the candlelight of Solomon's shop. It was hardly credible that the wearer of such a uniform could have travelled all the way from a continental battlefield. He therefore soiled the red coat all over with blacking taken from his boots, using a wet handkerchief as a dabber. He also rubbed and disfigured the embroidery and buttons and the lace of the cap. Then he sewed the star on the coat and made a dishevelled cockade of the white ribbon, which he also soiled.

Having enjoyed a good dinner de Berenger carried on with his preparations. He made a paper packet to resemble dispatches and he resolved not to remove this from his dispatch case, which was to be fixed to his sword belt, unless challenged. In that eventuality he would adopt a commanding tone, produce his dispatches, refuse to release them and defy anyone to impede his progress at his peril.

The next task was to reconnoitre the approaches to Dover from the sea so that he could identify a plausible landing spot. But before he did this he paid his bill at the Royal Oak in advance, not wishing to settle it as he left that night wearing his military costume. Then, departing the Royal Oak, he turned right into the market-place and found his way to the Ship Inn from where he walked along the seashore. Apart from identifying a location where he could claim to have been landed, he needed to find a secluded place where he could later splash himself with salt water so as to give the appearance of someone who had just crossed by boat.

De Berenger returned to the Royal Oak at about 10 p.m. and learned that the doors were locked at 11 p.m. However, the innkeeper said that he was willing to sit up for him if he wanted to be out later. De Berenger replied that he was going to visit a friend but said not to wait up for him beyond midnight since if he were delayed he could no doubt spend the night at his friend's house. The innkeeper, giving a knowing smile, was happy to oblige.

De Berenger could not leave the Royal Oak after 11 p.m. because this would involve asking someone to let him out when he was wearing all his paraphernalia. And since the appointed time for arriving at the Ship Inn was 1 a.m. he faced the prospect of walking about for two hours on a bitterly cold and frosty night. Preoccupied with this gloomy thought, de Berenger went up to his room and changed into his military costume, putting his old blue coat, the wig (which proved to be too small) and some linen into the portmanteau which he intended to leave behind.

De Berenger was now attired for his mission. He wore the bottle-green overalls over his Kerseymore breeches and jockey boots, and the black silk waistcoat under the aide-de-camp's uniform with its star and medallion. Over the uniform he placed his black swordbelt and a red sash, he had a black silk handkerchief round his neck and, for the time being only, he wore a round hat, concealing the foraging cap under his greatcoat. He carried his black dispatch case and his sword in its list case. Awkwardly encumbered, de Berenger descended the stairs, hurried past several customers drinking at the bar and went out into the cold night air.

Retracing his steps towards the seashore, he found that his plan to splash himself with water was thwarted by the presence of a number of soldiers and customs-house officers along the shoreline. He stood for some time listening to the murmuring of the sea, contemplating the risks of detection and the daunting task that lay ahead. Then he turned back towards the town and looked for fresh water to soak himself. After trying a roadside pump, which squeaked horribly and proved to be dry, and failing to break the thick ice in a water trough, he came upon a mill-stream. Dipping his hat into the stream, he poured the icy water over himself, and then threw the hat and his sword-case over a hedge. As he put on his foraging cap he noted that it was now approaching 1 a.m. and he therefore made his way through the streets of Dover towards the Ship Inn, loudly and impatiently asking for directions as he neared his destination. On arrival he adopted the commanding manner of military authority and banged loudly on the door with his sword.

The events that followed, witnessed as they were by those who testified at the trial, have already been described. Nevertheless, a few points of detail should be added. De Berenger did indeed write a letter while at the Ship but this was a dummy, the communication sent to Admiral Foley having already been written in advance by a third party. The 'true' letter was deliberately left on the table, wafered (stuck down) with a wet seal that had been marked. De Berenger used the excuse of feeling suddenly ill to leave the room for a couple of minutes. This gave any curious onlookers the opportunity to open and reseal the dispatch which, based on the evidence of careful marking, at least one person did. It was evidently the contents of that letter, as much as anything de Berenger said, that prompted the departure of express riders from the Ship Inn that night and the spreading of the news of Napoleon's death along the coaching road to London.

When de Berenger took his seat in the post-chaise he urged the postboys to make all possible speed, the reward for which would be a Napoleon each. However, their furious driving threatened to bring him to London much too soon, 9.30–10 a.m. having been agreed as the arrival time. Jolting over the rough and frozen road at a rate of 12–14 miles per hour was also extremely uncomfortable. Horses were changed at Canterbury, Sittingbourne and Rochester, and at Sittingbourne de Berenger got out briefly to warm himself by the horsekeeper's fire and dry his leather gloves, which in his great hurry he left behind.

On arriving at the Crown Inn at Rochester at around 5 a.m., de Berenger was surprised to find the landlord up and dressed. The reason, unknown to de Berenger at the time, was that Wright, the landlord of the Ship Inn, had already dispatched an express rider to precede du Bourg to London with the news. The rider had, en route, prepared the landlord of the Crown, who happened to be Wright's brother, to receive the 'messenger' from Dover. De Berenger's perception at this point was rather different, however. Unaware that any expresses could have preceded him, but fully expecting other messengers to be dispatched after his departure from the Ship, he anticipated being overtaken on the London road. This had not happened and now he feared that the news was not spreading far or fast enough. He therefore took the opportunity of disclosing to this Mr Wright the details of Napoleon's downfall. From the Crown Inn the coach went on to the Marquis of Granby at Dartford. It was now past 7 a.m. and while the horses were being changed de Berenger got out and once more recounted his news in some detail, to the landlord, a Mr William Tozier.

During the final stage from Dartford to London the fog increased considerably and it became obvious that the telegraph would not be operating that morning. Since de Berenger was still well ahead of his schedule he used this excuse to slow the progress of the coach. He explained to Shilling, the postboy, that since the telegraph would not work he need not reach town quite so soon: 'I have been racing all night to keep ahead of the morning telegraph so that I could be the first bearer of the happy news. But now you can let your horses breathe.'

While proceeding to the Marsh Gate, de Berenger drew up the coach blind because he was close to the boundaries of the King's Bench rules and was a familiar figure in the neighbourhood. Despite this precaution he did attract unwelcome attention at the Marsh Gate coach-stand from the banker's clerk, Barwick. Barwick's close scrutiny made de Berenger uneasy because he recognised him as someone he had seen frequently when living in Pall Mall and wondered whether he in turn might be recognised. His anxiety increased when Barwick made obvious efforts to keep up with his coach, sometimes coming parallel with the window and staring straight at him.

They proceeded together over Westminster Bridge in a direct line for Grosvenor Square where Crane, the coachman, had been directed to drive and where he, de Berenger, intended to change coaches as Cochrane had instructed him ('Come to my house in Green Street, but change the coach on your way'). But having eventually shaken off Barwick in Tichburn Street, he did not want to give this curious spectator the opportunity to catch up with him again. So, fatefully as it turned out, he ignored Cochrane's instruction and told Crane to drive on to Green Street. (For de Berenger's full account of what followed, see Exhibit 13.)

De Berenger pulled up at 13 Green Street slightly earlier than the planned 9.30–10 a.m. arrival time. Nevertheless, he expected Cochrane to open the door to him since the footman knew de Berenger slightly from a previous visit to Park Street and Cochrane had said he himself would be waiting in the parlour to let the visitor in. To de Berenger's dismay, it was the footman, Thomas Dewman, who opened the door to him and showed him into the parlour. Worse still, Cochrane's former black servant, Isaac Davis, who was well known to him, happened to be in the kitchen area at the time of his arrival and saw him clearly through the basement grille.

On learning to his further surprise that Cochrane was not at home and had gone to his uncle's at Great Cumberland Street, de Berenger considered for a moment whether he could go there himself but ruled it out because Cochrane Johnstone's servants all knew him very well. Instead he asked for pen and paper and wrote a short note to Cochrane expressing great surprise at his absence and requesting his immediate return. This he gave to Dewman to take to Great Cumberland Street. There being no wax readily at hand, the note was sealed with a wafer. Partly for that reason and partly because the message was self-explanatory, de Berenger declined to add his signature.

Dewman returned some fifteen minutes later to say that he had missed his master who had gone off with Butt and Cochrane Johnstone in the latter's coach. In an agitated state, de Berenger opened the note and added a few lines to the effect that he neither could nor would move until he had seen Cochrane. Dewman suggested Mr King's workshop as the most likely place to find Cochrane, and de Berenger urged the servant to trace him with the utmost urgency, wherever he might be.

Shortly after Dewman departed, the maidservant invited de Berenger to have breakfast in the drawing room with her 'mistress'. This he declined, conscious as he was of his filthy appearance after his travels, with his muddy boots, nearly three days of growth on his face and dishevelled, unpowdered hair. More to the point, he could not take off his greatcoat which he kept closely buttoned up for fear of incriminating himself by revealing all his regalia in front of the servants and other members of the household. A few minutes later the maidservant returned to the parlour bringing a basin of water and a towel and reiterating the invitation to breakfast. De Berenger again declined. Finally, he was summoned up to the drawing room in peremptory terms that left him no choice, the impression being given that his presence in the parlour was a little too public. In any event de Berenger ate his breakfast in the company of the lady of the house (whom we now know to have been Lady Cochrane) in a state of great embarrassment. He wore his closely buttoned greatcoat despite the comfort of a roaring fire and repeated invitations from his hostess to take it off and make himself at home. When breakfast was over the lady left the room and de Berenger, having refused her kind suggestion that he go and rest, was left to contemplate why the conspirators' plan had gone so badly wrong in its final stage.

Cochrane eventually returned alone to Green Street at around 11 a.m. He had deliberately left Dewman behind on an errand so that the transactions that were about to take place would not be witnessed. (Dewman did not return until early afternoon.) Cochrane was furious and wanted de Berenger out of the house as quickly as possible, and to this end he had kept the coach in which he had just arrived waiting outside. He also roundly criticised de Berenger for sending him a wafered note in such sensitive circumstances. Without further discussion he took de Berenger up to a second-floor back bedroom to organise a change of clothes. De Berenger wanted to leave his scarlet coat, cap and sword at Green Street and to go back to his lodgings wearing only his grey greatcoat over his green overalls, but Cochrane would have none of that. He took a large pillowcase from a chest of drawers and insisted that de Berenger put into it all his discarded clothes, including his greatcoat. These he arranged in such a way that the scarlet uniform was at the bottom and the greatcoat on top, thereby ensuring that not even a glimpse of red could be seen at the tying points. During this process Cochrane helped de Berenger pull off his scarlet uniform, after which he took off his own black longcoat and gave this and a wide-brimmed hat to de Berenger, who had now ceased to be du Bourg. Thus ridiculously attired in an Obadiah hat and a coat far too long for him (de Berenger was 5 feet 8 inches and Cochrane 6 feet 2 inches), de Berenger was hurried down the stairs without the attendance of a servant to depart furtively in the waiting coach, leaving nothing behind but his sword.

De Berenger was too embarrassed to arrive at his lodgings and meet his servants wearing Cochrane's exotic headgear. So he stopped at a hatter's and bought a round hat, a transaction which conveniently gave him the opportunity to change coaches. He arrived back at his lodgings at 2 Asylum Buildings to be met by his woman servant who took the bundle upstairs to his bedroom. Then, after washing and shaving and recovering his strength with a good lunch, de Berenger prepared himself to go to dinner at the longstanding invitation of the Honourable Basil Cochrane, a wealthy brother of the Earl of Dundonald, at his sumptuous house in Portman Square. Among the guests were Cochrane, who arrived late, and Cochrane Johnstone. The three conspirators exchanged knowing glances as the conversation during the evening focused exclusively on the great Stock Exchange hoax. For the first time de Berenger learned of the Holloway sub-plot which had been kept from him by Cochrane Johnstone. The atmosphere was one of general good humour. Those present showed some amusement and even admiration over the audacity of the frolic and no one referred to it as a 'crime' or a 'fraud'. At one point Cochrane Johnstone whispered to de Berenger that he was glad he had not made his excuses and had attended the dinner because his cheerful presence would remove any suspicions there might be.

Before the party broke up Cochrane Johnstone asked de Berenger to dine with him the following evening, 22 February, when they would be joined by Cochrane and Butt in addition to his daughter. The atmosphere on this occasion was the reverse of the previous night. The diners were pensive and gloomy, and after Cochrane Johnstone's daughter left the room the reason became apparent: the Stock Exchange was launching a full-scale investigation with a view to bringing proceedings against the culprits and punishing them severely, the main target being the impersonator, du Bourg.

The others suggested to de Berenger that he should stay put at his lodgings since to do otherwise would attract suspicion, and they also thought it would be a good idea if he were to discontinue his visits to Great Cumberland Street for the time being. In view of the hue and cry it was advisable that they and de Berenger should not be seen together. On a more positive note Cochrane Johnstone said that he would soon have some money to give de Berenger, representing profit on the stock they had purchased for him, though the receipt of the cash would have to be justified in some other way. At this point the dinner party broke up and de Berenger walked some distance with Butt who explained that the investment syndicate had cleared profits of only £1,600 each (£4,800 in all) on the temporary surge in stock prices. On the basis of that rather modest profit they proposed to give him £300 or £400 as a reward for his efforts. De Berenger was incensed by this offer since he understood that the profits would be equally shared. He also pointed out that even if the syndicate had made only the profits stated, the hoax had certainly saved them from ruinous losses.

On the morning of 23 February de Berenger wrote a note to Cochrane requesting a meeting at 9 a.m. the next day at Donithorne's house in York Street where de Berenger was supervising the completion of two large pieces of furniture for Cochrane Johnstone. The two men duly met there and in order to secure some privacy they paced around the garden, pretending to measure it up for some development work which Cochrane Johnstone, being the landlord, was planning for the property. They were able to use the seclusion of a summer-house to carry on a very sensitive conversation about the steps that should now be taken to avoid detection.

Cochrane proposed to de Berenger that if some witness or other should have observed him arriving in Green Street in his scarlet uniform and subsequently departing wearing a black coat, Cochrane would come up with an innocent explanation. He could say that the visitor was previously unknown to him but claimed to come from his brother – for no other purpose as it turned out, than that of swindling Cochrane out of a coat, hat, money and anything else he could lay his hands on. De Berenger objected to this explanation because if he were identified, it would expose him to a charge of felony for obtaining property under false pretences. De Berenger also declined to go along with an alternative suggestion that, if discovered, he should claim to have been employed in the hoax by Lord Yarmouth. As the son of the Prince Regent's mistress, Lady Hartford, Lord Yarmouth enjoyed many royal favours, including his appointment as aide to the Regent. Cochrane said 'anything about him will go down' because he was so unpopular.

De Berenger's outrage at the initial sum offered to him appears to have had some effect because on 24 February (the same day he met with Cochrane) Cochrane Johnstone left a note requesting that de Berenger call on him briefly at 9 o'clock that evening. At that meeting Cochrane Johnstone gave de Berenger £400 in £1 notes, neatly tied up in Bank of England parcels, explaining that this was on account only and that all were now agreed that de Berenger's share of the profits should be £1,000; £600 was therefore still owing. Before he left de Berenger was requested by Cochrane Johnstone to burn the scarlet coat and other incriminating articles, as well as the hat and coat belonging to Cochrane.

On returning home, de Berenger waited until his servants had gone to bed and then engaged in the laborious task of cutting up the scarlet coat and its trimmings into small pieces. Having determined that any attempt to burn this material would generate a smell that was bound to alarm his servants, de Berenger decided to sink everything in the Thames. For this purpose he deposited the shredded clothes in the pillowcase Cochrane had given to him and which he now intended to weigh down with old screws, lead and coals. The greatcoat, the black coat and the broad-brimmed hat, however, escaped destruction and were retained.

Two days later on Saturday 26 February at about 10 p.m. de Berenger took the bundle containing the mutilated red coat and carried it under a cape to Westminster Bridge, which even at that hour was far from deserted. The centre arch, being over the deepest water, was the selected target and after peering through the balustrades to ensure that there was no barge or boat passing underneath, he dropped the offending bundle into the water.

Cochrane Johnstone had meanwhile left a letter at the Asylum Buildings asking de Berenger to meet him at Donithorne's house in York Street at 9 a.m. on Sunday (27 February). Here Cochrane Johnstone warned de Berenger that matters looked bleak. Then, leaving the house to find greater privacy, the two men strolled along Willow Walk towards Chelsea. Cochrane Johnstone revealed that de Berenger had been identified, that a warrant was out for his arrest and that Bow Street runners would shortly apprehend him. There was, therefore, only one course of action – he must flee the country and he must do so that very night.

There followed a discussion about de Berenger's financial affairs. Cochrane Johnstone said he would pay de Berenger's sureties the £350 they would be liable for if he absconded, this to be taken from the £600 that was still owed to him by the syndicate.

Cochrane would also take an assignment from de Berenger of such property as he still possessed (these were illiquid assets in the form of patents and shares) and would in due course pay the proceeds of liquidation over to de Berenger. The legal arrangements could be made later. Cochrane Johnstone said that he himself would travel to Amsterdam on about 12 March where de Berenger should meet him: he should enquire from time to time at the banking house of Messrs Hope, where Cochrane Johnstone would write to him under the name of 'John de Beaufin'. Finally, Cochrane Johnstone handed over £90 in the form of a note for £50 and another for £40, saying that this was to cover the expenses of his flight abroad and was in addition to the balance still due.

It may be added that there was at this point no warrant out for de Berenger's arrest (according to the Stock Exchange, this was issued in early March) and de Berenger's later surmise was that the investment syndicate had decided by now to make him the scapegoat. They therefore wanted him out of the way fast, both for his sake and theirs. In any event he left London that evening after paying off his servant with the £50 note received from Cochrane Johnstone.

By now, one week after the hoax, the net was beginning to close in on the investment syndicate. Isaac Davis, Cochrane's former black servant, had witnessed the arrival of de Berenger at 13 Green Street that Monday morning wearing a red uniform and had also seen him depart wearing a black coat. There was no doubt gossip among the servants and Cochrane would have been aware of the risk of detection. On 28 February his fortnight's leave of absence expired and, having completed the specification for his lamp, he travelled down to Chatham to go on board the *Tonnant*. However, posters soon began to appear in London claiming that Colonel du Bourg had visited Green Street and linking his name to Cochrane's. As soon as he learned this, Cochrane obtained further leave of absence from the Admiralty and returned to London on 10 March in order to clear his name.

By this time the Stock Exchange Committee, in response to its advertised reward, had been approached in confidence by at least three witnesses who were able to identify du Bourg as de Berenger. Cochrane's servants would have been familiar with the rumours that were flying around, they would have been aware that Isaac Davis had identified de Berenger and they probably knew that Davis had claimed the £250 Stock Exchange reward. Cochrane realised that he must issue a statement that both acknowledged and accounted for the visit to his house by de Berenger and explained the fact that de Berenger had arrived in a military greatcoat and departed wearing Cochrane's own black coat. Hence the disclosures made in his affidavit issued on 11 March – which he later wrongly claimed were the first intimation that anyone had of du Bourg's identity.

It was not long after issuing his affidavit that Cochrane was alerted to the possibility of legal proceedings against him. He would have been anxious to see a potentially dangerous witness such as Davis out of the way and it is therefore no surprise that arrangements were made for his former servant to join Admiral Flemming on board the *Eurotas* which sailed for Gibraltar on 1 May. Cochrane was later able to claim that, ahead of the trial, he had written to Flemming, care of Admiral Bickerton in Portsmouth, requesting that Davis be made available as a witness in his favour, only to discover that the *Eurotas* had already sailed for Gibraltar.

Meanwhile, de Berenger, following his flight from London on 27 February, had spent six weeks in fruitless wandering, ostensibly in search of a passage to Holland. He intimated later that his plans were frustrated by an exceptionally cold winter which meant that extensive ice on the Continental shore was blocking the ports on that side of the Channel. First he went to Hull, where in the public library he was shocked to read Cochrane's affidavit identifying him as the visitor to Green Street. Then, he travelled to Newcastle,

Sunderland and, finally, Edinburgh where he had thoughts of residing permanently under his newly assumed name of Captain Brown. He eventually ended up at the Britannia Inn at Leith where, on 8 April he was apprehended and brought down to London, forced to travel for two days and two nights without sleep or basic comforts. Confined, in poor health, his hopes of a resumed military career in ruins and deserted by his former allies, de Berenger now faced his accusers alone.

Although de Berenger provided a very full account of the Stock Exchange fraud he failed to clear up several puzzling aspects of the story. He recounted what Cochrane wanted from him at their meeting at Donithorne's house on 24 February, but he omitted to say what he wanted of Cochrane – even though it was he who had requested the interview. Then, when de Berenger fled, there was an extraordinary delay in securing a passage to the Continent: he said there were problems with ice blocking the Continental ports, but this is hardly credible in late March/early April, especially when the *Gentleman's Magazine* for 1814 records that from 20 March through to mid-April the weather was very mild, with daytime temperatures regularly reaching the mid-50s Fahrenheit. Given that de Berenger was a most resourceful man, one has to ask: what was delaying him? There is also the mysterious letter written by de Berenger to his solicitor after his capture and while he was awaiting trial – a letter that later fell into Cochrane's hands and was published with a forged date in an attempt to discredit de Berenger's version of events. What was the underlying subject matter of this letter and why was it so sensitive? Finally there is the memorandum found on de Berenger at Leith:

To C.J. by March 1st 1814, £350 – £4–5,000 – assign one share of patent and £1,000 worth shares of Jn.de Beaufain at Messrs. H. to their care. – Believe from my informant £18,000 instead of £4,800 – suspicious that Mr B. does not account correctly to him as well as me. Determined not to be duped. No restrictions as to secrecy – requesting early answer.

According to de Berenger the £350 related to the money which would have to be paid by his sureties if he absconded and which Cochrane Johnstone had apparently agreed to pay on his behalf. The figures of £4,800 and £18,000 have already been explained as references to the profits made by the investment syndicate. The assignment of de Berenger's patent and shares refers to the understanding he had reached with Cochrane Johnstone for dealing with his remaining assets in England. This leaves unaccounted for the figure of '£4–5,000'.

There would appear to be a common link that can explain each of these mysteries. The clue is given by de Berenger himself in *The Noble Stockjobber*. He said that when dining with Cochrane, Cochrane Johnstone and Butt on the day after the fraud, and after being told by them that a criminal investigation had been initiated to identify Colonel du Bourg, he replied that he saw no reason why they should not all 'swim or sink together'. De Berenger hinted at a similar threat to implicate the Cochranes when Cochrane Johnstone was putting pressure on him to flee the country. He also reported the following assurance given to him by Cochrane Johnstone at their final meeting:

> Lord Cochrane and Mr Butt agree with me in the justice of your being taken care of <u>for life</u>, especially if, to answer our views, you abandon everything in this country, such as your prospects of success with your patents, and other inventions. . . . we have, therefore, agreed between us that I shall follow you to Amsterdam on purpose to convey to you the means to be raised between us.

It seems then that de Berenger, when he realised that the net was closing on him, demanded a substantial settlement to compensate him for what he had undertaken at huge personal risk on behalf of the others. There was also a clear hint that if the investment syndicate did not comply with this request, they might be implicated in the fraud.

Drawing the various threads together, the likely sequence of events can be easily imagined. At his meeting with Cochrane on

24 February de Berenger pressed for a substantial cash settlement, under the veiled threat that the Cochranes might be exposed if his demands were not met. Following this meeting the Cochranes decided that de Berenger was a danger to them and had to be got out of the country as quickly as possible. Cochrane Johnstone therefore gave him an initial payment, ensured that he destroyed the incriminating scarlet uniform, and then on 27 February cynically informed him he was about to be arrested and must immediately flee. As an added inducement, Cochrane Johnstone said that if de Berenger assigned to him his remaining assets in England the investment syndicate would make a substantial settlement in his favour to enable him to establish himself in another country.

De Berenger was persuaded to go but in Hull he wrote a letter to Cochrane Johnstone reminding him of the terms of the deal and drawing attention to the understatement of the syndicate's stock exchange profit. Berenger demanded £4,000–£5,000 to enable him to make a new life on the Continent. Aware that once he left the country his negotiating position would be severely weakened, de Berenger delayed his departure for Amsterdam until he could secure a legally binding settlement from the investment trio. When he was captured and brought to London he provided a helpful letter to Cochrane supporting the latter's voluntary affidavit, but behind the scenes he continued to press for a legal settlement backed by the implicit threat of disclosure. Hence the letter to his solicitor written while in prison, which Cochrane later published with a false date: it is typical of Cochrane that he should make public a letter that he regarded as an attempt at blackmail (the same treatment that he gave to Le Marchant).

After the trial de Berenger sent several unanswered letters to Cochrane appealing for his help. On 12 June he wrote:

Dreadfully as you are both [Cochrane and his uncle] situated, fate is not so cruel towards you as it is to me; for with your means you can live anywhere, but my want of means forces me to seek a living, which everywhere will be opposed by my debts and by the disgrace I suffer under, certainly on your account. . . . What is your intention as to me – how do you intend to heal my wounds, if healed they ever can be?

A letter dated 11 July is more explicit:

> I have already suffered much more than either of the other three. . . . It cannot be disputed that in the event of success you three would have cleared a very large sum of money, where the person who not only ran all the risks in the execution, but who also saved you three from inevitable ruin, would have received but a scanty remuneration.

And as a postscript de Berenger asks for the return of his Damascus sabre and belt 'which you persuaded me to leave at your house on the 21ˢᵗ February'. In this letter de Berenger also referred to an anonymous note he claimed to have received on 2 July from a source described as 'friends of Lord Cochrane' (Exhibit 14). De Berenger interpreted the message as an invitation to clear Cochrane and Butt by naming Lord Yarmouth as the instigator of the fraud, for which he could expect to be rewarded.

Finally, on 21 February 1815, the anniversary of the Stock Exchange fraud, de Berenger wrote to Cochrane openly referring to the pamphlet he was preparing against him and to his 'hour of retribution': 'I pledge myself to you, but more becomingly to the public, that I will, in a very short lapse of time, prove you are an artful, base and calumnious utterer of barefaced and infernally designing falsehoods.'

In *The Autobiography* Cochrane referred to this correspondence when he described letters from de Berenger 'the object of which was evidently the extortion of money'. He said that 'the whole of these letters were transmitted by me to the public press, without reply or comment, and were so published at the time'. When de Berenger's demands were not met he went public with his story in *The Noble Stockjobber*. Unfortunately for him, his literary ineptitude let him down and what was intended as a devastating revelation of Cochrane's involvement in the Stock Exchange fraud was easily dismissed as the bitter outpourings of a slightly deranged scoundrel.

ELEVEN

Recovery

After the traumas of the Stock Exchange trial, dismissal from the Navy and imprisonment, Cochrane had somehow to find another outlet for his talents and energy, as well as a new means of making money. The revolutionary wars then raging in South America presented an extraordinary opportunity for mercenary adventurers and he was quick to seize it. Chile and Peru had made considerable territorial gains in their struggle against Spanish colonial rule, but the revolutionaries were frustrated by long coastlines which gave the Spanish fleet a strategic advantage. Warships were able to supply fortified garrisons located along the seaboard, and as long as the Spanish navy had command of the sea, the revolutionaries' goal of national independence would be thwarted.

It was against this background that in 1817 the Chilean representative in London, Don José Alvarez, approached Cochrane to see whether he might be prepared to take command of his country's naval force with the objective of confronting the Spanish fleet. At a salary of $8,000 per annum and with the prospect of rich prize-money pickings, Cochrane agreed to his appointment as Vice Admiral of Chile and Commander-in-Chief of the Naval Services of the Republic. He was later to write to his brother William: 'I have every prospect of making the largest fortune which has been made in our days, save that of the Duke of Wellington.'

Towards the end of 1817 Cochrane sold his house at Holly Hill in Hampshire; in June 1818 he made his farewell speech in the House of Commons; and at the beginning of August that year he, with his wife Kitty and two sons, crossed from Rye to Boulogne in an open fishing boat. He then planned to sail to Valparaiso, stopping off at

St Helena en route. The purpose of this break in his journey was to meet Napoleon and discuss the possibility of Bonaparte becoming the crowned head of a new monarchy in South America. However, the urgency of the military situation in Chile prevented this diversion and the Cochrane family duly arrived in Valparaiso at the end of November.

The Spanish navy that Cochrane was to confront consisted of fourteen ships and twenty-eight gunboats. In contrast, Chile's naval forces were limited to seven ships, headed by the 50-gun flagship *O'Higgins*, named after the new Chilean republic's charismatic head of government, Don Bernardo O'Higgins. Cochrane began his campaign by sailing north to the adjoining coast of Peru in order to attack the Spanish naval base at Callao, the port of Lima. This planned surprise assault was frustrated by thick coastal fog and, having blockaded Callao, Cochrane spent several months raiding the stores of enemy shore bases, seizing vessels carrying money and bullion to pay the Spanish troops, and establishing an intelligence network based on patriots ashore.

Cochrane's next move in January 1820 was to sail south from Valparaiso to the Spanish military stronghold at Valderia. From his intelligence he knew that a new Spanish frigate was expected there and, coming in under the Spanish colours, the *O'Higgins* was taken into the navigation channels, enabling Cochrane to make a thorough reconnaissance of this reputably impregnable base. After capturing a sloop carrying $20,000 intended for the Valderia garrison, and picking up reinforcements from the nearest Chilean garrison at Concession, Cochrane returned to Valderia with the *O'Higgins*, accompanied this time by three other vessels, one with troops on board. The expedition faced near disaster, however, on the night of 29 January when the *O'Higgins* ran onto rocks some 40 miles from the mainland and began to fill with water. Cochrane, who had been asleep in his cabin, took control: he managed to prevent a panic evacuation, manoeuvred the ship off the rocks and, through his own technical skills, succeeded in getting the vessel's pumps to work sufficiently to reduce the level of water in the hold. Faced with a seriously damaged and leaking flagship, whose store of ammunition had been destroyed by flooding, Cochrane decided to carry on with the planned attack.

Valderia was served by a great natural harbour that had been heavily fortified on both sides by a series of forts. This enabled the defending forces to bring their heavy firepower to bear not only on the entrance to the harbour but at any point within it. Following his earlier reconnaissance, Cochrane had decided that the only sensible plan of attack was to land at a small bay a mile west of the harbour entrance which was guarded by the first of four forts on the western side. Attempting another deception, Cochrane used his two smaller ships as decoys; they came in under Spanish colours and used a Spanish-born officer to explain that they were part of a Spanish squadron that had become separated in a storm. Meanwhile out of sight on the seaward side they secured the ships' boats containing the landing force of troops and marines. The Spanish, however, were not to be taken in on this occasion and the landing had to be made prematurely against volleys of musket fire. Nevertheless, the Chilean forces, though starved of ammunition, succeeded in securing a foothold on shore after a brutal bayonet charge against the enemy. That night a detachment of the invading force managed to find its way around behind the fort, and the ensuing simultaneous assault from front and rear was too much for the defenders who fled. The gates of the second fort were opened to receive the fugitives but the Chileans, in close pursuit, poured in behind them. The story was repeated at the third fort and by daybreak all the Spanish defenders on the western side of the harbour were holed up in the one remaining bastion, Corral Castle. However, the Chilean forces had managed to capture Spanish artillery on high ground above the castle, and faced with the prospect of a heavy bombardment, those who had not already escaped across the water surrendered.

Having secured the western side of the anchorage, Cochrane brought his small ships into the harbour and prepared for an assault on the eastern forts. At this point he also allowed the crippled *O'Higgins*, which was slowly sinking and needed to beach, to appear for the first time for greater psychological effect. Mistakenly believing that this 50-gun warship was bringing reinforcements, the defenders in the eastern forts abandoned their positions and fled 14 miles up river to the town of Valderia. The panic continued and when Cochrane moved his ships upstream in preparation for a river attack on the town, the colonial governor retreated once more, along with the demoralised Spanish forces.

At the cost of seven dead and nineteen wounded, Cochrane had taken Spain's strongest military base in the southern half of the continent, along with tons of gunpowder, 10,000 cannon shot, 170,000 musket cartridges, 128 pieces of artillery and one prize ship. News of this astonishing feat of arms by 'El Diablo', as Cochrane was called by his enemies, soon travelled not only throughout the continent but also across the Atlantic. In Britain the reputation of the fallen naval hero began to rise once more.

After returning to Valparaiso at the end of February, Cochrane again turned his attention to Peru, where the Spanish garrison at Lima, protected by the port of Callao, presented a continuing threat to the cause of Chilean independence. In consultation with the Chilean government in Santiago, he proposed a joint attack on Lima and Callao using over 4,000 troops under the command of General San Martin and a naval force of which he would take charge. The expedition sailed on 21 August 1820, but San Martin, in Cochrane's view, showed excessive caution in insisting that his army should land 30 miles to the north of Callao.

Serving as a senior officer with San Martin was an Englishman, James Paroissien, who wrote from the general's camp with a critical assessment of Cochrane's character. After referring to the admiral's impetuosity and the need to have 'the patience of an angel' in dealing with him, Paroissien continued: 'He appears to be anxious about making money. Avarice and selfishness do certainly appear to form the groundwork of his character and from his speculative disposition he is often in great want of money to obtain which he is not so scrupulously exact in his word as every man ought to be, particularly a man of his rank and station.' Later Paroissien was to write: 'What a pity this man, who certainly does possess the elements of a hero, is so extremely avaricious.' These observations were made at a time of considerable tension between General San

Martin and his admiral, but they nevertheless throw an interesting light on how Cochrane was perceived by at least one compatriot.

Frustrated by San Martin's lack of enthusiasm for an immediate assault on Lima, Cochrane decided to take matters into his own hands. In early November he carried out a daring reconnaissance of Callao's defences, which consisted of a floating boom to protect the harbour entrance, the 44-gun Spanish flagship *Esmerelda*, lying within its protective escort of 27 gunboats, a powerful assemblage of 300 artillery pieces in the shore batteries and further assorted artillery mounted on block ships – all this manned by the best-trained sailors and marines in the Spanish service.

On 5 November Cochrane assembled the crews of the *O'Higgins* and its two support ships. He then selected 160 seamen and 80 marines from those who were prepared to volunteer to strike a 'mortal blow' against the enemy, the inducement being the prize money he offered for all ships captured by the expedition. The main objective was to 'cut out' and capture the pride of the Spanish fleet, the *Esmerelda*, and Cochrane ordered that once this had been achieved, the Chilean boarding force was to cheer 'Viva el Rey' in order to deceive the Spanish and gain time for capturing other vessels in the anchorage. (Were there echoes here of the French officers who had shouted 'Vive le Roi' in their dash through the City in 1814?)

The support ships were kept out of sight while Cochrane's flagship was anchored far enough offshore to lull the defenders into complacency. At 10 p.m. the volunteers set off in fourteen small boats with muffled oars, which had been assembled alongside the *O'Higgins*, Cochrane taking the leading boat. Around midnight the little flotilla reached the harbour and slipped silently through a small gap in the protective boom that earlier reconnaissance had identified. After silencing a gunboat that threatened to sound the alert, the lead boats managed to draw alongside the *Esmerelda* undetected. With the advantage of total surprise, Cochrane led the assault by climbing up the ship's main chains. He himself suffered a serious spinal injury when he was thrown back into his boat while boarding, and on resuming his attack, he was shot in the thigh, which forced him to direct operations while perched on a gun on the quarterdeck. Overwhelmed by the suddenness of the attack, 160 defending seamen and marines were cut down before the Spanish captain surrendered, no more than fifteen minutes having elapsed since the moment of boarding.

At this point the *Esmerelda* was dangerously exposed to the guns of the shore batteries, which began to fire into the darkened anchorage. However, Cochrane had one more trick up his sleeve. There were two neutral ships in the harbour, one American and one British frigate, and Cochrane guessed correctly that they would be carrying special identification lights to show the shore batteries where they were lying. He now hoisted lights of similar configuration and this had the desired effect of confusing the gunners on shore.

At around 3 a.m. Cochrane was forced by blood loss and faintness to withdraw to his flagship, appointing his second-in-command, Captain Guise, to take over in his absence. Cochrane's original plan had been to use the *Esmerelda*'s firepower to capture other Spanish vessels within the anchorage, thereby adding to the haul of prize money. However, Guise decided that this was too hazardous and put to sea with the *Esmerelda*. Although his plan had not been fully executed, Cochrane had succeeded in capturing the pride of the Spanish Pacific fleet, as well as its captain and officers, for the loss of eleven men killed and thirty wounded. The remnants of the Spanish naval force in the Pacific never ventured to show themselves again and left Cochrane undisputed master of the coast.

Cochrane followed up his *Esmerelda* triumph with a blockade of Callao while also carrying out a series of coastal raids around Lima with the aid of 600 troops borrowed from San Martin's army. Cut off by sea and harassed by land, Lima capitulated on 6 July 1821, Peru's declaration of independence following twelve days later.

Cochrane's military mission in the service of Chile was largely complete. There followed a prolonged and bitter dispute over his own emoluments, prize money and the settlement of his squadron's back-pay, all played out against the background of growing domestic political turmoil. Cochrane subsequently claimed that even after allowing for a belated settlement of some of the debts owed to him, the Chilean campaign had cost him £19,000. The truth of this will never be known.

Cochrane's role in the liberation of Chile and Peru was now acknowledged throughout the western world and towards the end of 1822 he received an invitation from the imperial court at Rio de Janeiro to take command of the navy in Brazil's struggle for independence from Portugal. After resigning his command in Chile, Cochrane and some of his officers set sail to undertake this new mission of liberation on the other side of the continent.

In 1821 Dom Pedro had been appointed by his father, King John VI of Portugal, as regent of Brazil, but a year later he yielded to popular pressure and declared independence, proclaiming himself emperor. Dom Pedro and the independence movement controlled the south of the country from Rio de Janeiro, but the provinces of the north, notably Bahia, Maranham and Para, remained subject to Portuguese colonial rule under the protection of the Portuguese fleet. As in the case of Chile and Peru, victory at sea held the key to autonomy for the new empire.

On arriving in Rio de Janeiro on 13 March 1823, Cochrane formally accepted command of the imperial fleet at an annual salary of $8,000 – the same terms that had been agreed for his Chilean command. The notional strength of the fleet was eight vessels, not far short of the dozen ships making up the Portuguese squadron, but only four of these, led by the 74-gun *Pedro Primiero*, were seaworthy. Worse still, the quality of the crews left much to be desired. After an early encounter with the enemy, during which his three supporting ships refused to engage, Cochrane decided to remove the American and European officers and seamen from two of the ships and transfer them to his flagship and the frigate *Maria de Gloria*, thereby reducing his effective fighting force to two. However, given Cochrane's personal preference for single- or double-ship actions, the limitations of the imperial navy in no way restricted his plan of campaign.

The Portuguese fleet lay 600 miles north of Rio de Janeiro, 9 miles up river from the port of Bahia. At the beginning of June,

Cochrane began a blockade with only two ships and then, on the night of 12 June when the Portuguese officers were attending a public ball, he navigated the *Pedro Primiero* up river in darkness to undertake a detailed reconnaissance of the anchorage. Cochrane had deliberately spread the word that he was preparing fireships to send into these confined waters, and when it became known that his flagship had been in the midst of the Portuguese fleet, there was a growing sense of alarm in the Portuguese command. Indeed, so great was the fear of the mayhem that might be caused by the hero of Basque Roads that both the army commander and the admiral at Bahia agreed on immediate evacuation to the northern city of Maranham before the blockade could be tightened to prevent escape.

On 2 July an armada of over seventy ships emerged at the river mouth, made up of thirteen warships, numerous transports with troops, and merchant vessels carrying fleeing families. With his tiny squadron Cochrane picked off the vessels at the tail end of the armada one by one. In the absence of sufficient prize crews, his instructions were that the masts of all troopships were to be cut away so that they would drift back before the wind to Bahia and it was not long before the Portuguese had lost half their army. Cochrane's flagship then harassed the Portuguese warships and broke off only when the mainsail split in two, leaving the much reduced and badly mauled evacuation fleet to proceed slowly to Maranham.

At the garrison town and port, the commandant was anticipating the arrival of the Portuguese fleet, as Cochrane knew from captured dispatches. Having carried out emergency repairs on the *Pedro Primiero*, Cochrane now raced ahead and came into Maranham under Portuguese colours. When a boat was sent out by the commandant to welcome him as the first of the expected Portuguese reinforcements, Cochrane revealed his true identity. He explained that he was the vanguard of a powerful and victorious Brazilian fleet and sent back a message to the effect that if the garrison were to surrender immediately before the invading force arrived, much bloodshed could be avoided. On 27 July the junta sent a deputation aboard under the protection of the local bishop to offer the submission of Maranham to the Brazilian emperor and to place the town with all its troops in the hands of his representative. As a final *coup de grâce* Cochrane 'allowed' the demoralised Portuguese garrison troops – who vastly outnumbered his own marines – to sail home to Lisbon in merchant vessels. At some point they would have passed the remnants of the evacuation fleet making its way to Maranham – where they would find that the town was flying the new flag of Brazil.

Following the double triumph of Bahia and Maranham, Cochrane sent one of his trusted senior officers to the neighbouring province of Para on board a captured ship. He was to practise the same kind of deception on the garrison town at the mouth of the Amazon. Having received news of the fall of the two provinces to the south, the junta at Para needed little persuasion that they should abandon the Portuguese cause and throw in their lot with the independence movement. It had taken Cochrane just three months to win for the emperor the three great northern provinces of Brazil.

On his return to Rio de Janeiro on 9 November Cochrane was greeted as a hero and created First Admiral of the Brazils and Marquess of Maranham. Yet, as in the case of Chile, the public accolades were soon blighted by disputes over pay and, above all, prize money. Cochrane's claims for himself and his men, based on the value of the property he had seized, were slashed by the Tribunal of Prizes. It was only a cash payment of £200,000 that induced Cochrane's squadron to resume its duties and put down a republican uprising in the north. In November 1824 Cochrane returned to Maranham to deal with growing civil disorder and political infighting, and after a wearisome six months he put to sea on his new flagship, the *Piranga*, heading east to arrive in Portsmouth on 25 June 1825.

Whether, as the Brazilian government claimed, Cochrane had deserted his post, or whether he had simply drifted north and east in search of cooler waters to alleviate the fever that allegedly afflicted him and his crew, no one can say for certain. But the result of this bizarre end to Cochrane's Latin American adventure was dismissal from his position as First Admiral and a protracted wrangle with the Brazilian authorities over what moneys were due to him.

Cochrane's return to England after nearly seven years' absence was a much happier affair than the dismal circumstances of his departure. He was widely acclaimed as a champion of democracy, the liberator of Chile, Peru and Brazil, and as a military hero who had displayed his genius in both the Napoleonic campaign and the South American revolutionary wars. Even so, as a radical, he was no friend of Lord Liverpool's Tory government and he was exposed to the risk of being prosecuted under the Foreign Enlistment Act of 1819 which prohibited British subjects from serving under a foreign power.

At the age of 50 Cochrane was once again looking for pastures new. He could expect no favours from the government and he needed to earn money, his haggling with the Brazilian authorities over pay and prize money offering little hope of a positive outcome. But an opportunity now presented itself to continue his military service in the cause of liberation. In the summer of 1825 he received an invitation from Prince Alexander Mavrokordatos, secretary to the Greek National Assembly, to take command of the Greek navy in the national struggle against Turkish occupation. He promptly accepted, the terms agreed being £37,000 on his signing as Admiral of Greece, with the prospect of a further £20,000 once Greek independence had been achieved.

As it turned out, Cochrane's glory days were over. In the four years he was to serve as Greek admiral he was involved with a major disaster on land and a fiasco at sea; his own endeavours were eclipsed by the brilliance of his second-in-command, Captain Frank Hastings, and he failed to endear himself to the Greeks or they to him.

From the outset Cochrane faced unexpected difficulties. He was forced to base himself initially in Boulogne to escape prosecution under the Foreign Enlistment Act. He was then obliged to move again, this time to Brussels in order to avoid arrest by France for illegally seizing a French ship during his Chilean campaign. Much more seriously, he encountered major problems in preparing a fleet of warships to join the fifty or so small vessels that constituted Greek's maritime force and take on the 135-strong Turco-Egyptian fleet. Given the urgency of the military situation, time was of the essence but Cochrane, with substantial sums at his disposal, decided to place orders for six steamships to be built in England and two heavy frigates to be built in the United States. Long delays in the completion and delivery of these vessels were to plague his campaign.

Before he could begin naval operations, Cochrane joined up with Sir Richard Church, who had been appointed commander of the Greek army, to try to lift the siege of Athens. The Turkish force had taken control of most of the city in August 1826. Both Greek defenders and citizens had withdrawn to the Acropolis where in the spring of 1827 they were in danger of being overrun by some 7,000 surrounding Arab troops. Cochrane and Church planned to land 3,000 troops by night. They would then move to a selected high point close to the Acropolis under cover of darkness. The rest of the Greek army, based south of Athens on either side of the Piraeus, was to launch a simultaneous diversionary attack on the Turks with the eventual aim of linking up victoriously in Athens.

The relieving force was duly disembarked on the night of 6 May but thereafter the planned assault unravelled rapidly. The disembarked Greek troops insisted on digging in instead of advancing, and the main Greek army refused to move. At daybreak the Turkish cavalry overran the beach-head, and of the 3,000 troops landed some 700 men were killed and many others taken prisoner before they could be re-embarked. The defenders of the Acropolis were left without hope of being relieved and on 5 June 1827 they surrendered to the Turks.

This tragedy on land was quickly followed by a major setback at sea. With only his flagship, a corvette and fourteen Greek gunships Cochrane planned a major attack on Alexandria where the Egyptian fleet of some twenty-five ships was based. Using his favourite device of fireships he succeeded in setting one vessel ablaze and forcing the Egyptian fleet to make for the open sea, but the response of his own squadron, believing themselves to be under attack, was to scatter in panic.

Thereafter events moved outside Cochrane's control. His naval operations were put on hold by the intervention of the great powers

– Britain, France and Russia – who were trying to broker a peace agreement between Turkey and Greece. The presence of a mercenary naval force operating independently of the Royal Navy was not acceptable and a message to this effect was brought to Cochrane from Sir Edward Codrington, Commander-in-Chief in the Mediterranean. However, the communication was too late to prevent Captain Hastings from inflicting some serious damage on the enemy: he succeeded in destroying seven Turkish ships and capturing three others before he heard of the peace initiative.

Turkish repudiation of the proposed peace agreement resulted in the combined fleets of the great powers, consisting of twenty-five warships, sailing to Navarino in the Pelopponese, where the Turkish fleet of eighty-two ships lay at anchor. The intent appears to have been to put on a show of strength rather than to attack but matters got out of hand when ill-disciplined seamen began to engage in musket fire. On the night of 20 October the Turkish fleet was effectively destroyed with the loss of 53 ships and 6,000 men, a military disaster for Turkey which enabled the great powers to enforce an armistice. After this there was little left for Cochrane to do.

At the beginning of March 1829 Cochrane rejoined his family in Paris. His own contribution to the Greek war of independence had been modest and he felt obliged to return the £20,000 contractually payable to him on the conclusion of hostilities. However, he had more than compensated for this by investing his entire front-end fee of £37,000 in Greek bonds which had soared in value. The speculator who had invested so heavily in British government bonds in 1814 had once again taken a big gamble on the outcome of a military conflict.

TWELVE

Vindication

Whether because of the threat of arrest under the Foreign Enlistment Act, his wife's delicate health or the lingering humiliation of the Stock Exchange trial, Cochrane did not immediately return to England, but travelled with Kitty in France and Italy during 1829–30. He was, however, determined to use his new-found fame to clear his name and overturn the 1814 verdict against him.

As early as 1825 Cochrane had written to Lord Melville, who was still First Lord of the Admiralty, to request a reinvestigation of his case. Lord Melville had replied that he did not feel able to recommend such a course to His Majesty. Then, in June 1828, Cochrane addressed an appeal to the Duke of Clarence, who, as Lord High Admiral, took a great interest in naval affairs. He asked the duke to represent his case to his brother, King George IV. The application was passed to the Prime Minister, the Duke of Wellington, who responded dismissively that 'the King's cabinet cannot comply with the prayer of the memorial'.

Then in 1830 events moved in Cochrane's favour. George IV died and the Duke of Clarence, a more amiable figure, became William IV. Furthermore, the Duke of Wellington's Tory government fell in November and was replaced by a Whig ministry under Lord Grey, which was likely to be much more sympathetic to Cochrane the radical. Returning to England, Cochrane submitted to the king and the cabinet a detailed 110-page printed statement of his case entitled *Review of the Case of Lord Cochrane*, which provided a very capable analysis of the evidence presented at the 1814 trial and in subsequent proceedings. Grey responded personally, expressing the hope that it might be possible to comply with the petition and referring back to earlier correspondence in which he had acquitted Cochrane of all blame 'except such as might have been incurred by inadvertence and by having suffered yourself to be led by others into measures of the consequence of which you were not sufficiently aware'. However, the king passed his copy of the review to the Home Secretary, Lord Melbourne, without comment, and in December 1830 Lord Melbourne informed Cochrane that 'His Majesty has returned the letter to him, but has not been pleased to signify any comments'.

On 1 July 1831 the 9th Earl of Dundonald died at his Paris lodging and Cochrane inherited the title but little else. He continued his lobbying of the government but it became clear that the Cabinet was split over the case. The breakthrough came when Kitty, as the new Countess of Dundonald, bypassed the government by approaching the king directly on behalf of her husband and persuading him to grant a free pardon, which it was within his prerogative to do. On 2 May 1832 the royal pardon was formally recorded by the Privy Council and on the same day Cochrane's name was restored to the Navy List as a Rear Admiral of His Majesty's Fleet, with immediate entitlement to half-pay.

However, the stain on Cochrane's character left by the trial verdict against him was not altogether removed, a matter of which he was keenly aware for the rest of his life and to which he alluded in his autobiography. The warrant for the pardon merely stated: 'Whereas upon consideration of some circumstances humbly represented to us on behalf of the said Thomas, Earl of Dundonald, We are graciously pleased to extend our grace and mercy upon him, and to grant him our free pardon for the said offences whereof he hath been convicted as aforesaid.'

Yet to the public at large, Cochrane, the naval hero and liberator of nations, had been vindicated. He could settle down in England with his professional and social status restored. Having acquired a new home at Hanover Lodge in Regent's Park, the Countess of Dundonald was able to indulge her taste for high society and entertainment, while Cochrane, who had little interest in partying, devoted his still considerable energies to inventions. He was particularly interested in harnessing the power of steam under pressure for use in tunnelling, ships and locomotives and on this he collaborated with Marc Brunel, father of the great Isambard. In 1834 he developed one of the earliest rotary engines, which attracted the interest of the London & Greenwich Railway. The company built two locomotives to his specification and trials were held. Numerous technical difficulties arose, however, and in 1837 the project collapsed amid mutual recriminations, a lawsuit and a personal loss to Cochrane of over £4,000.

Nothing daunted, Cochrane undertook further work at his own expense on engines, boilers and screw propellers designed to replace paddlewheels. In 1844 the Admiralty agreed to build a steam vessel to Cochrane's design and it was launched as HMS *Janus* at the end of 1845. However, in subsequent trials the *Janus* broke down and the Admiralty declined to carry out further development of the engines, on which Cochrane had spent over £16,000 of his own money.

While Cochrane's late career as an inventor was beset with problems, he was accorded further honours in his naval capacity. In 1841 he was promoted to the rank of vice admiral and granted a pension for meritorious service. Then on the birthday of Queen Victoria, 24 May 1846, he was invested once more as Knight Grand Cross of the Order of the Bath, Prince Albert sending him the insignia direct so that he could wear it at the queen's birthday celebration at St James's on 27 May. In July he was installed in the Chapel of the Order in Westminster Abbey when, ironically, it fell to Lord Ellenborough, son of the Chief Justice who had sentenced him in 1814, to act as one of his sponsors. The final mark of approval came eighteen months later when Cochrane received a letter from the First Lord of the Admiralty, Lord Auchland:

> I shall shortly have to name a Commander-in-Chief for the North American and West Indian Stations. Will you accept the appointment? I shall feel it to be an honour and a pleasure to have named you to it, and I am satisfied that your nomination will be agreeable to Her Majesty, as it will be to the country, and, particularly, to the Navy.

On 25 March 1848 Cochrane, at the age of 72, set sail from Plymouth on his flagship HMS *Wellesley*, having taken command of Britain's Atlantic Fleet. His tour of duty was to last just over three years but his peacetime role during this period was limited: it involved, *inter alia*, protecting British fishing interests, suppressing the slave trade and reporting on the state of British military and naval establishments throughout the region. He visited the Newfoundland fisheries and Nova Scotia, then sailed south to Bermuda, where he found the naval fortifications both extravagant and ineffective, before moving on to the Caribbean. In Barbados he recommended that the British troops stationed there be housed in barracks on high ground to reduce the high mortality rate due to fever and at Kingston, Jamaica, he recommended the appointment of a sanitary commission to address the filthy conditions in the local hospital and in Port Royal.

Cochrane had plenty of time to pursue his own personal interests when serving in the Atlantic and in Trinidad his entrepreneurial instincts were reawakened when he came across the island's famous 'pitch lake'. He carried out experiments to see whether the bitumen might be used as ship's fuel, obtained proprietorial rights in this potentially rich resource, and took a consignment of bitumen on board so that he could conduct further tests when he returned home. He was subsequently granted patents for the use of bitumen in sewers, tunnels, insulating wire and laying pipes below ground. He even had grandiose plans for the embankment of the Thames, using a kind of bituminous concrete to provide waterproofing. These were far-sighted ideas but once again Cochrane's hopes of personal enrichment were to be disappointed. One experience was particularly galling: when he obtained permission to lay an experimental asphalt surface on a street in Westminster, it was found that the horses slipped and much of the consignment of bitumen he had brought back on board ship was taken out to sea and dumped.

Cochrane had returned from his peaceful Atlantic tour of duty in June 1851. Yet within three years Britain was confronting Russia in what was to become the Crimean War and Cochrane put his name forward for the role of commander-in-chief of the Baltic fleet. When reporting the Cabinet's rejection of this proposal, the First Lord of the Admiralty paid a generous tribute to the old man of the sea while also pointing to the dangers of entrusting a fleet to someone with such a strong propensity for risk-taking:

> Lord Dundonald is seventy nine years of age: and though his energies and faculties are unbroken, and though, with his accustomed courage, he volunteers for the Service, yet, on the whole, there is reason to apprehend that he might deeply commit the Force under his command in some desperate enterprise, where the chance of success would not countervail the risk of failure and of the fatal consequences, which might ensue. Age has not abated the adventurous spirit of this gallant officer, which no authority could restrain and being uncontrollable it might lead to most unfortunate results. The Cabinet, on the most careful review of the entire question, decided that the appointment of Lord Dundonald was not expedient.

Cochrane, while seeking for himself an active role in the war, also revived two of his earlier ideas which he believed would quickly bring hostilities to an end. The first was a 'ship mortar', which was designed to scatter shells and projectiles over a mile-wide area. The second was a mechanism for the release of poison gas. A ship laden with sulphur would be towed to the windward of the target fortifications and ignited, the poison gas, carried on the wind, then expelling or destroying the enemy.

Cochrane's ingenious ideas for weapons of mass destruction and chemical warfare were seriously considered by the Admiralty but not pursued. Yet Cochrane never quite gave up the hope of playing a major role in the Crimea. After being turned down for the Baltic command he wrote to the First Lord, Sir James Graham:

> The unreasoning portion of the public have made an outcry against all old admirals (as if it should be expected that they should be able to clear their way with a broadsword) but . . . were

it necessary – which it is not – that I should place myself in an armchair on the poop with each leg on a cushion, I will undertake to subdue every insular fortification at Cronstadt within four hours from the commencement of the attack.

Cochrane's days of command were over but in 1855 he was consoled with a further promotion to the largely honorary title of Admiral of the Fleet. With his reputation and honours restored and his professional standing within the Royal Navy unchallenged, it might be thought that Cochrane would be able to live out his remaining years with peace of mind and pride in what he had achieved in the service of five countries over the course of a naval career spanning some sixty years. Yet behind the outward appearance of dignity, Cochrane's last years were far from happy.

In the first place, his personal financial affairs remained a matter for concern. He had demanded £26,000 in settlement of his claims against Chile but was eventually forced to accept £6,000. He claimed £100,000 from Brazil but nothing was to be paid during his lifetime. He was also lobbying the British government to pay him £4,000 in compensation for the loss of half-pay during the eighteen years he was struck off the Navy List. On the expenditure side, he had spent £20,000 or more on inventions which had yielded nothing in return, and his family were putting a further heavy strain on his finances.

Writing to her son Arthur in September 1854, Kitty expressed her own frustrations over her husband's financial mismanagement:

For forty years and more I have been your Father's wife and I have seen two noble fortunes spent, and not one penny of money spent ever returned: £10,000 lost in lamp concerns, nearly as much in copper rolling machinery, then came the famous *Janus* [the steamship built to his design] of ruinous memory, and now those most dreadful Pitch affairs. Oh Arthur, it is fearful, to say nothing of £70,000 spent in the Elections in younger days, our little place at Holly Hill for which he paid £13,600 was sold for £8,000. The house, Hanover Lodge cost £16,000 besides nearly

£5,000 laid out upon it, was sold to pay for the outlays for that hateful *Janus*. That home was sold over my head for (I think) £7,500.

No doubt some of these figures were inaccurate but there is insight here into Cochrane's extraordinary tendency to gamble away his money in speculative projects. In this letter Kitty also throws light on her relationship with Cochrane, as well as his own state of mind:

I do not believe a more miserable man breathes upon earth, dissatisfied with himself and everyone else he moans over the years which are past in perfect uselessness, money squandered without any real friends or supporters he is left to end a life which might have been the brightest that mortal man ever had a chance of possessing.

As her outpourings to her youngest son suggest, Kitty's marriage had broken down. The home that Cochrane had hoped to establish at Hanover Lodge was not to be. Kitty now lived her own life in Boulogne and when she visited her husband in London, she took separate lodgings. He, however, appears to have remained devoted to his wife and settled on her the whole of the capital sum he had obtained from his service in the cause of Greek independence – a further source of financial strain.

Cochrane's children were another cause for anxiety in his later years. His two eldest boys, Tom and Horace, both ended up in the hands of moneylenders. Tom, who at one point owed £4,800, had to be bundled off to Hong Kong where he was safe from his creditors. He later redeemed himself but Horace allowed his unpaid debts to mount up to £8,000 and was forced to hide from his creditors under an assumed name. In Horace's case there was also a suggestion of fraudulent misuse of funds. Cochrane's only daughter, Lizzie, also experienced financial difficulties when she left her husband and adopted a bohemian lifestyle that shocked her parents and peers. Cochrane used whatever spare resources he had to assist his wayward children but when his youngest son, Ernest, asked for help he replied, shortly before his death, that 'I cannot supply you with money, there not being above ground wherewith to put me below it.'

While Cochrane's financial and domestic concerns blighted his twilight years there was another matter that returned to torment him: the Stock Exchange trial of 1814. As far as the general public was concerned their great naval hero had been vindicated, but as he approached death Cochrane's anguish on this subject was evident. What mattered to Cochrane was to have the slate wiped clean, which meant nothing less than restoration to the position he would have been in had the case against him never been brought. Accordingly, he wrote to Lord Palmerston on 26 May 1856 stating that although he had been restored to the Navy by William IV, he should surely as a matter of justice be entitled to receive his half-pay for the period during which he had been wrongly struck off the Navy List. This he calculated at £4,000. In addition he suggested that the government should repay the £1,000 fine that had been imposed on him, plus his legal costs. Palmerston replied that there were no Treasury funds available for the repayment of fines and no precedent for such restitution, while he found 'on enquiry, that pay or half-pay has not been granted to any naval officer for any period during which he may have been out of the service.'

While Cochrane continued to lobby the government for reimbursement of his half-pay he fought to justify himself to posterity with *The Autobiography of a Seaman*, the first volume of which was published in 1859. The last chapters of this work deal with the Stock Exchange fraud in some detail and Cochrane makes clear from the outset the huge pall this episode had cast over the last forty-five years of his life:

I now approach a period of my life in which occurred circumstances beyond all others painful to the feelings of an honourable man. . . . But when an alleged offence was laid to my charge in 1814, in which, on the honour of a man now on the brink of the grave, I had not the slightest participation, and from which I never benefited, nor thought to benefit one farthing, and when this allegation was, by political rancour and legal chicanery, consummated in an unmerited conviction and an outrageous sentence, my heart for the first time sank within me, as conscious of a blow, the effect of which it has required all my energies to sustain. . . . It may be thought that after the restoration to rank and honours by my late and present sovereigns – after promotion to the command of a fleet when I had no enemy to confront – and after enjoyment of the sympathy and friendship of those whom the nation delights to honour – I might safely pass over the day of deep humiliation. Not so. It is true that I have received those marks of my sovereign's favour and it is true that from that day to the present I have enjoyed the uninterrupted friendship of those who were then convinced, and are still convinced, of my innocence; but *that unjust public sentence has never been publicly reversed, nor the equally unjust fine inflicted on me remitted*; so that if I would, it is not in my power to remain silent and be just to my posterity.

The defence of his conduct presented in *The Autobiography* is a rather sad affair. With his powers failing, it is perhaps not surprising that there should be misstatements of fact as well as contradictions of his earlier versions of events, particularly regarding the circumstances in which he published his affidavit ahead of the Stock Exchange trial. But whether from a burning sense of injustice, a simple desire to protect his reputation after his death or an inner fury at his own reckless misjudgement which, all those years ago, had changed the course of his life, Cochrane was determined to dig over yet again the events of that fateful Monday morning in February 1814.

Cochrane's last years were therefore characterised by public acclaim on the one hand and private grief on the other. Financial worries, desertion by his wife, the failings of his children and, above all, the open sore of the Stock Exchange scandal, prevented one of Britain's finest warriors from enjoying in old age the peace of mind which he surely deserved. He lived frugally and alone in lodgings in unfashionable Pimlico, first in Victoria Square and then in Belgrave Road, writing regularly to Boulogne where lived the wife he had always loved.

In *The Autobiography* he railed against the prosecution witness Crane and against Lord Ellenborough, and time and again intimated that he was framed either by his enemies in the government or those in the Admiralty or both in order to put him out of the way: 'It is clear that the influence and vindictiveness with which this most unjustifiable prosecution was carried out against me, arose from motives far deeper than the vindication of stock-jobbing purity, viz. from a desire in more influential quarters to silence, if possible, an obnoxious political adversary.' And again: 'my unjust conviction of having participated in a trumpery hoax, which common-sense might have convinced them was beneath my notice, was converted into the means of preventing the future exercise of my abilities as a naval officer.'

In 1858, when his health was failing, Cochrane moved into the house of his eldest son, Lord Thomas Cochrane, in Prince Albert Road, Kensington, where he died on 31 October 1860. There was no state funeral but he was buried with great pomp and ceremony in Westminster Abbey, his banner and insignia being restored to Henry VII's Chapel at the command of the queen just one day before the funeral. His memorial tablet in Westminster Abbey provides a fitting epitaph:

Here rests in his 85th year Thomas Cochrane, Tenth Earl of Dundonald, Baron Cochrane of Dundonald of Paisley and of Ochiltree in the Peerage of Scotland, Marquess of Maranham in the Empire of Brazil, GCB and Admiral of the Fleet who, by the confidence which his genius, his science and his extraordinary daring inspired, by his heroic exertions in the cause of freedom and his splendid services alike to his own country, Greece, Brazil, Chile and Peru, achieved a name illustrious throughout the world for courage patriotism and chivalry.

It was only after his death that Cochrane was to be rehabilitated in a manner that would have satisfied both his purse and his pride. In his will he had bequeathed to his eldest grandson his claims against the British government for his back-pay and repayment of the fine imposed in 1814. In 1864 his successor in the title applied for payment of these sums as well as a pension, but was turned down. Twelve years later Cochrane's grandson, having reached his majority, presented a petition to the queen, praying that she would be 'graciously pleased to order that compensation might be made to him, as the legatee of the late Earl of Dundonald, in respect of the loss of pay and allowances of the late Earl as a naval officer in the Royal Service, for a period of eighteen years'. This submission, too, was rejected on the grounds that the matter had been fully considered in 1848 by the government of the day.

However, in 1877, Cochrane's supporters in the House of Commons proposed that a select committee be appointed to enquire and report upon the petition and this was voted through. In July of that year the committee produced its report which referred back to the free pardon granted to Cochrane, his reinstatement in the Navy and the honours restored to him: 'It appears to your Committee that these steps could not have been taken by responsible advisers of the Crown, who believed that Lord Dundonald was guilty of the crime of which, in 1814, he was convicted, and the course pursued towards him amounts to nothing less than a public recognition by those Governments of his innocence.' The committee went on to say that no technical rule should stand in the way of full reparation and concluded that 'this is a case peculiarly exceptional in its character, and deserving Her Majesty's most gracious and favourable consideration'. This recommendation was acted on and in 1878 a grant of £5,000 was made by the government to Lord Cochrane 'in respect of the distinguished services of his grandfather, the late Earl of Dundonald' – a sum that was said to be equivalent to the arrears of half-pay without interest.

Cochrane's vindication was now complete. Of all the great battles that he fought this was the most prolonged, the most bitter and the most fiercely contested. It was also, in one sense, his greatest triumph. For here was a man who, in mid-career, had committed a reckless act that threatened to bring ruin on himself and his family. He had fought back, as if engaged in war, using every means available to clear his name, restore his honour and secure his reputation for posterity. In the end he succeeded and whatever one's views on the Stock Exchange fraud, one must admire his tenacity.

But if it can now be shown that Cochrane was almost certainly guilty of the fraud, surely he was guilty of much worse. After all, the implication is that he perjured himself in court, manipulated his servants' evidence and possibly obtained false affidavits from others – all this while solemnly protesting his innocence to the world. Worst of all, he was arguably guilty of a second fraud when he made repeated representations that he was blameless to successive governments in order to obtain financial compensation for the loss of his navy pay.

However, this would be a very harsh judgment of the man. To begin with we need to view Cochrane's original offence in the context of the time. The Stock Exchange in 1814 was only beginning to establish its respectability and from today's perspective it was something of a snakepit. Rumours and counter-rumours of great military events were deliberately planted, and the London newspapers, in the absence of hard facts, reported these rumours as lead items. A typical example is to be found in the *Morning Chronicle* of 9 March 1814:

> various reports were made yesterday of new battles but we believe without any foundation. The rumour was, however, that Blucher had been attacked by Bonaparte, and that though he was himself slightly wounded, it had terminated greatly to his advantage. . . . We believe that this was the mere fabrication of the day.

The Stock Exchange conspirators took rumour-mongering one dangerous stage further by adding colour to their story – unacceptable and reprehensible, yes, but not quite the outrage that it would be in today's tightly regulated financial markets. When the cry went up and the Stock Exchange launched its investigation, Cochrane no doubt appreciated the gravity of what he had done and the danger he was in. At this point he *could* have come clean. As he himself wrote when protesting his innocence to Cochrane Johnstone's daughter, Elizabeth: 'The deception may have originated in thoughtless levity; in that case, though I might not have published the fact to the world, I would not have denied it.' But others were involved and owning up would expose them too. More critically, once Cochrane came under attack the paranoid side to his character was provoked and his instinct then, as a fighting man through and through, was to reach for his sabre. He no doubt convinced himself that his enemies in the Admiralty and the political establishment were out to get him by indicting him for an offence that to his mind was no more than a piece of mischief.

War against him having been declared, Cochrane was prepared to go to any lengths to extricate himself. And once he had started down that road and had committed his reputation and honour to his defence, there was no going back. After the trial verdict the only way he could rehabilitate himself was by convincing the world at large that the verdict was wrong. That involved him in further subterfuges, culminating in his claim for back-pay, not so much perhaps for the sake of the compensation itself, but in order to wipe the slate clean. Perhaps the last thing that should be said on the subject is this: men make mistakes, and even great men make mistakes. Cochrane made his mistake, but the rest of his active life in the service of independence and freedom around the world was itself a form of redemption, for which we can all be grateful.

While Cochrane was eventually restored to rank and fame, the other Stock Exchange miscreants were less fortunate. After the trial Cochrane Johnstone fled to Calais and from there made his way to Dominica where he tried in vain to prevent the sale of his property there to satisfy creditors. A few years later he moved to Demarara and later to Paris where he died as a fugitive in 1833. Butt fared worse, apparently losing his bearings completely after his release from prison in 1815. He first pursued Cochrane Johnstone to the West Indies in a futile attempt to obtain repayment of a debt of some £4,000 allegedly owing to him. On his return to London he was imprisoned again in 1817 for fifteen months for claiming that Lord Ellenborough had corruptly misappropriated the £1,000 fine he had paid into court in 1814. He was in prison once more in 1830–1, this time as a debtor, and in 1847 he was still pestering

Cochrane for money, having on his own admission spent fourteen years in various prisons since the Stock Exchange fraud.

De Berenger demonstrated greater resourcefulness and resilience than either Cochrane Johnstone or Butt. He maintained his connection with the Duke of Cumberland's Sharpshooters and there is reference to him living in Kentish Town in 1827. Then in 1831 Cramorne House, Chelsea, was opened to the public as a sports stadium under the management of none other than Baron de Berenger, who taught shooting in the butts erected there. De Berenger held an 'Olympic Festival' at his Chelsea stadium in 1832 and to commemorate Queen Victoria's coronation he staged another festival in 1838 which included archery, gymnastics, cricket, fencing, rowing, sailing and target shooting with rifle and pistol. These grand sporting occasions are now regarded as a precursor of the modern Olympic Games and de Berenger can therefore claim his place in history for reasons other than the Stock Exchange fraud. He also published in 1835 *Help and Hints: How to Protect Life and Property* in which he set out the criteria he had established in the Duke of Cumberland's Sharpshooters for grading the qualified shot (e.g. six shots at a 30 inch target at 200 yards to attain first class). Despite these achievements, de Berenger was again getting into financial difficulties by 1840, a year in which he directed that the profits of Cremorne House be held in trust for a lady named Beatrix Chowder. The colourful life of Baron de Berenger, alias Baron de Beaufain, alias Colonel du Bourg, alias Captain Brown finally passed away in 1845.

Postscript

Towards the end of his life Cochrane was acclaimed as one of the greatest naval commanders of his age. He had proved himself in a series of extraordinary engagements against the navies of France, Spain and Portugal in the Pacific, Atlantic and the Mediterranean; he had terrorised the enemy on shore with brilliantly conducted lightning raids on communications, fortifications and garrisons; and he had wrought havoc against enemy ships and fleets with few resources at his disposal. As one contemporary observed, his career 'was distinguished above all others by the attainment of great results with small means'. And although he took great risks, he always valued the lives of his crew, as was observed by Marryat who served with him on the *Impérieuse*: 'I never knew anyone so careful of the lives of his ship's company as Lord Cochrane, or anyone who calculated so closely the risks attending any expedition.'

Cochrane was a true hero in the eyes of his men, his country and the liberated peoples of Latin America. Following his burial with full honours in Westminster Abbey, a statue was erected to his memory in Valparaiso in 1873 and in 1901 the Brazilian ambassador conducted a ceremony at Cochrane's grave to mark 'the first pilgrimage from our continent to the tomb of the South American Lafayette'. Cochrane's exploits have since been immortalised in literature, first through Captain Marryat, then by C.S. Forrester's Captain Hornblower and most recently by Patrick O'Brian whose hero, Jack Aubrey, is also loosely modelled on Cochrane.

Yet despite these accolades Cochrane is not today a household name, ranking alongside the great figures of British naval history as, surely, he deserves to be. Part of the reason, no doubt, is that having commanded squadrons rather than great fleets, he is not associated with any particular victory or encounter. Another explanation is that some of his greatest exploits were undertaken while in the service of foreign governments rather than under the national flag. It is also fair to say that the Royal Navy could never be entirely comfortable with such an unconventional figure who had much of the buccaneer about him. And, finally, there are the events of February 1814 which still cast their long shadow over Cochrane's brilliant career.

After Cochrane's death the controversy over his trial for the Stock Exchange fraud persisted. In *The Autobiography of a Seaman* Cochrane had quoted with approval Lord Campbell's *Lives of the Chief Justices of England* (1857), which severely criticised Lord Ellenborough for his handling of the Stock Exchange trial. Lord Campbell's assessment carried considerable weight, coming as it did from the pen of the Lord Chancellor and former Lord Chief Justice. The key passage reads as follows:

Lord Cochrane (since Earl of Dundonald) was one of the most gallant officers in the English navy, and had gained the most brilliant reputation in a succession of naval engagements against the French. Unfortunately for him, he likewise wished to distinguish himself in politics, and, taking the Radical line, he was returned to Parliament for the City of Westminster. He was a determined opponent of Lord Liverpool's administration, and at popular meetings was in the habit of delivering harangues, of rather a seditious aspect, which induced Lord Ellenborough to believe that he seriously meant to abet rebellion and that he was a dangerous character.

It so happened that Lord Cochrane was then in London, living in his uncle's house, and was much in his company, but there is now good reason to believe that he was not at all implicated in the nefarious [Stock Exchange fraud]. However, when the fraud was detected – partly from a belief in his complicity, and partly from political spite – he was included in the indictment preferred for the conspiracy to defraud the Stock Exchange.

The trial coming on before Lord Ellenborough, the noble and learned Judge himself being persuaded of the guilt of all the defendants, used his best endeavours that they should all be convicted. He refused to adjourn the trial at the close of the prosecutor's case about nine in the evening, when the trial had lasted twelve hours; and the jury as well as the defendants' counsel were all completely exhausted, and all prayed for an adjournment. The following day, in summing up, prompted no doubt by the conclusion in his own mind, he laid especial emphasis on every circumstance which might raise a suspicion against Lord Cochrane, and elaborately explained away whatever at first sight appeared favourable to the gallant officer. In consequence the jury found a verdict of Guilty against all the defendants.

Next term Lord Cochrane presented himself in Court to move for a new trial but the other defendants convicted along with him did not attend. He said truly that he had no power or influence to obtain their attendance, and urged that his application was founded on circumstances peculiar to his own case. But Lord Ellenborough would not hear him because the other defendants were not present. Such a rule had before been laid down, but it is palpably contrary to the first principles of justice, and it ought immediately to have been reversed.

Lord Cochrane was thus deprived of all opportunity of showing that the verdict against him was wrong, and, in addition to a fine and imprisonment, he was sentenced to stand in the pillory.

Lord Campbell's account, which misrepresented the circumstances in which a retrial was refused, helped to foster the notion that Cochrane had been set up by Lord Ellenborough because of his radical political views. However, Lord Ellenborough's family was not prepared to let this version of events go unchallenged and one of the judge's descendants, Edward Law, commissioned a very able lawyer, J.B. Atlay of Lincoln's Inn, to examine the trial in great detail with a view to exonerating his illustrious forebear. Atlay's scholarly treatise, *The Trial of Lord Cochrane before Lord Ellenborough*, was published in 1897 and became the basis of a further work by John Law, the 5th Baron Ellenborough, entitled

The Guilt of Lord Cochrane in 1814, which was published in 1914. These works defended Lord Ellenborough's conduct of the trial and implied that Cochrane's defence was a sham. Thus was battle joined between the families of Dundonald and Ellenborough.

Since then Cochrane's colourful career has been the subject of a number of biographies, all of which without exception proclaim his innocence of the Stock Exchange fraud. This wave of literary absolution does credit to Cochrane's presentation of his own case but it no doubt also reflects the fact that the general reading public prefer their heroes to be untarnished by fraud.

Apart from Atlay's book, there have been few studies of the Stock Exchange trial itself. William Townsend in his *Modern State Trials* (1850) pointed to the 'very strong' circumstantial evidence connecting Cochrane to the facts charged but nevertheless expressed his opinion that Cochrane was innocent. On the other hand, the most careful modern analysis of the trial which is to be found in Henry Cecil's *A Matter of Speculation* (1965), concluded that on the basis of the then published evidence, Cochrane was clearly guilty. Cecil drew parallels between Cochrane's diversionary tactics in making wild allegations against all and sundry – his lawyers, the Stock Exchange, the government, the Admiralty, hostile witnesses – and his highly successful diversions of the enemy at sea. Cecil's final word on Cochrane's campaign to clear his name still has relevance today: 'What is extraordinary is the extent of its success. . . . The myth of Lord Cochrane's innocence has been so fully implanted in the mind of each generation since his pardon in 1832 that proof of his guilt is simply ignored and the old stories blandly repeated.'

The pattern of repetition goes on. The three latest biographies of Cochrane (published 1978, 1978, 2001) dismiss the idea that he could have been involved in the fraud, as does the introduction by Richard Woodman to the latest edition of *The Autobiography of a Seaman* (2000). Patrick O'Brian, in his novel *The Reverse of the Medal* (1986), also supports the traditional view of Cochrane's innocence. Jack Aubrey is here innocently embroiled in a Stock Exchange scandal closely modelled on the events of February 1814. O'Brian, while acknowledging the provenance of the story in a carefully worded introduction to his book, disclaims any attempt to form a judgment as to Cochrane's guilt or innocence. He also refers to Atlay's study, which he describes as a 'fully documented and closely reasoned book [that] might shake all but the most determined of Lord Cochrane's supporters'.

However, some modern historians have been less kind to Cochrane. Professor Richard Glover, in his study of Britain's defence against Napoleon (1973), condemns Cochrane as 'just a plain and shameless liar'. A scholarly but unpublished work by John Sugden (1981), which focuses exclusively on Cochrane's early career, concludes that so far as the Stock Exchange prosecution is concerned 'there is no doubt that it was a far stronger case than Cochrane's biographers have generally admitted'. And the naval historian, Professor Nicholas Rodger, in his acclaimed *Naval History of Britain* (2004), goes further in suggesting that Cochrane had a well-established reputation for dishonesty which culminated in his conviction for the Stock Exchange fraud. This, he says, was passed off by his radical friends as a political prosecution, although the evidence against him was very strong. Rodger also asserts that Cochrane's *Autobiography of a Seaman* is 'a mendacious work of self-justification, to be used with extreme caution'.

The present study, drawing on hitherto unavailable sources, suggests that Cochrane, with amazing audacity and resourcefulness, hoaxed the world twice over: first with a military masquerade that duped investors, and then with a campaign of self-vindication that persuaded the world of his innocence. The story may be one of mischief and deception but it does portray a man with remarkable fighting spirit in adversity. It is also a tale about the poignantly contrasting high and low points of a career that progressed from inauspicious beginnings to public adulation and honours, through humiliation and dismissal, to restoration of rank, renown and dignity.

While Cochrane's life at sea was marked by a succession of glittering achievements, his life ashore was full of misjudgments, both political and financial, among which the Stock Exchange fraud stands out as an act of extreme folly. As one contemporary remarked: 'Take him out of a profession in which he is without rival and all is inconsistency.' The fact is that Cochrane's restless energy was ideally suited to his daring naval exploits but got him into deep trouble as soon as he was away from the water. Thomas Cochrane has, however, left a magnificent naval legacy and while this book has attempted to put the record straight regarding a moment of recklessness in February 1814, he will always be remembered as a fearsome commander and liberator of nations.

APPENDIX

Exhibits

March 11, 1814

13 Green Street

I, Sir Thomas Cochrane, commonly called Lord Cochrane having been appointed by the Lords Commissions of the Admiralty, to active service (at the request, I believe, of Sir Alexander Cochrane) when I had no expectation of being called on, I obtained leave of absence to settle my private affairs previous to quitting this country, and chiefly with a view to lodge a specification to a patent to a discovery for increasing the intensity of light. That in pursuance of my daily practice of superintending work that was executing for me, and knowing that my uncle, Mr Cochrane Johnstone, went to the city every morning in a coach.

I do swear, on the morning of the 21st February (which day was impressed on my mind by circumstances which afterwards occurred) I breakfasted with him at his residence in Cumberland Street, about half past eight o'clock, and I was put down by him (and Mr Butt was in the coach) on Snow Hill, about ten o'clock: that I had been about three quarters of an hour at Mr King's manufactory, at No. 1, Cock Lane, when I received a few lines on a small bit of paper, requesting me to come immediately to my house: the name affixed, from being written close to the bottom, I could not read. The servant told me it was from an army officer, and concluding that he might be an officer from Spain, and that some accident had befallen to my brother; I hastened back, and I found Captain Berenger, who in great seeming uneasiness, made many apologies for the freedom he had used, which nothing but the distressed state of his mind,

185

arising from difficulties, could have induced him to do. All his prospects, he said, had failed, and his last hope had vanished of obtaining an appointment in America. He was unpleasantly circumstanced, on account of a sum which he could not pay, and if he could, that others would fall upon him for full £8,000. He had no hope of benefiting his creditors in his present situation, or of assisting himself. That if I would take him with me he would immediately go on board and exercise the sharpshooters, (which plan Sir Alexander Cochrane, I know had approved of). That he had left his lodgings and prepared himself in the best way his means allowed. He had brought the sword with him which had been his father's, and to that and to Sir Alexander, he would trust for obtaining an honourable appointment.

I felt very uneasy at the distress he was in, and knowing him to be a man of great talent and science, I told him I would do every thing in my power to relieve him: but as to his going immediately to the *Tonnant* [the ship of which Lord Cochrane had been appointed Captain], with any comfort to himself, it was quite impossible, my cabin was without furniture, I had not even a servant on board. He said he would willingly mess anywhere. I told him that the wardroom was already crowded, and besides I could not with propriety take him, he being a foreigner, without leave from the Admiralty. He seemed greatly hurt at this and recalled to my recollection certificates which he had formerly shown me, from persons in official situations, Lord Yarmouth, General Jenkinson, and Mr Reeves, I think, were among the number. I recommended him to use his endeavour to get them or any other friends, to exert their influence, for I had none, adding that when the *Tonnant* went to Portsmouth, I should be happy to receive him: and I knew from Sir Alexander Cochrane, that he would be pleased if he accomplished that object.

Captain Berenger said, that not anticipating any objection on my part from the conversation he had formerly had with me, he had come away with intention to go on board and make himself useful in his military capacity;– he could not go to Lord Yarmouth, or to any other of his friends, in this dress, (alluding to that which he had on) or return to his lodgings where it would excite suspicion (as he was at that time in the Rules of the King's Bench) but that if I refused to let him join the ship now, he would do so at Portsmouth. Under present circumstances, however, he must use a great liberty, and request the favour of me to lend him a hat to wear instead of his military cap. I gave him one which was in a back room with some things that had not been packed up, and having tried it on, his uniform appeared under his greatcoat; I therefore offered him a black coat that was lying on a chair, and which I did not intend to take with me. He put up his uniform in a towel, and shortly afterwards went away in great apparent uneasiness of mind; and having asked my leave, he took the coach I came in, and which I had forgotten to discharge in the haste I was in.

I do further depose, that the above conversation is the substance of all that passed with Captain Berenger, which, from the circumstances attending it, was strongly impressed upon my mind, that no other person in uniform was seen by me, at my house, on Monday 21st February, though possibly other officers may have called (as many have done since my appointment;) of this, however, I cannot speak of my own knowledge, having been almost constantly from home, arranging my private affairs. I have understood that many persons have called under the above circumstances, and have written notes in the parlour, and others have waited there in expectation of seeing me, and then gone away, but I most positively swear that I never saw any person at my house resembling the description, and in the dress stated in the printed advertisement of the members of the Stock Exchange.

I further aver that I had no concern, directly or indirectly, in the late imposition and that the above is all that I know relative to any person who came to my house in uniform on the 21st day of February, before alluded to. Captain Berenger wore a grey greatcoat, a green uniform, and a military cap. From the manner in which my character has been attempted to be defamed, it is indispensably necessary to state that my connection in any way with the funds, arose from an impression that in the present favourable aspect of affairs, it was only necessary to hold stock in order to become a gainer without prejudice to anybody: that I did so openly, considering it in no degree improper, far less dishonourable; that I had no secret information of any kind, and that had my expectation of the success of affairs been disappointed, I should have been the only sufferer.

Further I do most solemnly swear that the whole of the Omnium on account, which I possessed on the 21st day of February 1814, amounted to £139,000 which I bought by Mr Fearn (I think) on the 12th ultimo at a premium of 28¼, that I did not hold on that day any other sum on account in any other stock directly or indirectly, and that I had given orders when it was bought to dispose of it on a rise of one per cent, and it actually was sold on an average at 29½ premium, though on the day of the fraud it might have been disposed of at 33½. I further swear, that the above is the only stock which I sold of any kind on the 21st day of February, except £2000 in money which I had occasion for, the profit of which was about £10. Further, I do solemnly depose, that I had no connexion or dealing with any one, save the above mentioned, and that I did not at any time, directly or indirectly, by myself or by any other, take or procure any office or apartment for any broker or other person for the transaction of stock affairs.

Cochrane

EXHIBIT 2: JAMES LE MARCHANT'S CORRESPONDENCE WITH
COCHRANE, APRIL 1814

Glo'ster Hotel, Piccadilly
6th April 1814

My Lord,
Although I have not the honour of your acquaintance, I beg leave to
address you, to solicit an interview with your lordship, for the
purpose of explaining a conversation I had with Mr de Berenger, a
few days prior to the hoax of the 21st February last, and which must
be interesting to you. If your lordship will condescend to appoint an
hour, I will not fail attending punctually at your house, or elsewhere.

I have the honour to be my Lord,
your Lordship's most obedient and
humble servant,

Js. Le Marchant

Rt Hon Lord Cochrane

Glo'ster Hotel, Piccadilly, London,
7th April 1814

My Lord,
I had the honour yesterday to address your Lordship, for the sole
purpose of giving you that information you are not aware of; and
knowing my letter was delivered (your lordship being at home when
it was presented at the door), I beg to say, that I am now justified
from your silent contempt and defiance thereof, *to make my
information public* and which I should not have done before
consulting you on that head, my sole wish being to state facts and
not be considered acting underhand. As I feel exonerated from the
last charge, and being in a certain degree called on to give my
evidence relative to 21st February last; and as the rank I hold in
society will *give weight* to my *testimony, with the witnesses* I shall
bring forward on the occasion, I feel justified in the steps I am about
to take, nor can your lordship blame me for doing so, understanding
the business in question will be brought before Parliament on a

future day. I am sorry to have intruded myself on your lordship's notice, by addressing you yesterday: but, to be correct, I thought it my duty to inform you by this, what have been and are my intentions.

> I have the honour to be, my Lord,
> Your Lordship's most obedient
> Humble servant,
>
> J. le Marchant

Rt Hon Lord Cochrane, MP
No. 13 Green Street, Grosvenor Square

13 Green Street
April 8th 1814

Sir,

I should have hoped, circumstanced as I am, and attacked by scoundrels of all descriptions, that a gentleman of your understanding might have discovered some better reason than that of 'silent contempt', to account for the delay of a few hours in answering a note; and more particularly as your note of the 6th led me to conclude, that the information offered to me was meant as a mark of civility and attention, and was not on a subject in which you felt any personal interest.

> I am, Sir,
> Your obedient servant,
>
> Cochrane

Colonel le Marchant
Glocester Hotel

Glo'ster Hotel, Piccadilly,
8th April 1814

My Lord,

I ask your Lordship's pardon for my letter of yesterday, and which was written under the supposition of being treated with silent contempt. To convince you of the high respect I have for your

Lordship, I have the honour to enclose to you a statement of what I know relative to the 21st February; and I also now declare solemnly, that no power of consideration shall ever induce me to come forward as evidence against you, and that all I know on the subject shall be buried for ever in oblivion. Thus much I hope will convince you I am more your friend than enemy; as my testimony, corroborated by the two officers, would be of great importance, not (believe me) that I myself doubt in any wise your Lordship's affidavit; but de Berenger's conversation with me would to your enemies be positive proof; as for my part, I now consider *all that man told me to be diabolically false*. If my conduct meets your approbation, can I ask for a reciprocal favour, as a temporary loan, on security being given. – I am just appointed to a situation of about £1,200 a year, but for the moment am in the greatest distress, with a large family; you *can* without risk, and have the *means* to relieve us, and I believe, the *will* of doing good. Necessity has driven me to ask your Lordship this favour. Whether granted or not, be assured of my keeping my oath now pledged, of secrecy; and that I am with the greatest respect,

My Lord,
Your Lordship's most
Obedient, humble servant.
J. le Marchant

Right Hon Lord Cochrane

[Enclosed with the letter was the following statement:]

I became intimately acquainted with de Berenger about eighteen months ago, and have continued so till a few days prior to the hoax of 21st February last. He was in the habit of calling on me at the Glo'ster Coffee House, Piccadilly; and did so frequently, between the 10th and 16th of last February. He generally called late in the evening, saying he had dined with Lord Cochrane. Once he called about noon, stating he had breakfasted with his Lordship, had been with him on particular business, and was to return to dinner; he mentioned being very intimate with Lord Cochrane and the Hon. C.

Johnstone; that they were kind friends to him, with whom he frequently dined. In his apartments, in the rules of the King's Bench, he showed me the devices he was drawing for Lord Cochrane's lamp invention. The last time he called upon me, it was very late; he appeared elated somewhat by drinking, having (as he said) dined with his Lordship; and in consequence of there being company, he could not then show Lord Cochrane a copy of a memorial he had written to the Duke of York, praying to be given field officer's rank, and to be appointed to be sent out under Lord Cochrane, for the purpose of instructing the marines in rifle exercise; that his Lordship was very anxious to have him on board of his ship, that he objected going, unless with field-officer's rank, hoping to procure a majority; and that Lord Cochrane had said he would try and get him a lieutenant-colonelcy.

De Berenger shewed me his memorial to the Duke, the head of which not being in propria forma, I corrected, it was very long, and related to the losses his family had sustained as American loyalists; also on the cause of his first coming over to England. On my asking him, if the Duke of York was to appoint him, how he could extricate himself out of his difficulties and leave the Bench, he answered, 'all was settled on that score; that in consequence of the services he had rendered Lord Cochrane and Mr C. Johnstone, in devising, whereby they had and could realise large sums by means of the funds or stocks, Lord Cochrane was his friend, and had told him a day or two ago, that for these services his Lordship had, unknown to him (de Berenger) kept a private purse for him, placing therein a certain per-centage on the profits Lord Cochrane had gained through his stock suggestions; and that now this purse had accumulated to an amount adequate to liberate him from the Bench.' When he said this, he appeared overjoyed, and said it in such a manner as to make me credit him. He remained with me this said evening, drinking hollands and water, till near two o'clock in the morning.

On his leaving me, I thought of the conversation, especially that part which related to the funds, and conceived, from the numerous stock-jobbing reports, whereby the funds raised or were depressed, that he must have been deeply concerned in it. A few days after the

21st February, it was whispered that Lord Cochrane was concerned in the hoax. Immediately, de Berenger's former conversation with me forcibly occurred to my mind, and I then mentioned to two friends, with whom I was in company, *(and this prior to Lord Cochrane's affidavit, or de Berenger's name being mentioned)*, that I would lay my existence de Berenger was the sham Colonel du Bourg, and I stated my reasons for supposing so.

Recollecting myself afterwards, I made them, as officers, pledge their oath and word of honour, that what I had said on the subject they would never repeat, or even hint at; and I am most fully persuaded they have not. The same day, but prior to the conversation above mentioned, the hoax being the topic in the coffee-room, I said I thought I knew more than any one relative thereto, except the parties concerned, but I never mentioned any name whatever; yet some days after, I received two anonymous two-penny-post letters, recommending my giving up my information, either to Ministers or the Members of the Stock Exchange Commission; that I might depend on their secrecy, and an ample reward, in proportion to my report; of course these letters were left unnoticed. As soon as I suspected de Berenger to be Colonel du Bourg, I called twice on him, but could not get admittance; I also gave one of the officers above alluded to, a letter of introduction to de Berenger, for him to gain information on the rifle manoeuvres; he called; was not admitted; left the letters; and, as well as myself, has heard nothing since of de Berenger.

To the whole of this I can solemnly make oath; and I am sure I can bring the two officers in question to swear to what I said to them, and *the time when*, although I have never since spoken to them on that subject.

J. le Marchant

EXHIBIT 3: TRACING OF NOTES

Date	Cheque	Form of payment	Transactions	End use
10 Feb.	£56 5s drawn by Fearn on Bond & Co., payable to Butt	£50 note plus cash		£50 note found in de Berenger's possession
19 Feb.	£470 14s 4d drawn by Smallbone on Jones, Lloyd & Co., payable to bearer and given to Cochrane	£200 note	24 February exchanged for 2 £100 notes which then exchanged for 200 £1 notes	25 £1 notes traced to de Berenger's use, 67 found in his possession
		2 £100 notes	24 February exchanged for 200 £1 notes	47 £1 notes traced to de Berenger's use, 48 found in his possession
		£50 note plus cash		£50 note paid by Cochrane to his coal merchant

Date	Cheque	Form of payment	Transactions	End use
25 Feb.	£98 2s 6d drawn by Lance (clerk) on Prescott & Co., payable to Butt	£50 note		£50 note given by de Berenger to William Smith, his servant
		£40 note plus cash		£40 note paid by de Berenger in Sunderland

Note: de Berenger appears to have received £400 in £1 notes, paid notes of £50 and £40 and had in his possession at Leith a remaining £50 note. The total of £540 is consistent with a memorandum contained in his papers referring to a sum of £540 received.

EXHIBIT 4: EXTRACTS FROM THOMAS SHILLING'S EVIDENCE

Thomas Shilling, examined by Mr Adolphus

    A. *Shilling*. Then he asked me 'which was the first hackney cab stand?' I told him, at the Bricklayers Arms, was the first.

    Q. *Mr Adolphus*. Did he say why he asked that question?

    A. Not a word; he said that would not do, for that was too public; he was afraid some body would cast some reflections, and he should not like that. I told him, I did not think anybody would do that, that they would be so glad to hear of the news. Then he asked me, if there was not a hackney coach stand in Lambeth Road? I told him yes. Then he said 'Drive me there, post-boy, for your chaise will go faster than a hackney coach will, and so you may drive me there.' I drove him to the Lambeth Road, and when I came there, there was no coach on the stand.

    Q. Where about in the Lambeth Road?

    A. I went from the Dog and Duck by the Asylum; this coach-stand was at the Three Stags, there was no hackney coach there; but there was a coach stand at the Marsh Gate, and if he liked to get in there, I dared to say nobody would take any notice of him – I drove him up along side of a coach.

    Q. Did he do anything about that?

    A. I think he pulled up the side-blind as I came round the corner.

    Q. Was the side-blind up?

    A. Yes, it was up when I came there; I saw it up, but I did not see when he pulled it up.

    Lord Ellenborough. Having been down before, it was up when you got there?

    A. Yes, when I got there I pulled up alongside of a hackney coach.

    Mr Adolphus. How many hackney coaches were there there?

    A. Only one; I called the coachman, and the waterman opened the coach door, and I opened the chaise door.

    Q. Did the gentleman go into the coach?

    A. Yes he did.

    Q. How?

A. He stepped off my step on to that, for he stepped on the body of the coach, or on the step of the coach; I cannot say he never stepped on the ground, the coach and the chaise were too nigh together.

Q. Did he make you a present for your trouble?

A. He then held his hand down, and gave me two Napoleons; I have them here now; he did not say one was for my fellow-servant and the other for myself, but I supposed it was so. (The witness produced the Napoleons.) . . .

Q. How was this gentleman dressed, that you drove to town?

A. He was dressed with a dark fur cap – a round cap, and with white lace, of some sort, round it; whether it was gold or silver, I cannot say; he had a red coat on underneath his outer coat.

Q. What sort of coat was his outer coat?

A. I think it was a dark coat, a kind of brown coat – but I will not swear to that.

Q. You saw a red coat underneath it?

A. Yes, I saw a red coat down as far as the waist; I did not see the skirts of it. . . .

Q. As you conversed so much with that gentleman, do you think you should know him again?

A. I should know him in a moment.

Q. Have you seen him since you have been in Court?

A. Yes, that is the gentleman *(pointing to de Berenger)*.

EXHIBIT 5: WILLIAM CRANE'S EVIDENCE

William Crane, examined by Mr Adolphus

Q. *Mr Adolphus*. Do you drive a hackney coach?

A. *Crane*. Yes

Q. What number?

A. 890

Q. On a Monday morning in February do you remember taking up a fare at the Marsh Gate?

A. Yes

Q. What day of the month was it?

A. The 21st of February.

Q. Where did the fare come from?

A. From Dartford.

Q. Out of what?

A. A post chaise and four – a Dartford chaise.

Q. Where were you directed to drive to?

A. To Grosvenor Square.

Q. Where to there?

A. He did not say where in Grosvenor Square.

Q. Where did you set him down?

A. I drove him into Grosvenor Square, and then the gentleman put down the front glass and told me to drive to No. 13 Green Street.

Q. Did the gentleman get out there?

A. Yes.

Q. Did you hear whom he asked for?

A. He asked for Colonel or Captain somebody, I did not hear the name, and they said he was gone to breakfast in Cumberland Street.

Q. What did the gentleman say then?

A. The gentleman asked if he could write a note to him.

Q. Did he go in?

A. Yes, he went into the parlour.

Q. Were you discharged then?

A. Yes, the gentleman gave me four shillings before he went in, and I said, I hoped he would give me another shilling: he took out a bit of a portmanteau that he had, and a sword, and went in, and came out into the passage and gave me another shilling.

Q. What sort of portmanteau was it?

A. A small leather one, big enough to wrap a coat in.

Q. What sort of leather?

A. I think black leather, as well as I can recollect.

Q. Do you see [the gentleman] in court?

A. I think this is the gentleman, here *(pointing to de Berenger).*

Cross-examined by Mr Richardson (counsel for de Berenger)

Q. *Mr Richardson.* You do not pretend to be able to recollect every person you carry in your hackney coach every day?

A. *Crane.* No, but this gentleman that I took from a post chaise and four, when he got out at Green Street I saw that he had a red coat underneath his great coat.

Q. You did not open your coach to him, the waterman did that?

A. Yes, the post boy ordered me to get on the box.

Lord Ellenborough. When he got out you opened the door to him I suppose?

A. Yes I did.

Mr Richardson. Did you open the door, or the footman at the house?

A. I opened the door.

Q. And he paid you and passed into the house?

A. Yes, he did.

EXHIBIT 6: COCHRANE'S LETTER TO HIS SOLICITORS REGARDING
MARY TURPIN'S EVIDENCE

June 7. To Parkinson Esq, Farrer & Co.
I have questioned Mary Turpin on the two points in her statement to
you which appeared to me to give an impression that de Berenger
was the hoaxer beyond the possibility of doubt; and I do declare to
you upon my honour that she informed me that she never said that
she saw any part of de Berenger's undercoat, said to be red, except
the collar of the coat which was green – a fact which she stated in
her first affidavit. This, therefore, ought to be expunged from the
brief, and made known to the Counsel. As to the water to wash she
knows nothing of her own knowledge, it was Cotton [Busk] who is
said to have taken water into the Parlour, and you know the reason
for her discharge from my service. She is a most infernal faggot.
I shall find out however, whether such was the fact or not if
possible.

Yours very sincerely,
COCHRANE

EXHIBIT 7: COCHRANE'S STATEMENT BEFORE THE COURT OF KING'S
BENCH, 20 JUNE 1814

Your Lordships having listened to those who had any thing to offer
which they considered material for their defence, emboldens me to
trust that your Lordships, though I do not address you by counsel,
will grant me a similar indulgence, and even that you will extend
that indulgence further to me on account of my not appearing by
Counsel, for the reasons which I had the honour to state to you
upon a former occasion. In order that those feelings which must
agitate me on the present occasion, may as little as possible enter
into what I have now to state, I have judged it proper to reduce it to
writing; and in order to give the Court as little trouble as possible,
to make my statement as short as the circumstances of the case
appear to me to admit of.

It has been my very great misfortune to be apparently implicated
in the guilt of others with whom I never had any connexion, except
in transactions, so far as I was apprised of them, entirely blameless.
I had met Mr de Berenger in public company, but was on no terms
of intimacy with him. With Mr Cochrane Johnstone I had the
intercourse natural between such near relatives. Mr Butt had
voluntarily offered, without any reward, to carry out stock
transactions, in which thousands, as well as myself were engaged, in
the face of day, without the smallest imputation of anything
incorrect. The other four defendants were wholly unknown to me,
nor have I ever, directly or indirectly, held any communication with
them. Of Mr de Berenger's concerns in the fraud, I have no
information, except such as arises out of the late trial. With regard
to Mr Johnstone and Mr Butt, I am willing to hope that they are
guiltless. They repeatedly protested to me their innocence. They did
not dare to communicate any such plan to me, if such was projected
by them, or either of them. Be they guilty, then, or be they, one or
both, erroneously convicted, I have only to lament, that, without the
most remote suspicion of their proceedings, if they, or either of
them, were concerned in the fraud, I have, through my blameless
intercourse with them, been subjected to imputations which might,

with equal justice, have been cast upon any man who now hears me. Circumstanced as I am, I must keep myself wholly unconnected with those whose innocence cannot be so clear to me as my own. Well had it been for me if I had made this distinction sooner.

I do not stand here to commend myself – unhappily, I must seek only for exculpation; but I cannot exist under the load of dishonour which even an unjust judgment has flung upon me. My life has been too often in jeopardy to make me think much about it; but my honour was never yet breathed upon; and I now hold my existence only in the determination to remove an imputation, as groundless as it is intolerable.

The evidence which I now tender to your Lordship, will aid me in performing this duty towards myself, my rank and my profession. I first offer the affidavit, which I have repeated at a risk which I formerly had no opportunity of encountering. I have been told, that I then incurred the moral guilt of perjury, without exposing myself to the legal penalties. I know nothing of such distinctions. I have repeated the statement upon oath – and I am now answerable to the laws if I have falsely sworn. The affidavits of three people who saw de Berenger at my house on the 21st February, fully confirm my statement, and I have only been prevented from bringing forward a fourth, by his sailing to a distant situation, before I could possibly stop him for this purpose.

The grounds upon which I have been convicted are these: That notes were found in de Berenger's possession which had been changed for others, that had once been in mine. That de Berenger came to my house after returning from his expedition; and that my account of what passed at this visit is contradicted by evidence.

The first ground has been clearly explained away; it amounts to nothing more than that which may happen to any man who has money transactions. Mr Butt voluntarily made purchases and sales of stock for me, and having received a small loan of money from him, I repaid him with bank notes which he used for his own purposes. He says that he exchanged these notes, and that a part of the notes which he received in exchange he paid to Mr Cochrane Johnstone, who states, that he gave them to Berenger in payment of some drawings; but with this story, whether true or false, I have no manner of concern, and consequently no wish to discuss it. In what way soever the notes which were received in exchange for mine reached de Berenger, I can only say, that mine were given to Mr Butt in discharge of a bona-fide debt; and I have no knowledge whatever of the uses to which he applied them.

De Berenger's coming to my house, I before accounted for upon the supposition of his being unconcerned in the fraud; but is it not obvious that he might have come there to facilitate his escape, by going immediately on board of my ship, with the additional prospect of obtaining employment in America? It has been said that there was a suspicious degree of familiarity in his treatment of me and my house. I can only observe, that over his conduct I had no control. But he knew, it seems, of my change of abode, which had occurred within a few days. I trust it will be recollected, that he is proved to have left town three days after such change, and that though not intimate with me, he had the means of knowing where I resided, even if he should not have enquired at my former lodgings, where my address was left. Indeed, if taking refuge in my ship, in order to facilitate his escape, was part of his scheme, it was very likely that he would have ascertained the precise place of my abode, previous to his quitting London. Again, I am said to have left the tinman's (where I think I should hardly have gone had I expected such a messenger) as soon as I heard of the officer's arrival, I was in apprehension of fatal news respecting my brother then in France, from whom I had received a letter but three days before, with the intelligence of his being dangerously ill; and I now tender you his affidavit, with the surgeon's certificate, dated the 12th February, which he brought home with him. And therefore, on receiving the note from de Berenger, whose name I was unable to decypher, and as that note announced that the writer, whom I learnt from my servant had the appearance of an officer in the army, who was desirous of seeing me, I hastened to learn intelligence so anxiously expected; nor had I the least doubt that it related to my brother. When, however, I found that the person was de Berenger, and that he had only to speak of his own private affairs, the apparent distress he was in, and the relief it gave my mind to know that he was not the bearer of the news I dreaded, prevented me from feeling that displeasure which I might otherwise have felt at the liberty he had taken or the interruption it had occasioned. Comments have been made on my saying so little to the servant who brought that note; but the fact is, I did ask him several questions, as appears by his affidavit. That I did not learn the name of the writer from the note itself, I have truly accounted for, by its being written so close to the bottom of the paper that I could not read it. This assertion is said to be contradicted by the circumstance of the writer having found room to add a postscript, as if there was only one side to the paper. Of the postscript, I have no recollection, but it might have been written even opposite the signature. That I did not collect from the handwriting, that it was addressed to me by de Berenger, is nothing extraordinary; my acquaintance with that person was extremely slight; and till that day I had never received more than one or two notes from him, which related to a drawing of a lamp. I was too deeply impressed with the idea that the note was addressed to me by an officer who had come with intelligence of my brother, to apprehend that it was written by de Berenger, from whom I expected no communication, and with whose hand-writing I was not familiar. All that I could afterwards recollect of the note, more than what is stated in my affidavit is, that he had something to communicate which would affect my feeling mind, or words to that effect, which confirmed my apprehension that the writer was the messenger of fatal news of my brother.

If de Berenger had really been my agent in this nefarious transaction, how I should have acted or where I should have chosen to receive him, it is impossible for me to say: but I humbly apprehend that my own house was not the place I should have selected for that purpose. The pretended du Bourg, if I had chosen him for my instrument, instead of his making me his convenience, should have terminated his expedition and have found a change of dress elsewhere. He should not have come immediately and in open day to my house. I should not so rashly have invited detection and its concomitant ruin.

But this is not the only extravagance of which I am accused. What supposition short of my absolute insanity will account for my having voluntarily made the affidavit which has been so much canvassed, if I really knew the plot in which de Berenger appears to have been engaged? Let me entreat your Lordships consideration of the situation in which I stood at the moment in which that affidavit was made; I was suspected of being connected with the pretended du Bourg; if I had known that de Berenger was the person who had assumed that name, could I possibly have betrayed him, and consequently myself, more completely than by publishing such a detail to the world? The name of de Berenger was never mentioned till brought forward in my affidavit; which affidavit was made, as sworn by Mr Wright, a witness at the trial, with the circumstance present to me, and remarked by me at the time I delivered it to him to be printed, that if de Berenger should happen to be du Bourg, I had furnished a clue to his detection. The circumstance of his obtaining a change of dress at my house, never could have been known if I had not voluntarily discovered it; and thus I am represented as having brought him publicly to my own house, of being the first to disclose his name, and of mentioning a circumstance, which, of all others, it was the most easy to conceal, and, if divulged, the most certain to excite suspicion! Is it not next to impossible, that a man conscious of guilt, should have been so careless of his most imminent danger?

My adversaries dwell upon some particulars of this affidavit, which they pretend to find contradicted in the evidence. The principle one is my assertion that Berenger wore a green coat. I have repeated this assertion upon oath, under all the risks of the law; and I also solemnly affirm, upon my honour, which I regard as an obligation no less sacred, that I only saw him in that dress. The witnesses on the part of the prosecution have asserted, that he wore a red coat when he arrived in town. Granted. But may he not have changed it in the coach, on his way to Green Street? Where was the difficulty, and for what purpose was the portmanteau? My own fixed opinion is, that he changed his dress in the coach, because I believe that he dared not run the risk of appearing in my presence till he had so changed it. I tender affidavits of those who saw him, as I did, in his green coat, at my house. That he should have changed his dress before I saw him is most natural, upon the supposition of his wishing to conceal from me the work he had been about; but it is like many other confirmations of my innocence, fated to excite no attention in the minds of those who only seek food for their suspicions. Much is said of the star and other ornaments, as if any proof had been given of his wearing them in my presence. He took especial care, I doubt not, to lay them aside on his way, when he had divested himself of his official capacity, long before I saw him. The small portmanteau before-mentioned, which it is admitted he brought with him, in all probability furnished him with the green coat, and received the red coat and its ornaments, and very possibly for this reason no remark has been made upon it. A good deal of observation has been bestowed upon de Berenger's unwillingness to appear before Lord Yarmouth in uniform, and the inference was, that this uniform could not have been the green dress of his corps, otherwise he must have felt the reverse of uneasy at being seen in it by his Colonel. Does any volunteer officer go out of a morning to make calls in his regimentals? Could so unusual a circumstance have failed to excite remark from Lord Yarmouth? To me, indeed, he had explained himself – he had of necessity told me his nearly desperate state, in asking me to receive him on board my ship; but is there any thing so very incredible in the statement that he was unwilling to tell his whole case to everybody? It may now doubtless be perceived, that he might have had other reasons for disliking to go out in a green dress.

Let it however, be recollected, that my statement was, that he only asked me for a hat in lieu of his military cap, and that the black coat was my own voluntary offer. The idea of his applying to Lord Yarmouth, or to any other of his friends, originated with me, and I proposed it in consequence of his calling to my recollection the certificates he had received from them. I then had no suspicion awake, and I believed what he told me. In what manner the disguise was ultimately disposed of I can only conjecture, as any one else might, from the evidence given at the trial. He presented himself to me in a grey great-coat and a green under coat; and if the person whose affidavits I now tender had been examined at the trial, and they did attend for that purpose, I do feel persuaded that a very different impression would have been made on the jury and the world at large, than that which they appear to entertain; and that your Lordships might have been disposed to take an opposite view of the case as it affected me. Those witnesses would have corroborated the particulars of my affidavit relative to de Berenger's dress, when I first saw him at my house, namely, a grey great coat, and a green under coat and jacket. Unfortunately, through some mistake or misconception, not on my part, they were left unnoticed, and, of course, were not examined. I have now to offer their several affidavits to your Lordships.

I would further submit to your Lordships, that my affidavit was made at the impulse of the moment, as soon as I heard that placards had been posted, stating that the pretended Colonel du Bourg had gone to my house; and in the conscious rectitude of my own conduct, I not only introduced the name of the only officer I saw at my house on the day stated, but narrated every occurrence that took place, and all the conversation that took place at the interview, to the best of my recollection. If I am censured for having been too ingenuous in my communication, I trust it will be admitted, that as ingenuousness disclaims all connexion with guilt, it is indicative only of my innocence.

If your Lordships will be pleased to reflect on all that I have offered respecting de Berenger, and to bear in mind the avowed intercourse which I had with two other defendants, respecting whose conduct I have been compelled to speak at last upon a supposition of their guilt, I am confident you will perceive how easily any man living so circumstanced might have been placed in the very situation. But waiving the supposition of de Berenger acting under the direction of either of the other defendants, I do still contend, that any man who had stock concerns, and was slightly known to de Berenger, ran the same risk with me, of being driven into the ruin, which undeservedly, as I am still willing to hope, has befallen the others.

The artifices which have been used to excite so much prejudice against me, I unfeignedly despise, in spite of the injury they have done me. I know it must subside, and I look forward to justice being rendered my character sooner or later: It will come most speedily, as well as most gratefully, if I shall receive it at your Lordships' hands. I am not unused to injury; of late I have known persecution; the indignity of compassion I am not yet able to bear. To escape what is vulgarly called punishment, would have been an easy thing; but I must have belied my feelings by acting as if I were conscious of dishonour. There are ways, even of removing beyond the reach of ignominy, but I cannot feel disgraced while I know that I am guiltless. Under the influence of this sentiment, I persist in the defence of my character. I have often been in situations where I had an opportunity of showing it. This is the first time, thank God, that I was ever called upon to defend it.'

EXHIBIT 8: AFFIDAVITS OF COCHRANE'S SERVANTS

No. I

I, THOMAS DEWMAN, do swear, that I was hired by Lord Cochrane expressly for the purpose of going to the country, and that about two days before I went down to relieve his Lordship's steward, several gentlemen called upon his Lordship, as was the case daily. And further, that to the best of my recollection and belief, on Monday, the 21st day of February, a gentleman came in a hackney-coach, and finding his Lordship out, desired to go in and write a note, which he did in the parlour. He asked when his Lordship had gone out, and I told him he had gone to Cumberland-street to breakfast. I came back and acquainted the gentleman that his Lordship had gone into the city, and that it was most likely he would not be back before dinner-time. He said, his business was pressing, and asked if it was possible to find him; I replied, I was not certain, but I thought I might; and I went to Mr King's tin manufactory in Cock-lane, where I delivered the note to his Lordship. The officer who sent me to the city wore a grey regimental great-coat buttoned up; I saw a green collar underneath it; he had a black silk sock or handkerchief round his neck; he was of middle size, and rather of a dark complexion. Several gentlemen called in the morning, but this was the only one that I saw in uniform at his Lordship's house, in which no man lived (as I have seen stated by Sayer, the police-officer,) except his Lordship and his servants. And I further depose, that I never saw Mr Cochrane Johnstone or Mr Butt in his Lordship's house, at No. 13, in Green-street, from the time he entered it, until the time I left London, nor any person dressed as described by Crane, the hackney-coachman. And this deponent also swears, that the above statement contains all that he knows about the matter.

THOMAS DEWMAN
Sworn at the Mansion-house, London,
This 21st day of March, 1814,
W. Domville, Mayor

No. II

I, ISAAC DAVIS, do swear, That I was in Lord Cochrane's service. That when his Lordship was appointed to a ship, I received warning to provide myself with a place; and that on the 21st day of February, when the month's warning had expired, I was in his Lordship's house in Green-street, where several gentlemen called in the morning, one of whom was Captain Berenger. He had on a grey great-coat, buttoned, and a green collar under it. I knew him, having seen him when his Lordship lived in Park-street. And I do further swear, that no man lived in his Lordship's house but his servants; and that I did not see any man dressed, or answering the description of Crane, the hackney-coachman, at his Lordship's house on the day above-mentioned.

ISAAC DAVIS
Sworn at the Mansion-house, London,
This 21st day of March, 1814
W.Domville, Mayor.

No. III

I, MARY TURPIN, do swear, That I lived as cookmaid with Lord Cochrane, and that I saw an officer in the parlour at Lord Cochrane's house in Green-street, on Monday morning the 21st of February last, when I went into the parlour for the purpose of mending the fire, and that the said officer had on a grey great-coat and a sword, and that his under-coat or his great-coat had a green collar to it. And that he stayed in the said house (as I verily believe) until his Lordship's return. And I further swear, that no men whatever have lived in the said house with Lord Cochrane except his servants. And this is all that I know as to the above matter.

MARY TURPIN
Sworn at the Mansion-house, London,
This 21st day of March, 1814.
W. Domville, Mayor.

EXHIBIT 9: AFFIDAVITS OF TWO 'RESPECTABLE TRADESMEN' RESIDING
NEAR MARSH GATE

The following AFFIDAVITS *are the voluntary and disinterested Acts
of the respective Deponents*

James Miller of Marsh-gate, Westminster-bridge-road, in the county
of Surrey, butcher, maketh oath and saith, That on the 21st day of
February last, between eight and nine o'clock in the morning, as he
was standing at his door in the said Westminster-bridge-road, he saw
a Dartford chaise-and-four stop at the coach-stand opposite to his
house, when several persons assembled and inquired of the postboys, whom they had brought in the chaise? They answered, 'A
messenger from France, and the bearer of dispatches that
Buonaparte was killed, and cut to pieces by the Cossacks.' That
deponent saw the supposed messenger, dressed in green with a grey
great-coat, get out of the said chaise into a hackney-coach; and
deponent positively declares he saw no red upon any part of his
dress. That deponent asked the waterman who attends the coach-
stand, where the gentleman was going to? and he replied, 'the
coachman is ordered to drive over the bridge.' And this deponent
further saith, that about seven o'clock in the morning of the said 21st
of February, as he was going to market, one of the collectors of the
tolls at the said Marsh-gate told him that a chaise-and-four, with a
messenger, went through the said gate towards town, between six
and seven o'clock that morning.

(Signed) JAMES MILLER

Sworn at the Mansion-house, London
The 22nd day of July 1814
(Signed) WM. DOMVILLE, Mayor

Joseph Rayment, of the Westminster-bridge-road, in the county of
Surrey, fishmonger, on his oath, saith, That to the best of his
recollection, on the morning of the 21st of February, about nine
o'clock, he saw a post-chaise-and-four pass his house, which is near
to the Marsh-turnpike-gate, and was informed that it brought

intelligence that the French army was cut in pieces and Buonaparte killed; on which he went out to learn the fact; when he saw the said post-chaise draw up along-side of a hackney coach, and a person got out of the chaise into the hackney-coach; that on getting out, his great coat, partly open, enabled deponent to see the coat underneath, and it appeared to him to be dark green: deponent fancied he was a foreign officer, as the dress was like that of the sharp-shooters. When deponent returned to his house, he mentioned to his wife the intelligence, and described to her the dress in which the person appeared, which fact she is ready to testify.

(Signed) JOSEPH RAYMENT

Sworn at the Mansion-house, London,
This 22d day of July 1814
(signed) WM. DOMVILLE, *Mayor*

EXHIBIT 10: LETTER FROM JAMES HULLOCK TO BUTT REGARDING
COCHRANE'S WINE BILL

Fenchurch Street, 4th July 1814

Sir,

In answer to your letter of this date, addressed to Messrs Wilkinson
& Co., I have to give the following statement of what occurred, to
my own knowledge, relative to the transaction you allude to:–

I well recollect that, a few days previous to the 29th day of
January last, you ordered of my employers Messrs Wilkinson and
Crosthwaite, for Lord Cochrane, a quantity of wine, amounting to
24/- (a copy of the bill of particulars of which is inclosed) to be
delivered at his Lordship's house in Park-street, Grosvenor-square,
and which I believe was delivered there accordingly, on the 29th.

On or about the 19th of February last,* Lord Cochrane and
yourself called at the counting house in Fenchurch-street, and you
paid us your own bill of 24*l*.0*s*.6*d* as appears by an entry in my
writing in our books. Afterwards I took an order from Lord
Cochrane himself for wines, amounting to 675*l*.9*s* (after allowing a
discount of 35*l*.11*s*.) as set forth in the copy of the bill of particulars
enclosed, which his Lordship desired might be sent on board his
Majesty's ship *Tonnant*, without loss of time. I believe his Lordship
and yourself were engaged in our cellars upwards of two hours in
tasting wines, before his Lordship gave me the order.

A few days after the last wine was so ordered, you called at the
counting-house again to ask if it was sent as it was your wish to
settle the bill as soon as you heard the wine was received on board,
and desired the bill to be sent to you.

The wine was accordingly shipped about the 26th of February last,
and on the 2d of March following, I sent the bill of parcels, directed
to Lord Cochrane, on board the *Tonnant*, at Chatham.

---

* It is important to shew that it was on that particular day. Mr Hullock
  says '*on or about*' but he adds, that Mr Butt paid his own bill at that
  time; and fortunately, Mr Butt has preserved the receipt, which bears
  date February the 19th. [Cochrane's postscript]

About the same day I left another copy of the bill for yourself at Mr Fearn's counting-house, in Shorters-court, Throgmorton-street.

On the 8th of March you called at our counting-house, and paid the two bills, amounting together to 699*l.* 0*s.* in the following Bank-notes, viz.

A Bank-note,	No. 3095, dated Feb. 16th, 1814,	for	£100.	0. 0.
Another,	No. 3040, 16th " "	for	100.	0. 0.
Another,	No. 4540, 4th " "	for	<u>500.	0. 0.</u>
			£700.	0. 0.
Gave change			<u>0.11.	0.</u>
			£699.	9. 0.

which notes, on the same day, I paid into Messrs Lees and Co. the bankers, as appears by their books.

I am, Sir,

Your obedient, humble servant

JAMES HULLOCK

To R.G. Butt Esq

EXHIBIT 11: COCHRANE'S CHARGES AGAINST LORD ELLENBOROUGH
BEFORE THE HOUSE OF COMMONS

1. Of compelling the Counsel for the defendants to enter upon the defence at or near midnight, when they complained of great fatigue from long attendance, and *assigning insufficient and artificial reasons for so doing.*

2. Of confounding the different cases of Lord Cochrane, Mr Cochrane Johnstone and Mr Butt,, and untruly representing their respective transactions in the funds on and prior to the 21st February, 1814, to be so far similar in manner and amount as to indicate that each of them had speculated with a view to that particular day.

3. Of untruly alleging such a communication between Lord Cochrane, Mr Cochrane Johnstone and Mr Butt, as to render it impossible for the jury to say from whom the draft of 170/- and a fraction, or such part of the ultimate produce as was found in the possession of de Berenger, ultimately proceeded.

4. Of unwarrantably insinuating that a connection between Lord Cochrane and the bank notes found in De Berenger's possession had been proved by evidence, and expressly instructing the jury to consider, as a circumstance, against Lord Cochrane, the evidence given in order to prove such a connection, and unjustly evading the consideration whether the evidence so given was not negatived by evidence of a memorandum found in the handwriting of de Berenger.

5. Of unduly and repeatedly insinuating to the jury that Lord Cochrane in disclosing the name of de Berenger was influenced by an opinion that he had quitted the kingdom.

6. Of unwarrantably and untruly insinuating to the jury that the reason assigned by Lord Cochrane for obtaining leave of absence in Feb. 1814 was introduced by him as a colour to draw off their attention from other matters.

7. Of misrepresenting the disclosure voluntarily given by Lord Cochrane on the subject of his seeing and being in the company of Mr Cochrane Johnstone and Mr Butt on the morning of Feb. the 21st. and unwarrantably applying it as evidence that they

215

met together to communicate on some business in common to be transacted on that day.

8. Of unwarrantably controverting the declaration upon oath of Lord Cochrane that the note received by him on Feb. the 21st was signed close to the bottom, and that he could not read the name; and of repeating with commendation the fallacious argument of the Counsel for the prosecution that the name could not be written at the bottom because the writer, after closing the note, opened it again and wrote something more.

9. Of repeatedly, unwarrantably, and unjustly representing to the jury that the reason assigned by Lord Cochrane upon oath for returning home, in consequence of the note he received on the 21st of Feb., was unworthy of credit, because he did not communicate it to the servant who brought the note.

10. Of devising unwarrantable and unfounded objections to Lord Cochrane's declaration upon oath that he received a letter from Major Cochrane, his brother, acquainting him with his dangerous state of health previous to the 21st of Feb., 1814 and of treating it as unworthy of credit, though supported by circumstances and by the affidavit of Major Cochrane himself, stating that he wrote such a letter early in that month.

11. Of unjustly representing that the evidence adduced on the part of Lord Cochrane that application had been made to obtain an appointment for de Berenger connected with the service in America was immaterial to corroborate the narrative contained in Lord Cochrane's affidavit; of untruly insinuating that Lord Cochrane himself had suggested the application, and of applying it as evidence of guilt against Lord Cochrane.

12. Of injuriously passing over, without comment or observation, that part of Lord Cochrane's affidavit which stated that when he objected to take de Berenger to America, without leave from the Admiralty, he recalled to his recollection certificates which he had formerly shown him from Lord Yarmouth and others in official situations; and of misrepresenting the evidence of the Hon. Alexander Murray, on the subject of Lord Cochrane's acquaintance with de Berenger.

13. Of repeatedly, unwarrantably, and unjustly conveying and enforcing an opinion that de Berenger appeared before Lord Cochrane on the 21st of Feb., 1814, in the red coat, star, and order in which he had committed the fraud; of suppressing evidence corroborative of Lord Cochrane's declaration upon oath that he wore in his presence a green uniform; and of supplying evidence in opposition thereto, and passing without pause or remark the solemn declaration of Lord Cochrane upon oath, that he had no concern, either directly or indirectly, in the fraud that had been committed.

EXHIBIT 12: DE BERENGER'S SOCIAL ENGAGEMENTS WITH THE
COCHRANES IN JANUARY 1814.

Sunday 9th Jan. – I paid a morning visit to *Lord Cochrane*, in Park
Street, but most assuredly *not* on business, I found him at home, and
I have strong grounds to think, that on *this* morning, I met the
Hon. Basil Cochrane there.

Sunday, 9th Jan. – Dined in Great Cumberland Street, with
Mr Cochrane Johnstone, Miss Johnstone, Col. George Cochrane,
and *Lord Cochrane*.

Saturday 15th Jan. – Dined in Great Cumberland Street with
Mr Cochrane Johnstone, Miss Johnstone, Admiral Sir Alexander
Cochrane, Lord Balgownie, Sir George Jackson, several other
gentlemen (whose names I have incorrectly), Lady Cochrane, Lady
Trowbridge, Mr and Miss Cochrane (Sir Alexander's son and
daughter) and *Lord Cochrane*.

Wednesday, 19th Jan. – Dined in Great Cumberland Street, with
Mr Cochrane Johnstone, Miss Johnstone, Admiral Sir Alexander
and Lady Cochrane, Mr and Miss Cochrane, Hon. Basil and
Mrs B. Cochrane, Lady Trowbridge, Colonel Dillon, Colonel
George Cochrane, and *Lord Cochrane*, with some others unknown
to me.

Friday 21st Jan. – Dined in Portman Square, with the Hon. Basil and
Mrs B. Cochrane, Admiral Sir Alexander and Lady Cochrane, the
Hon. Cochrane Johnstone, and Miss C. Johnstone, Admiral Hope,
Miss Hope, Lady Trowbridge, Colonel Dillon, Colonel George
Cochrane, Mr Turton, and *Lord Cochrane*, with several other
gentlemen.

Saturday 22nd Jan. – Breakfasted at Admiral Sir Alexander
Cochrane's, with a large part of naval gentlemen whose names I did
not retain; *Lord Cochrane* was also there.

N.B. The admiral left London on the 25th of January; I visited Sir Alexander additionally on the 24th, and I breakfasted again with him on the 25th, meeting *Lord Cochrane* there each time.

Here, then, in a short period of only *fourteen days*, out of *twelve months*, previous to the trial, during which I had very frequent intercourse with Lord Cochrane; so much so, that my proof alone shews, that in *fourteen successive days* I have met him *six times*, and, in *sixteen successive days, eight times*.

EXHIBIT 13: DE BERENGER'S ACCOUNT OF HIS ARRIVAL AT 13 GREEN STREET

In Grosvenor Square, I told the coachman to drive to No. 13 Green Street, where arriving, I was not a little surprised to see the door opened, not slyly by Lord Cochrane, for it had been preconcerted that he should remain at home; that he should send his man servant out, who knew me; and that for once he should condescend, on such an occasion, to become his own porter, by being ready in the parlour, at given time, to which I was punctual to let me in without shewing himself. Whether avarice to direct his own sales, or a weak idea that his absence would prove the impossibility of preconcerted measures, or any other similar motive, caused his non-performance, I cannot take upon myself to determine, but this is certain, that my perplexity was great when I saw Thomas Dewman open the door. . . . I said, 'Is *your master* at home?' to which he replied in the negative, whereupon I asked leave to write a note, carrying my supposed dispatch-case, as well as my sabre, *myself* into the house: he shewed me into a parlour.

I had never been in this house before, and was not a little surprised that a nobleman's residence should be so ill supplied, as to furnish me but a small scrap of paper, on my asking for pen and ink, etc. to write a note to Great Cumberland-street, where I had been told Lord Cochrane had gone, and where I could not follow, as Mr Johnstone kept several men servants, who all knew me perfectly well.

After penning a short note to Lord Cochrane, conveying, in rather *touchy* terms, (to use which I felt entitled, because unnecessary perplexities were added to my task,) great surprise at his absence, and requesting his undelayed return; I dispatched this same man with it to Great Cumberland-street: it will hardly be expected that at such a crisis a copy was taken, but I perfectly remember NOT to *have subscribed any name whatever*, though Lord Cochrane states on oath that he could not read 'the name' because it was written 'close to the bottom' of the note, 'on a small bit of paper.' – And why did I not subscribe a name? – for a variety of solid reasons. The note itself spoke only of my disappointment occasioned by his absence; it therefore afforded no new suspicions to a servant had he even perused it for my looks and manner had already but too forcibly betrayed my disappointment. – No wax was at hand, and a wafer was used, not to lose a moment, anxious as I was lest Lord Cochrane should be gone to the city before my messenger could reach Mr Johnstone's – and so it proved. To a note *with a wet wafer* it was not likely that, thus situated, I should sign my name particularly since Dewman did not appear to recognise me. . . .

The servant was desired to use all possible speed to Great Cumberland-street: and his return apprised me that Lord Cochrane had gone off in Mr Johnstone's coach with him and Mr Butt – where to I knew too well; and I could immediately have told the servant where to find him, the impolicy of avowing such knowledge struck me so forcibly, that I resolved on endeavours to obtain the information from him instead. Opening the note again, some few lines were added, (as Dewman admits on the Trial . . .) being in substance, *that I neither would or could move* TILL I HAD SEEN LORD COCHRANE, *and that his absence had caused me much unnecessary pain.* . . .

Very shortly after Dewman had left me, I received an invitation to breakfast from the Lady whom Cochrane calls his 'Housekeeper'; though certainly not from the basement story, but from the drawing room; the maid servant so sent also expressed her 'mistress's' regret that Lord Cochrane's absence should have disappointed me. It will require little persuasion to convince my reader, that this civil offer was thankfully declined, although a breakfast just then would not have been a needless refreshment; the lady, however, was determined to urge her hospitable civilities with firm perseverance, so much so, that it embarrassed me beyond conception; for how could I appear in a dining room, before a lady, tired out, and far from clean, with a large great coat on? In accepting the invitation, I had but one of two alternatives, either to display my glaring dress to her and to her servant's scrutiny, and which certainly was not likely; or to be so rude, and so inconsistently eccentric, as to make my bow to a *lady closely buttoned up in a full military great coat, worn over an under coat; hereupon to sit down with her in this unmannerly trim to a breakfast table and by a good* FIRE, *without any plausible reason that could be offered for my so doing.* To avoid these pressing invitations, I stated my inability on grounds of my being dirty and fatigued with a long journey, my being sleepy, and perfectly unfit for female society; and so terrified was I, lest no denial would be taken, that as soon as the maid left the room, I laid my head down on a table pretending to be fast asleep, hoping thereby to escape these civil importunities. Not many minutes elapsed before the same female returned, bringing a basin of water, towel etc; believing me asleep, she quitted the room, probably to make her report; she, however, returned almost directly, and shaking me forcibly, for I chose to be obstinate, hoping she would give up her object; she did not quit me till I acknowledged her success, by listening to a very polite, but *positive* message, that I must come up stairs; that breakfast was then ready, which had been prepared on purpose for me; that she had brought me water to wash; and that after I had breakfasted by a much better fire than *the parlour* could boast of, I should either lay down on a sofa in the drawing-room, or that a mattress, pillow, and blanket, should be added: all these attentions prove either the greatest possible kindness and consideration for Lord Cochrane's friend, or they were employed to withdraw me to a room less exposed to intrusion; whichever object they sought, how could I refuse, without appearing the most ill bred being in existence; and what grounds were left me for declining? – Returning thanks for the basin of water (which it will thus appear I did not *ask for*, as Lord Cochrane artfully insinuated) I said she was assured that I would use it, but that really I felt no inclination whatever for breakfast. Scarce were the ablutions over, when the servant, if such she was, *peremptorily* summoned me up stairs: for I hardly dare to describe the rank of any of Lord Cochrane's inmates, after breakfasting in his drawing-room with his 'house-keeper' who, nevertheless, *there* seemed to be perfectly at home.

Arriving in the drawing room, I began by very awkwardly mixing thanks and apologies, on purpose, that my excuses for continuing to wear my bulky great coat might be received, unaccompanied by any reason for such extraordinary conduct; for all that could be learnt from me was, that I neither could or would take it off though invited so to do, to be 'more comfortable, as there was a good fire,' which strange appearance, as well as incoherent address, induced the Lady some time after to describe me as being 'deranged'. After repeated, and certainly most obliging and considerate entreaties to go to rest after my fatigue, the breakfast being over, the Lady quitted the room, where I remained some time, ruminating on Lord Cochrane's pointed absence, when it occurred to me, that my not having sent my servant with a hat and coat, as had been determined, might have induced him to imagine that I had substituted some different plan for ridding myself of my paraphernalia, than that of calling on him in Green-street.

To the best of my recollection, it was a little after eleven o'clock when Lord Cochrane arrived; he came to me in the drawing-room, where I was alone, and immediately to say, 'How could you be so imprudent as to send me a wafered note?' which was retorted with – 'Had your Lordship attended to your promise, and staid at home, this trifling uneasiness to you, as well as many greater to me, would have been spared': he ran out of the room, and immediately returned, desiring me to follow, with my sabre, cap, and lock leather case! – he took me to a back bed-room on the *second* floor, there to talk to me while I packed up my dress. Now, if Lord Cochrane's affidavit was correct, what occasion could there be to take me up into the *second* floor? And that he did so I can prove, if required, without having before or since been in the Green-street house, by drawing an exact plan of that room, and the situation of its furniture; yet the affidavit carefully conceals our going up stairs. Attempts to relate my adventures were interrupted, for he was too anxious about my being gone; my request to leave the *scarlet* coat, sword, and cap there, (for I proposed to go home in my grey great coat and green overalls, after a round hat had been procured from a hatter,) Lord Cochrane positively declined; and he said, that having sent his man servant out of the way, he could not send for a hat, which, besides, would be recollected; but that he had *purposely* kept the coach that brought him, to carry me and my bundle away; and that, therefore, I might go home in one of his hats, though they were very remarkable; he then went to some drawers, and taking out a large pillow-case, not unlike the French pillow-cases, (not the 'cover of a chair bottom', as stated on the trial) he persisted in my putting up every thing, even my great coat, *and very obsequiously and much flurried*, THE NOBLE LORD LENT AN HELPING HAND TO PULL OFF THAT VERY **SCARLET** COAT WHICH HE SWORE NEVER TO HAVE SEEN, *and which, to his agitated vision, must have appeared* **GREEN!** – He next, (instead of taking a coat that was 'laying on a chair', as stated in his EXTRAORDINARY AFFIDAVIT) eclipsed even St Martin, for, not content with sheltering me under his hat of hats, he voluntarily offered me, not half his cloak, but he actually forced on me the *whole* of his *long* coat, taking it from *his own back*; and perfectly positive am I in this, for it felt warm, and caused a disagreeable, and in me insurmountable sensation. Thus ridiculously equipped, I departed in *his* coach, leaving nothing but my long sabre behind.

EXHIBIT 14: ANONYMOUS LETTER DE BERENGER CLAIMED TO HAVE
RECEIVED WHILE IN PRISON

COPY of an ANONYMOUS LETTER *sent by the Twopenny Post July
2, 1814, and received by* C.R. DE BERENGER *early the next day; with
his* COMMENTS *interlined.*

'Sir,
A few friends of Lord Cochrane are of Opinion that you are a
person who can explain the late fraudulent Transaction. It does
appear to them that you are fully proved to be Colonel du Bourg –
and if so you can inform his Lordship and the Public who employed
you in this Business, who was the person who supplied you with the
Napoleons?'

> *Does this not decidedly say, you have no chance of persuading the
> world that you are not du Bourg, for it has been brought home to
> you most unquestionably, but there still remains a hope of
> extricating Lord C. if you will but impeach any body else?*

'It is understood that you are or have been a particular Friend and
under Obligation to the Cochrane family now you have a fair
Opportunity of boldly stepping forward and declaring his innocence
to the world. Mr Butt is presumed to be equally innocent with Lord
Cochrane.'

> *This in other words means, – remember the friendship and
> obligations which you, de Berenger, have experienced from the
> Cochrane family. Now is your time, – do not 'boggle', but step
> forward without fear, with as much falsehood as is requisite to
> save me. It next is evident that Mr Butt sits in council at the
> manufacturing of this morceau, for he says, – and me too, my
> Lord. It must be clear to every capacity that 'a few friends of
> Lord Cochrane', would not have bargained for Mr Butt also, had
> they been by themselves.*

'Some people suppose that the real persons concerned in this Transaction are of high rank in Life and that you have a handsome Annuity or provision secured to you for your Silence.'

Oh, the cloven foot! – Lord Cochrane, at a meeting which, he gave me clandestinely at Donithorne's, after the 21ˢᵗ of February, 1814, as described in the pages concluding the First Part, said: 'Should they ever find you out to be Du Bourg, and should you be unable to deny it any longer, could you not then say, that you had been employed by Lord Yarmouth? – It would go down with the public, at all events.' Here then is a plain repetition of that advice; and the supposed annuity is clearly brought in with a view to offer me one in a cautious manner.

'But Sir you should recollect that Lord C——— and Mr B——— have it in THEIR power to remunerate you for your Services and no doubt would willingly and handsomely contribute towards your future Support provided their Characters were through your means cleared from this infamous charge.

You Sir have now an Opportunity of doing a good Action, if you will between this time & 12 o'clock on Tuesday next declare all you know of this Business in writing to Lord C——— the party of Friends privy to this Letter will consider him innocent otherwise they will consider both him and Mr Butt guilty.'

Mr Cochrane Johnstone always said, that, to save Lord Cochrane would be doing a 'good Action', as he was a great naval officer, etc. Being at that time abroad, he could not have been 'privy' to this Letter; but the prompter of that argument, and of the word 'good' was present without doubt – therefore it comes out once more. – Now for plausibility and consistency. Would a few of Lord C's friends have directed my hoped for assistance to be sent to Lord C. and by a given hour? But it suits Lord Cochrane and Mr Butt, deficient of an address of these phantasmagoria 'friends', and not inclined to run the risk of exhibiting my foreseen indignant answer to other eyes; thus situated, they prefer to become the receivers of the infamies which, under false colours, they had proposed themselves. Mr Butt here again is present; for surely no such partnership anxiety could have been manifested by 'a few friends of his Lordship.'

'You will please to observe that this declaration made by you will in regard to your sentence not place you in a worse situation than you are at present.'

Dated – 'Saturday 24 July.'
    And addressed,
'To the Baron De Berenger
    Kings Bench Prison'

The above plainly observing – do what you will, your sentence, horrible as it is, cannot be made worse by such doings, nevertheless your 'future support' may be improved, if you will but forge, lie, and swear, all that we require of you.

Bibliography

PRIMARY SOURCES

The primary sources listed below, other than the Dundonald family papers, can be found in the British Library; those marked with an asterisk can also be found in the Inner Temple Library.

Manuscripts and documents

Dundonald family papers: trial documents previously held by Cochrane's solicitors, Farrer & Co., and now deposited by the Earl of Dundonald with the National Archives of Scotland, Edinburgh (classification GD/233/199); family correspondence

Published works

Calumnious Aspersions contained in the Report of the Sub-Committee of the Stock Exchange exposed and refuted in so far as regards Lord Cochrane, K.B. and M.P., the Hon Cochrane Johnstone, MP, and R.G. Butt Esq., The (London, 1814)

Cochrane, Thomas, A Letter to Lord Ellenborough (London, 1815)*

——, De Berenger Detected, including The Letter of C.R. de Berenger to his solicitor dated 17th February 1814 (London, 1816)

——, The Autobiography of a Seaman (originally published in 2 vols, London, 1860; new edition, London, 2000)

de Berenger, Charles Random, The Noble Stockjobber (London, 1816)

Gurney, William, The Fraud on the Stock Exchange: Trial of De Berenger, Lord Cochrane, and others, June 1814 (printed transcript of shorthand note of the trial, London, 1814)

M'Rae, Alexander, A Disclosure of the Hoax practiced upon the Stock Exchange, Feb 21 1814 (London, 1815)*

228

Bibliography

Remarks on the Case of Lord Cochrane, by a Near Observer (London, 1814)*

Review of the Case of Lord Cochrane, 1830, as presented to King William IV

Three Reports of the Sub-Committee of the Stock Exchange, 1814–15 *

Periodicals

Courier, The
Morning Chronicle
Times, The

SECONDARY SOURCES

Atlay, James Beresford, *The Trial of Lord Cochrane before Lord Ellenborough* (London, 1897)

Campbell, Lord, *The Lives of the Chief Justices of England*, 3 vols (London, 1857)

Cecil, Henry, *A Matter of Speculation: The Case of Lord Cochrane* (London, 1965)

Cochrane, Douglas Fiennes, *The Case of Lord Cochrane: Henry Cecil Examined* (London, 1965)

Glover, Richard, *Britain at Bay: Defence against Bonaparte, 1803–14* (London, 1973)

Grimble, Ian, *The Sea Wolf: The Life of Admiral Cochrane* (first published London, 1978; revised edition, Edinburgh, 2000)

Harvey, Robert, *Cochrane, the Life and Exploits of a Fighting Captain* (London, 2000)

Law, Edward Downes, *The Guilt of Lord Cochrane in 1814, a criticism* (London, 1914)

Lloyd, Charles Christopher, *Lord Cochrane, Seaman-Radical-Liberator. A life of Thomas, Lord Cochrane, 10th Earl of Dundonald* (1947)

Mallalieu, Joseph Percival William, *Extraordinary Seaman* (London, 1957)

O'Brian, Patrick, *The Reverse of the Medal* (London, 1986; reprinted 2003)

Rodger, Nicholas A.M., *The Command of the Ocean: A Naval History of Britain 1649–1815* (London, 2004)

Sugden, John, 'Lord Cochrane, Naval Commander, Radical, Inventor (1775–1860): A study of his Earlier Career, 1775–1818' (Sheffield University PhD thesis, 1981)

Thomas, Donald, *Cochrane, Britannia's Sea Wolf* (London, 1978; reprinted 2002)

Townsend, William C., *Modern State Trials* (London, 1850)

Tute, Warren Stanley, *Cochrane, A Life of Admiral the Earl of Dundonald* (London, 1965)

Twitchett, Eric Gilbert, *Life of a Seaman: Thomas Cochrane 10th Earl of Dundonald* (London, 1931)

Index

Notes

1. Page numbers for **chapters** are emboldened.
2. Sub-entries are arranged in *chronological order* where significant.
3. The following abbreviations are used: TC (Sir Thomas Cochrane); ACJ (Andrew Cochrane Johnstone); dB (de Berenger)

231